6/09

D0844449

We Are All
Moors

We Are All Moors

Ending Centuries of Crusades
against Muslims and Other Minorities

ANOUAR MAJID

UNIVERSITY OF MINNESOTA PRESS

MINNEAPOLIS • LONDON

WITHDRAWN FROM
...DES PARISH LIBRARY

c.1
RAPIDES PARISH LIBRARY
ALEXANDRIA, LOUISIANA RS MN

Copyright 2009 by the Regents of the University of Minnesota

All rights reserved. No part of this publication may be reproduced, stored in a retrieval system, or transmitted, in any form or by any means, electronic, mechanical, photocopying, recording, or otherwise, without the prior written permission of the publisher.

Published by the University of Minnesota Press
111 Third Avenue South, Suite 290
Minneapolis, MN 55401-2520
http://www.upress.umn.edu

Library of Congress Cataloging-in-Publication Data

Majid, Anouar, 1960-
We are all Moors : ending centuries of crusades against Muslims and other minorities / Anouar Majid.
p. cm.
Includes bibliographical references and index.
ISBN 978-0-8166-6079-7 (hc : alk. paper) — ISBN 978-0-8166-6080-3 (pb : alk. paper)
1. Christianity and other religions—Islam—History. 2. Christianity and other religions—Judaism—History. 3. Islam—Relations—Christianity. 4. Judaism—Relations—Christianity. 5. Muslims—America—History. 6. Jews—Islamic countries—History. I. Title.
BP172.M28 2009
305.6'97—dc22
2008048891

Printed in the United States of America on acid-free paper

The University of Minnesota is an equal-opportunity educator and employer.

18 17 16 15 14 13 12 11 10 09   10 9 8 7 6 5 4 3 2 1

Our troubled age has sometimes mirrored medieval Spaniards at their very worst: killing the innocent in God's name, expelling the "infidel," rallying coreligionists by slandering other faiths, refusing to understand our neighbor's sacred beliefs, and infringing his or her right to worship God freely. Wherever such acts trample human dignity and freedom, no just and lasting peace can be possible.

—CHRIS LOWNEY, *A Vanished World*

We are all the direct descendants of Columbus; it is with him that our genealogy begins, insofar as the word beginning has a meaning.

—TZVETAN TODOROV, *The Conquest of America*

CONTENTS

PREFACE

In November 2005, I gave a talk at the National Hispanic Cultural Center (NHCC) in Albuquerque, New Mexico, titled "Moors Redux." The talk was a variation on my chapter "Other Worlds, New Muslims" in *Freedom and Orthodoxy: Islam and Difference in the Post-Andalusian Age* (2004), but the enthusiastic response from the audience, including from New Mexico's luminaries Tomás Atencio, E. A. "Tony" Mares, and Enrique Lamadrid, that Sunday evening, together with the eloquent comments of Carlos Vásquez, the cultural director of the center, encouraged me to think about a book-length project. An invitation from the medievalist Ibtissam Bouachrine to share my views on the "post-Andalusian condition" at Smith College and the generous feedback of Roberto Márquez of Mount Holyoke College further convinced me that this book is worth writing. Other friends and colleagues along the way kept the flame of interest burning. A special note of thanks must, however, be reserved, yet again, to my friend Michael Morris for arranging the NHCC event, including a moving performance by the musical group Crisol Luz, led by Tomás Lozano. Tomás, a talented musician and historian, was born near Barcelona to a family from Granada, and his study of New Mexico's musical traditions has been quite enlightening and helpful. Not only did Tomás and his band honor me with "A la una," a haunting medieval Sephardic song from my native city of Tangier, but also, during the question-and-answer session, he stood up and proudly declared that he, too, is a Moor when he is in northern Spain. By suggesting that even a Spaniard in the wrong part of Spain could be treated as a Moor (as a Muslim was, and still is, commonly known in that country), Tomás provided the strongest and most ironic confirmation of this book's thesis— that since the defeat of Islam in medieval Spain, minorities in the West have become, in some ways, reincarnations of the Moor, an enduring threat to Western civilization.

With such encouragement (and much thanks), I sallied forth, expanding on the Moorish connection to Africans and Hispanics in America, Jews in Europe, and nonwhite immigrants on both continents. I owe my interest in the shared destiny of Jews and Muslims almost entirely to Gil Anidjar, whose article for the magazine *Tikkun* (based on his extensive body of scholarship) on the semantic, to say the least, conflation of both religions in Nazi Germany I came across some years ago. That small article set me on a path of what was to me uncharted terrain, which turned into a totally engrossing voyage of discovery. Coming across Tom Reiss's book *The Orientalist* was also a delightful surprise, one that brought to life a long-vanished world of Jews and Muslims that existed for me only in the hazy fables of childhood.

In September 2008, inspired by Max Harris's sure-to-be-classic study of the popular festivals of mock battles between Moors and Christians, *Aztecs, Moors, and Christians: Festivals of Reconquest in Mexico and Spain,* and supported by a grant from the College of Arts and Sciences at the University of New England, I attended the fiesta of *moros y cristianos* in Villena, a small town in the region of Alicante, Spain. There, armed with a press pass and camera, I was able to capture not only what seem to me the cultural origins of the long conflict between the West and Islam but also, as I shall indicate in the Conclusion, the possibility for living together in our troubled world. (A full discussion of the fiesta, which I attended after this book had gone into production, would simply take too long to discuss here.) For that successful trip, which included a quick visit to Santa Fe and Granada, I need to thank, first and foremost, my brother Rami, who worked scrupulously to arrange for my stay and work in Villena. I got all the help I needed from Antonio Martínez and Manolo Muñoz Hernandez, public relations manager and president, respectively, of the Junta Central de Fiestas de Moros y Cristianos; José Fernando Domene Verdú, probably the foremost historian and local expert on the fiesta of Villena; Francisco (Paco) Domenech Ferriz, a long-standing member of the Moros Realistas and now a good friend; and, finally, the gracious Rachida, known locally as Racha, who opened her home to me and my wife and allowed us to stay for a few days. A few *festeros* from one of the Christian companies, the Students, were equally gracious by sharing drinks, history, and memorabilia. Although this book deals only briefly with Villena, its title is, in some ways, a tribute to that town. When Max Harris attended the fiesta in 1992, it was one of his friends from Villena who told him, "We are all Moors."

My trip to Spain was made richer by the help of my childhood friends from Tangier—Abdellatif (Tifo) Bouziane, of Málaga, and Mustafa Akalay, of Granada. Mustafa, who secured us entrance to the fabled Alhambra Palace at the last minute; hosted us at his restaurant, Tragaluz, deemed, by one account, the best Moorish restaurant in the city; and gave us a brief intellectual tour of the challenges and promises of coexistence in Spain, was quite generous with his time. It was also good to see that the diplomatic representation of my native Morocco in Spain was in the able hands of a very old friend from Tangier, Farid Aoulouhaj. Finally, the hospitality and love of my Spanish nephews Omar and Ismael, as well as those of Rosa and the whole Rodríguez family, reminded me of what we all have in common.

When I returned to Spain the following month for more explorations, my suspicion that Spain offers the way out for the hardened positions on both sides of the conflict between Islam and the West was further confirmed by my discussions with prominent Moroccan and Spanish scholars and activists in Granada, all introduced to me by my friend Mustafa. Professor Manuel Barrios Aquilera was kind enough to tell me about his scholarship on the Moriscos of Granada, whose plight is wonderfully captured in the title of one of his many books, *La convivencia negada* (Coexistence denied). Even more gratifying was my encounter with the Socialist Party's representative in Catalonia's parliament, Mohammed Chaib Akhdim, the first Muslim ever elected to high public office in Spain in modern memory. The Tangier native is a new Morisco, a proud Catalan and Spaniard who also cherishes his Moroccan Islamic heritage. If there is any promise of a new positive *convivencia* and productive assimilation, no one represents it better than this politician. By the time I left Barcelona, a glimpse of promise was in the air, not least because DNA studies continue to reveal the presence of indelible Jewish and Moorish traits in the Spanish body.

Part of the reason I wrote this book is to commemorate the quadricentennial of the royal decree to expel all Moriscos (forcibly baptized Muslims or Spaniards of Muslim descent) from the self-proclaimed Catholic nation. So significant was this tragic event that one Spanish commentator, Rafael Torres, declared 2009 "el año morisco" or "the Morisco year." The approaching anniversary of this dark episode in our history had been constantly on my mind as I read and wrote. The encouragement of Nabil Matar, the indefatigable scholar of British–Muslim relations in the early modern period, strengthened my conviction that this was indeed a timely project. The long, critical comments I received from several readers and from members of the University of Minnesota Press's faculty board, together with Tammy Zambo's careful reading and excellent editorial skills, not only provided further affirmation but also helped turn my manuscript into a much better book. In the end, I remain mostly indebted to my editor Jason Weidemann for his critical engagement. Jason and his colleagues at the Press have made my intellectual pursuits so rewarding in the past few years. For an author to work with such a group of talented professionals is no small blessing. To them, and all the people mentioned here, I humbly extend my gratitude.

When I started working on this project at least three years ago, I suspected that part of the anxiety surrounding the issue of Muslim and Hispanic immigraton in Europe and America had something to do with the impending end of the age of Euro-American dominance in global affairs. Since then, a number of publications have emerged to confirm this assumption. In November 2008, soon after Barack Obama was elected president of the United States, the U.S. National Intelligence Council issued a report forecasting the decline of the United States in an increasingly multipolar world. In his book *On Empire* (2008), the veteran historian Eric Hobsbawm simply noted that, with the end of the classical age of empire, "we shall have to find another way of organizing the globalized world of the twenty-first century." I hope this book helps us think further along that path.

I should note that my references to Samuel Huntington, whose work I discuss at some length in the book, are in the present tense. The world-renowned political scientist passed away on Christmas Eve, 2008. His ideas are very much alive and will continue to stimulate debate and discussion across disciplines, ideologies, languages, and even nations. I wonder how Huntington, who warned against the Hispanic menace and credited the Anglo-Saxon genius for the making of the United States, might have responded to the increasingly precarious economic and political situation of the United States today. What, for instance, do Hispanics have to do with the collapse of the U.S. and global financial structure in 2008? However much I disagree with his views, I have always read his work with much interest and, more importantly, engagement. Huntington's death is a loss to all of us.

One last thought that I probably ought to share with readers familiar with my work, particularly my last book, *A Call for Heresy*, on the vital necessity of cultivating dissent in Islam and America: If that book was quite critical of Islamic thought and traditions, this book looks at the ways in which the West has been unable to overcome its old animosities toward Islam. When I tried to understand what drove me to work on seemingly unrelated projects, I realized that I am ultimately interested in liberalizing thought and politics, not in substituting new systems for old ones. This is, I think, the thread that runs through my whole work. All political and cultural traditions, however liberating at first, eventually turn into closed systems if there are no strong countermeasures to avoid this grim outcome. We do need generous heretics to help keep our vistas broad and our hearts capacious. Religions, cultures, and nationalities are boundaries of our own making. If we can't undo them, we can at least enlarge their scope. By alienating those who are different, we end up alienating ourselves and diminishing our own lives. Heresies of the right kind may, in fact, set us free.

Specters of the Moor

More than ever before, light needs to be shone on the long Andalusian
aftermath that is pressingly with us now.

—DAVID LEVERING LEWIS, *God's Crucible*

As the first decade of the twenty-first century comes to a close, western
Europe seems to be, once again, struggling with its old Muslim problem.
About four hundred years ago, Spain, the southwestern frontier of the continent, expelled all its citizens of Muslim or Moorish descent, closed a nine-
century history of living with Islam, and reveled in the purity of its faith
and the racial homogeneity of its people. The Moor became, over time, a
bad memory from the past. But Europe's expansion across the Atlantic in
1492, and eventually in Africa and Asia, upset the world order and threw
all nations into the vortex of a European-defined globalization. Soon, the
Muslims who had come to Europe first as conquering warriors in 711, then
as grand chiefs and caliphs who turned marginal Iberia into the most advanced nation in western Europe, returned to the continent as lowly immigrants, determined to eke out a living but resolute in their commitment
to their faith and ways. As Europe's population continues its downward
trend, and as more immigrants are needed to fill jobs, the Muslim presence on European soil is being depicted as a major challenge to European
identity even though polls have shown that the vast majority of Muslims
in nations such as the Netherlands and France subscribe to the republican,
secular model of government.

It is nearly impossible to keep track of the mind-bending furor swirling
over the future of Europe in the age of Muslim minorities. Whether it's

I

Muslims erupting into violence to condemn cartoons that defame their faith and their Prophet, protesting the pope's selective allusion to the image of Islam in the medieval period, complaining about the beheading of the prophet Mohammed in an opera, condemning the selection of a Muslim woman for Miss United Kingdom, objecting to Britain's political leaders for their views on the *niqab* (the head-to-toe veil that shrouds the Muslim woman's body), a week rarely goes by without the West being reminded about the Muslims' strange costumes and customs. As if this were not enough, the problem of violence and terrorism complicates the controversy, because now, as in the decades and centuries following 1492, the Moors—all Moors—are suspected of being potential fifth columnists, members of sleeping cells, or secret agents of nebulous organizations in the rocky and rugged mountains of central Asia.

Even if there were no threat of terrorism, Muslim minorities and non-Muslim majorities would disagree loudly. Europeans would express the same anxieties over the upsetting of a familiar way of life and their diminishing control over the shape of their societies. In the last half millennium or so, most of the world has experienced such disruptions from European colonial powers; but when most of the world's nations obtained their political independence and were gradually incorporated into the process of globalization, Europe lost the ability to manage the global game of human movement and national destinies. It is, therefore, not inconceivable that what we are witnessing today is the last phase of the classical Reconquista, when first Spain and then the rest of Europe emerged out of their long war against Islam as the masters of the modern world. Moreover, if the rise of the West started in the fifteenth century, as Fareed Zakaria has shown in his recent book *The Post-American World* (2008), the leading Western power, the United States of America, is being challenged on every front—economic, cultural, and even political—by the ascendancy of non-Western nations that, only a few decades ago, had no resonance whatsoever. Nowadays, these emerging markets account for almost 40 percent of the global economy. By 2040, China, India, Brazil, Russia, and Mexico "will together have a larger economic output than the G-7 countries, the seven Western nations that have dominated global affairs for centuries." Ours may well be a new historical era as Europe and Anglo America are frantically trying to come to terms with the steadily collapsing tenets of the ideologies that have given them absolute power since 1492. "The descent of the West," wrote the historian Niall Ferguson in *The War of the World* (2006), is "the most important development of the twentieth century."[1]

In other words, as the myths of Europe's crusading, conquistador, and settler cultures are being challenged by the rise of new, nonwhite powers abroad and new demographic realities at home—the "blowback" or "boomerang" effect of relentless economic dispossession and endless military crusades—Western nations are understandably concerned about a future of diminished control over people of non-European heritage. Since the defeat of the Moors in Spain and the conquest of the New World, Euro-Americans have simply not had to worry about their racial and cultural hegemony. Now that they do, they are beginning to sound like the conquered and colonized of yesterday. Tensions keep mounting and, barring the massive deportation of more than 15 million Muslims from Europe, there is no clear path ahead. This is the dilemma hanging over Europe's future.

The United States is in the same situation in relation to both its Muslim immigrants and, especially, its Hispanic ones. As Mexicans and Hispanics keep pouring into the country, a growing and outspoken chorus of U.S. nationalists are describing their country as besieged and threatened by cultural changes that might very well imperil the republic. The United States, for them, is the unalloyed product of Anglo-Saxon ingenuity and has no option but to hold on to this legacy if it is not to go the retrograde way of Latin America. This view of the foundations of the nation often implies that American greatness was achieved by white Europeans and might very well be undermined by a Hispanic population still upset over the loss of their lands to Anglos in earlier centuries. A nation is great, according to them, only when it is culturally and racially unified. Thus, with a much smaller Muslim immigrant population and a much larger Hispanic one, the United States is wrestling with the same dilemmas besetting its European counterparts.

Indeed, anyone watching the events unfolding in Europe and the United States in recent years cannot help but be struck by the confluence of the two overriding concerns of these two continental states: the mounting anxiety over coexisting with Muslims and the seemingly unstoppable waves of illegal and nonassimilable immigrants. All sorts of explanations have been offered about these twin elements fueling the global crisis—bookshelves are filled with books about Islam, minorities, and questions of immigration—but no one seems to be reading the intense debate over immigration and minorities who resist assimilation as the continuation of a much older con-flict, the one pitting Christendom against the world of Islam. We are often being asked to ponder "what is wrong with Islam" and "what is wrong with the West," as if these two abstract, ideological entities suddenly bumped into each other in their travels and were jolted by the shock of discovery. The West encountered an archaic Islam stuck in the primitivism of pre-modern cultures, whereas Muslims discovered a dizzying, fast-dissolving secular West that is guided by the fleeting fantasies of materialism. All of this is by now amply documented. Yet what I propose in this book is that a secular, liberal Western culture and Islam were never really parted, that they have been traveling together since (at least) 1492, despite all attempts to demarcate, first, zones of Christian purity and, later, national homogeneity.

Without Islam, there would be no European identity to speak of, and no America, with all the consequences the "discovery" of this continent has entailed for the future of human civilization. By authorizing Christopher Columbus's mission to the East via the western Atlantic route, the Spanish monarchs King Ferdinand and Queen Isabella sponsored what amounted to a crusade whose ultimate goal was nothing less than the recapture of Jerusalem.[2] Even before the Renaissance, especially during the fifteenth century, when the Moor emerged as the foil against which Europe would define itself, the vexed relationship (or confrontation) with Islam had been the primordial element in the constitution of an unconscious form of Europeanness.[3] In his recently published history of the early encounters of Christians and Muslims in Europe, the Pulitzer Prize–winning historian David Levering Lewis shows that the term *Europenses,* or *Europeans,* was coined by Isidore Pacensis, an eighth-century Andalusian priest, to describe the new identity of Christians who defeated Muslim armies near Poitiers in 732. So significant was this confrontation in the formation of a sense of common European identity that early twentieth-century historians such as the French Ernest Lavisse and the German Hans Delbrück could still claim that this was the most decisive battle in the history of Europe or the West.[4] Christendom's conflict with Islam appeared so permanent that, as Samuel Huntington notes in *The Clash of Civilizations and the Remaking of the World Order* (1996), the "term *guerra fría* [cold war] was coined by thirteenth-century Spaniards to describe their 'uneasy coexistence' with Muslims in the Mediterranean."[5] Islam, in other words, whether in medieval

Christendom or in the secular West, has consistently maintained its troubling strangeness. Its specter has never vacated the West's unconscious.

Because of his or her quintessential difference in the long European imagination, the Moor, I want to show in this book, is not only someone who is religiously Muslim; even more importantly, he or she is also a figure that stands for anyone who is not considered to be part of the social mainstream. It is only in this *symbolic* or *metaphorical* sense that minorities living in the West after 1492 are the descendants of the Moors. Given that the archetypal Other of Europe *before* 1492 was the Muslim, the world's non-European natives or religions were all stamped with the taint of Muslim impurity. The Moor was, in the words of Emily Bartels, "first and foremost a figure of uncodified and uncodifiable diversity."[6] The West's minorities, whether Native Americans, enslaved Africans, Jews, or non-European, particularly Hispanic, immigrants (legal or illegal), would become indispensable for the expanding European and American, or Euro-American, sense of self after 1492, just as the Moor had been for Christian Europe up to that time. Not only this, but African Americans and Jews would embrace their Moorish heritage to fight back their exclusion or forced assimilation, whereas others, such as Hispanics and nonwhite immigrants of all sorts in the United States, would simply be invested with the Moor's quintessential attributes without anyone's making the connection between the Christian Crusades against the Moor and national policies to stem immigration.

My purpose, therefore, is to make those connections more visible by showing that, despite all our claims to modernity, we are far from having overcome medieval animosities and that the West and Islam are still locked in the fatal embrace that has been the distinguishing feature of their identities. This is not to give a one-dimensional interpretation of the long histories of discrimination against Jews, blacks, people of darker skin, and immigrants, nor to attribute such discrimination to Europeans and people of European descent only. Not at all. Most Arab nations, for instance, are more xenophobic in their immigration policies than even the least enlightened European country. Entire generations of a single family can live in an Arab country without qualifying for citizenship. The genocidal behavior toward minority groups in some parts of Africa, for another instance, dwarfs anything that is happening today in Western nations.

To the extent that minorities have been crucial in forging modern national identities, one needs to take into account—among other contributing factors—Christian Spain's pivotal role. So indispensable were Jewish and Muslim minorities to the nascent Castilian state that it instituted what amounted to racial safeguards against assimilation. Almost fifty years before Granada was taken by Catholic forces, a new law stressing purity of blood *(limpieza de sangre)* was promulgated in Toledo to avoid integrating converted Jews into the main professions and occupations. In this way, the state could unite the nation around a faith that would never, in theory, be accessible to descendants of Jews and Muslims. Minorities in this new scheme (which the church rejected, at first, because it undermined the redemptive powers of baptism) would serve as a rallying point for consolidating national unity, but these very useful minorities would also have to suffer permanent exclusion and harassment. The modern nation that was emerging in Catholic Iberia both depended on and deliberately punished its Others. This double contradiction, in some ways, has been the defining fate of nations ever since.

One simply cannot fully appreciate the precarious position of minorities in the modern world without having some sense of the historic clash between Christianity and Islam, and without seeing modern-day minorities as latter-day Moors—Muslims in disguise, as it were, wearing the masks of different religions and speaking different languages. Ideologically speaking, then, all minorities in the modern West can trace their genealogical origins to the Moor in Christian-ruled Spain. To say so is not to obviate the fact that the plight of the outsider is a universal and timeless condition, but only to propose that, to the extent that the condition of minorities today is coterminous with the rise of nation-states with membership ideologies and exclusion policies, the place of Islam in post-Reconquista Spain can no longer be ignored.

One might argue that the tragedy of the Moors is not a major concern to nations founded on the vilification of Islam, but how could one think about the long history of Western racism, the atrocities committed by the Nazi regime, the horrors of the Holocaust (ironically, it was Spain, as we shall see, that devised the first concentration camp, in Cuba), and the dreadful Communist police apparatuses without thinking about Spain's anti-Moorish legacy? The rise of a surveillance society in the last few decades and the steady encroachments on the right to privacy as necessary undertakings to protect nations against terrorists and immigrants are elements of a story that was promoted by the Inquisition in early modern Spain to maintain Iberia's cultural purity. By worrying about their national homogeneity and the integrity of their civilization, many conservative and right-wing Europeans and Americans unwilling to contemplate the fact that mixing is often the inevitable lot of nations, particularly in an age when national boundaries are too porous to allow for dreams of insularity, are replaying an old story, one that is full of pain and sorrow.

Muslims don't do much better in taking stock of this tragic episode, leading one of the most prominent scholars of Morisco culture to suggest that Muslims are more interested in promoting (ad nauseam, I might add) the legacy of great medieval Muslim philosophers or "the heroic conquerors of earlier periods."[7] It often appears as though Muslims spend more time reminding the West of the diminishing glories of the past than meditating on the failures and tragedies of their own history. When Muslim fanatics, for instance, recall Muslim Spain, or al-Andalus, it is often in terms of loss accompanied by the violent threat to reclaim their western outpost. But such remembrances and threats somehow disguise the fact that Spain had been Christian *before* it was conquered by the Muslim troops led by Tariq ibn Ziyad, the Moroccan Berber, in 711. This selective memory—often emanating from the Middle East and beyond, almost never from next-door Morocco, except in the case of the Spanish enclaves on Moroccan territory proper—doesn't help us think better about the problems facing Muslim minorities in non-Muslim states.

In many ways, Samuel Huntington was right to point out, in his era-defining book *The Clash of Civilizations and the Remaking of the World Order,* that the persistence of cultural memories is at the root of the problems besetting the world today. A whole range of literature exists to confirm the enduring and primordial importance of civilizations—sprawling, large, geographically imprecise, and evolving agglomerations of peoples, nations, and states sharing religion, language, ancestry, and values—and it would be utter folly, as Fernand Braudel suggested, to overlook this fact.[8] In this sense, Huntington provides a healthy counterbalance to Edward Said's broad-brush theory of *Orientalism* (first published in 1978), whose effect—although it was not necessarily Said's intention—is to present a one-dimensional story of (Western) villains and (Muslim or Arab) victims. Daniel Martin Varisco's exhaustive study of Said's book, as well as of its reception and influence, shows clearly that Said was too selective and polemical to have given us a good sense of the vexed history of East and West.[9] But if Said was speaking as a third-world pugilist fighting back against a West that had trampled on his tradition back in Palestine and the Middle East as a whole, Huntington is speaking as an American realist, one who despite being aware of the vicissitudes of history still wants to hold on to Western supremacy for as long as possible. He knows that the West is fighting against the odds of globalization and the inevitable rise to power of unfriendly nations. As the West's share of world populations and territories is receding, the only options it has left to contain its diminished influence are to restrict the dissemination of technology to non-Western civilizations (a policy that is now being vigorously pursued by the United States in relation to Iran, for instance) and to implement anti-immigration policies.[10] This is where Huntington's realism went astray in the 1990s, and it continues to muddle his thinking in his more recent book on Hispanic immigration, *Who Are We?* for such stopgap measures have the effect of maintaining violence at the heart of global relations and poisoning the promise of cultural goodwill without, in the long term, yielding the sought-after outcomes. To think that a society or civilization can be frozen into an essence is exactly the trouble with the kind of nationalism pursued by the anti-immigrant patriots of all nations.

To disagree with Huntington's shortsighted solutions is not to deny that religions and cultures have a tendency to clash. The persecution of Moors and Moriscos is part of a complex history that began with the advent of Islam in the seventh century and the long struggle for supremacy between the two contending faiths. Each party had reason to suspect and mistrust the other. Moreover, highlighting the Christian injustices committed against Muslims (and Jews) in Spain after 1492 in no way implies that Muslims have been innocent bystanders or that they are not capable of similar behaviors. There is no denying that Islam and Christianity had been at war—hot or cold—since the birth of the younger faith, just as there is no overlooking the real tensions arising today among devout Muslims who inhabit the West's liberal and secular spaces. The dictates of Islam's strict and rigorous monotheism *do* hamper successful integration into culturally pluralistic societies, which is, in my mind, a far more pressing issue to resolve than the overtrumpeted idea of a clash of civilizations. Two or more cultural tendencies can and do coexist within a single nation, which is why many Muslim fundamentalists—as well as their Christian peers in the United States—target their own national institutions with the same passion that they malign rival faiths and civilizations. If Moors, therefore, appear as victims in this book, it is only because they are essential to understanding the cultural origins of minorities in the West. Given that minorities presume the existence of a nation united around a common heritage (whether such heritage is primarily ethnic, religious, racial, or any combination of the three), they are, like the Moors of old, both indispensable sacrificial bodies (burnt offerings) and the target of exclusionary policies ranging from expulsion to genocide.

It is the Moors' religious and cultural difference that allowed sixteenth-century Castilian monarchs to forge a slippery notion of identity, one that sounds ominously modern in its racist assumptions, even though, strictly speaking, it was not informed by the scientific notions of race that led to the genocidal policies of colonial powers and fascist regimes in the modern age. Spain's purity-of-blood statute was a departure from classic forms of exclusion and discrimination, because, at least semantically, faith and blood were united in an indivisible whole. Modern racism would seemingly separate these terms to privilege one (biology) over the other (religion); but in late medieval Spain, the combination of blood and faith formed the cornerstone of a new apartheid regime, one whose consequences were quite tragic. The expulsion of Moriscos in 1609—what the eminent historian of Spain Henry Kamen called "the biggest ethnic cleansing to have been carried out in western history" until the twentieth century[11]—was, then, part of a Castilian political philosophy whose aim was to conflate religious and political unity into an undifferentiated ideology, one that would enable Castilian monarchs (in alliance with the Aragonese ones, joined in marriage since 1469) to seek imperial ventures overseas and at home. The Moors and Moriscos turned out to be an invaluable device to unite the fragmented Iberian Peninsula around this vision; by doing so, Spain inadvertently defined the role of minority communities in post-Reconquista nation-states, and so shaped the destiny of the modern world—our world—in profound ways.

Chapter 1 of this book, "Pious Cruelty," named for the phrase Niccolò Machiavelli used to describe King Ferdinand's cynical treatment of his Moorish vassals, shows how the effects of the Spanish notions of nation, race, and minorities have led to the worst horrors of our own times. If Spain didn't invent modern racism, it certainly was the first to racialize religious and cultural difference on a massive scale. Only in the nineteenth century did it rescind its purity-of-blood policy, by which time a more insidious form of racism was taking hold of Europe's imagination.

Obviously, the expulsion of Moors and Moriscos from Spain and the multiple decrees to prevent Muslims from residing anywhere in Spain's empire across the Atlantic did not eliminate Muslim presence from either continent. Despite authorities' repeated attempts to prevent their presence in the New World, both Jews and Muslims (among other undesirable groups) were part of the sixteenth-century transatlantic culture. The Moorish legacy was introduced to the Americas by the Spaniards themselves, for Spain was so hopelessly multicultural that neither the Inquisition nor the expulsion of Jews and Moors was sufficient to cleanse its heritage from centuries of cultural borrowing and influences. Islam was, thus, paradoxically carried to the Americas in the arms of Christian conquistadors.

Christian Spain's long history of clashes with the Moors was encoded in the names and design of new towns and expressed in a variety of cultural practices. America's indigenous people, makers of some of the greatest civilizations in history, were treated like Moors and subjected to a relentless war of extermination. "The conquest of the Indians," wrote Francisco López de Gómara in his *Historia general de las indias* (1552), "began after that of the Moors was completed, so that Spaniards would ever fight the infidels."[12] Indians were seen as less than human, unworthy of much except total submission to European rule. "God has never created a race more full of vice and composed without the least mixture of kindness or culture," the Dominican Tomás Ortiz told the Council of the Indies, the king-appointed body that had ultimate authority over Spain's extensive dominions.[13] The crusade against Indians was devastating, but the persecuted natives resisted as best they could, thereby extending the Christian-Muslim war, at the symbolic level, to our times.

The Moors also arrived in America as black slaves who set out to fight for their rights from the moment they landed. Like their coreligionists in Spain, the Moriscos, Muslim slaves in the Americas resisted oppression and held on to their faith and languages in spite of isolation and the passing of time. Because Islam reconnects many contemporary African Americans "with a heritage of Afro-Islamic identity that was broken by the Atlantic slave trade," Robert Dannin has called the conversion of African Americans to Islam (which turns the converts into a "double minority") a "black pilgrimage to Islam."[14] As late as 1964, Malcolm X could still provocatively claim that he was not an American but "one of the 22 million black people who are victims of Americanism."[15] The story of African Muslims in America is the subject of "New World Moors," the second chapter of this book. Although this aspect of American history still requires a more systematic academic approach, I take heart in the admirable pioneering scholars whose work has guided me in my own explorations.

Muslims found their way to the New World and Islam survived in European culture, either through its extensive cultural legacy or, in one of the most remarkable episodes of Semitic solidarity in the face of an upstart European civilization, through many Jews' identification with Islam and Moorish traditions. Many Jews, or "Mosaic Arabs" in the expression of Britain's legendary prime minister Benjamin Disraeli, adopted their Islamic heritage to better resist Europe's design on the Orient and its people. Thus, as Africans were struggling against slavery and racism in the United States, and America as a whole, by relying on the strength that Islam provides, Jews in Europe were proudly displaying their Moorish heritage to counter European anti-Semitism with the claim that they belonged to the far grander stock of the Arab nation. Not only did many prominent Jews, including Disraeli, see themselves as Arabs or admire the Islamic faith, but also many Jewish communities used Moorish designs to build their synagogues, some claiming that Moorish architecture was the closest to the original model of their ancient temple in Jerusalem. The U.S. government, recognizing the close cultural bonds of Jews and Muslims, deliberately appointed the former to important ambassadorial and consular posts in Muslim nations such as Turkey. When the Jewish Simon Wolf, biographer of Mordecia Noah, was appointed consul in Cairo in 1881, right in the midst of Ahmad 'Urabi's revolt against the corrupt khedive and his Western masters, Wolf sympathized with the revolt and expressed a not-uncommon view: "As an Israelite, a brother of the Arab branch of the human family, I fully appreciate all [the Egyptians] long for. I feel grateful for Mahammadens for their shelter and protection and [the] freedom my brethren enjoyed for years in Moslem countries."[16] I examine such affinities in chapter 3, titled "Muslim Jews," by looking at the common fate of Jews and Muslims as Christian Europe's Others since the Middle Ages. As the Christians launched the Crusades against Muslims, Jews came to be seen as "Muslims" at home and therefore were persecuted as the natural allies of the crusaders' Muslim enemies. To cite but one example: in 1321, one year before they were expelled from

France, French Jews were accused of conspiring with Moors in Spain and Morocco to poison wells and were burned.[17]

Indeed, Jews and Arabs were rather indiscernible in the European imagination well into the modern period, partly because, as Gil Anidjar points out in his book *Semites* (2008), race and religion operated in one and the same register. Religion, a nineteenth-century European concept, was simply a cover for race. This explains why the prominent French philologist Ernest Renan's declared war on *la chose sémitique* (the Semitic thing) targeted Jews and Arabs indiscriminately: both religious communities represented "the Semitic spirit" in its purest form. In this reading, ancient Israel is part of Arab culture—a defective part, to be sure, as the eighteenth-century German philosopher Immanuel Kant stated in his description of Jews as Palestinians. Thus, in Renan's quest for a higher social order, the "eternal war" on the Semite "will not cease until the last son of Ishmael has died of misery or has been relegated to the ends of the desert by way of terror."[18] Reading through this history makes us wonder how things ended up the way they are now, especially if Zionism itself would not have been conceivable without the Jews' strong consciousness of their oriental heritage.[19] Even the atheist Karl Marx, the dark-featured descendant of German Jews, was called "Moor" by his family and close friends. It was as a Moor that the man who announced the specter of communism signed his last letter to Friedrich Engels in January 1883.[20]

It is within this broad historical context that the current debate over Muslim and Hispanic immigration in Europe and the United States (the subject of chapter 4, "Undesirable Aliens: Hispanics in America, Muslims in Europe") begins to appear to be another instance of Spain's crusading medieval spirit, another anxious quest for national purity, even as the world's communities are increasingly aware of the instabilities generated by a global economic system that pays no heed whatsoever to such archaic sentiments. With the assimilation of the Jews and their migration to Israel, the Moors of old returned to Europe as immigrants unable to fully assimilate into European culture. Anti-Semitism, which condemned Jews to exclusion because of their racial unfitness during the high age of nationalism, has now given way to Islamophobia, the new political platform of the European Right, allowing right-wing movements to shed their old, untenable hatred of Jews and replace it with the condemnation of Islam as a culture that is incompatible with the principles and high aspirations of a European civilization.[21] (*Islamophobia* is a term that is assumed to be of recent coinage but was, in fact, used as early as 1966 by the Peruvian scholar Rafael Guevara Bazán to describe sixteenth-century Spain's fear of Muslim immigration to the New World.) These immigrants, like their Hispanic counterparts in the United States, are now triggering the free rein of ancient prejudices. In the chapter I will read Samuel Huntington's book on Hispanic immigration, *Who Are We?* (2005)—a natural follow-up to his *Clash of Civilizations and the Remaking of the World Order*—within this context and the long history of nativism and Anglo-Saxon racism in the United States. With the idea that nations and civilizations have immutable cultural and racial characteristics being given such academic legitimacy, no wonder journalists and pundits who preach the same message are finding receptive audiences in both Europe and, particularly, the United States.

Europe, in the Spenglerian pessimism and doomsday predictions of anti-Muslim immigrant advocates, has turned into Eurabia, a concept borrowed from the title of a newsletter founded in 1975 and given ominous connotations by the Egyptian-born, Switzerland-based British citizen Bay Ye'or (the pen name of Giselle Litmann), author of *Eurabia: The Euro-Arab Axis* (2005). Such conspiracy-laden views were once associated with the neofascist fringe but have now entered the cultural mainstream, not only diffused by pundits and journalists such as the late renowned and controversial Italian journalist Oriana Fallaci ("the grand dame of Eurabian discourse," in Matt Carr's expression)[22] and the Canadian conservative Mark Steyn, but also invoked by scholars such as Bernard Lewis, the historian Niall Ferguson, and Winston Churchill's biographer Martin Gilbert. It is in this sense that the fear of European cultural and racial extinction dovetails seamlessly with Samuel Huntington's thesis in *Who Are We?*

Consider, for instance, the warnings of Fallaci following the attacks of 9/11. During her self-imposed exile in Manhattan, she witnessed the tragedy from close range and decided to embark on a "crusade of words" and fight back the "nazifascism" of Islamic fundamentalism—a laudable goal, if that's what Islamic fundamentalism is—and take on any challenges that might result. In *The Rage and the Pride* (2002), her initial salvo (or "sermon," as she called it) against Islam in the West, Fallaci downplays the Muslim contribution to world civilization, because she is far more concerned about the assault of Islamic fundamentalism on Western culture and traditions.[23] With a few exceptions, such as the medieval Aristotelian philosopher Averroës,

as well as "some poets and some mosques and the way of writing the numbers," Islam, she asserts, doesn't even come close to matching the achievements of the West.[24] Yet it is this backward civilization, blindly praised and
defended by a host of politically correct or liberal westerners, that is now
threatening the great achievements of Europe. Little do these duplicitous
"cicadas," as Fallaci calls the self-defeating Western liberals, know that only
the United States could save the West from the Muslim barbarians.[25] These
are the same views advanced by Canadian conservative Mark Steyn, whose
doomsday warning about the Islamic takeover of the West in the book
America Alone (2006) not only made the *New York Times* best-seller list but
also was read and recommended by President George W. Bush. "You can't
win a war of civilizational confidence," the witty, tough-minded Steyn commented, "with a [European] population of nanny-state junkies."[26]

   Predictably, the ailing Fallaci's uncensored comments turned her into the
"Orhyena" of the liberals she dismissed—as the Italian newspaper *La Repub-
blica* dubbed her, an ignorant "exhibitionist posing as the Joan of Arc of
the West"[27]—but she also became a darling of political conservatives who
shared her views. While the author's courage for writing *The Rage and the
Pride* and denouncing Islam after 9/11 was suspected by the French intellectual Bernard-Henri Lévy to be a new form of anti-Semitism, it was
praised by French philosophers such as Alain Finkielkraut and American
conservatives.[28] In a speech she gave in New York to the Center of the
Study of Popular Culture on November 28, 2005, during which she was
awarded the Annie Taylor Award in recognition of her "resistance to
Islamo-fascism," whose Qur'an is the "*Mein Kampf* of a religion which has
always aimed to eliminate the others," she was once again unsparing in her
hatred of liberals and members of the "Caviar Left," the new Torquemadas
such as Noam Chomsky and the filmmaker Michael Moore, people she
hated "as much as I hated Mussolini and Hitler and Stalin and Company."
She reminded her admirers in New York that they were a truly embattled
group, "outlaws-heretics-dissidents" fighting, against overwhelming odds,
a mostly Islamophilic, Westphobic, and anti-American media. (Before she
gave this speech, she had been indicted by an Italian judge for *vilipendio,* or
defamation, and expected to stand trial in June 2006.)[29] Neither of the Left
nor of the Right, and considering herself a mere "revolutionary" struggling
for "the No," Fallaci was already seeing the time when Europeans would
become "natives," the "indigenous" or the "aborigines" of the continent.[30]

Fallaci's New York speech capped a fascinating, Cassandra-like warning in *The Force of Reason* (2006), a book she again translated herself, from the Italian *La Forza della ragione,* as if the betrayals of translation pertaining to such life-and-death matters as the Muslim invasion of Europe were somehow attenuated by the use of awkward idiomatic and syntactic English. Feeling persecuted by a new, secular inquisition that tortures the soul, not the body, the "Christian atheist" Fallaci was bent on alerting a somnolent Europe to the fact that, like Troy, it is burning, because Europe is becoming a province, a "colony" of Islam. Remember, she said, had Charles Martel not won the battle of Poitiers in 732, the French also would be dancing the flamenco. Because of this historical precedent, the tens of millions of Muslims living in Europe (however defined) today constitute the new armies of Muslim reconquest. The eighth-century French, as Mark Steyn suggests, had the unshakable will to repel the marauding Muslim armies, but "today, a fearless Muslim advance has penetrated far deeper into Europe than Abd al-Rahman."[31] Consequently, Europe has become a real Eurabia with pure Arab or Maghrebian cities such as Marseilles. The case of Spain is even worse, for in this border zone "Islamization [*sic*] occurs with more spontaneity," as if Islam were in the blood. The Muslim Albaicín quarter in Granada is literally a state within a state, even with its own currency! (Fallaci didn't seem to realize that Albaicín is the old *morería,* or Muslim ghetto, of post-Reconquista Granada.)

In Italy, too, Fallaci finds attempts to carve out similar Muslim spaces. Not only that, but Muslims in Fallaci's country are trying to ban the teaching of Dante Alighieri's *Divine Comedy,* Saint Francis of Assisi's *Canticle of the Creatures,* and Voltaire's works (because of his *Le Fanatisme ou Mahomet le prophète*), as well as to erase offensive frescoes in cathedrals, bury their own against health regulations, build mosques against zoning laws, and so on—all with the sheepish complicity of liberals and leftists. Of course, there are now grand mosques in all the major capitals of Europe, let alone the hundreds of smaller ones that dot the continent.[32] Don't self-hating Europeans know, Fallaci asks, that Constantinople was desecrated by Muslim rapists and pedophiles, and that the Crusades were a "counter-offensive," and don't Italians remember when their ancestors, on the lookout for marauding Ottomans, screamed, "Mamma, li turchi!" (Mother, the Turks!)?[33] Despite such views, Fallaci insists that she is not a right-wing conspiracy monger, particularly given that what passes for Right and Left today are mere semantic fictions, for the "filthy, reactionary, obtuse, feudal Right" has not been a feature of Europe since the American and French revolutions; this Right has survived only in Latin America ("where western civilization is a dream never achieved") and, especially, in the world of Islam.[34] Thus, in one inadvertent stroke, Fallaci manages to conflate Muslims and Latinos as anti-Euro-American and invites us to consider the two social groups as a serious threat to the West.

While Europe's high culture is being besieged by the invasion of Muslim hordes, unchecked Hispanic immigration, the conservative commentator Patrick Buchanan warns in his *State of Emergency* (2006), is hastening the death of the United States and the end of Western civilization. If Europe has become Eurabia, California is already Mexifornia, paving the way for further inroads into the nation's Anglo identity. Enthralled by the god of markets and influenced by the elites' empty talk about diversity and multiculturalism (since, unlike the anti-immigrant working classes, elites rarely have to live next door to poor Spanish-speaking immigrants), U.S. political leaders have lost all will to defend their nation and heritage, even when an intifada has already erupted at the U.S.-Mexican border. Though his treatise is devoted mostly to the United States, Buchanan takes some time to reflect on European affairs, calling the presence of 20 million Muslim immigrants Europe's "return of the Moor." He displays a sense of history that is central to the argument of this book, namely, that the Western civilization that emerged in the aftermath of the defeat of Islam in Spain is coming to an end: "From 1492 to 1914, Europeans went forth to conquer, colonize, and command the peoples of this earth. Then, between 1914 and 1945, Europe's imperial powers indulged themselves in two of the bloodiest wars in all history, on their own continent. Comes now the closing chapter: the colonization of the mother countries by the children of the subject peoples that Europe once ruled."[35] Let us be clear, says Buchanan in the last chapter of his book, "Last Chance": "The existential crisis of Western civilization does not come from Islamic terrorism" but from the West's "paralysis" on the issue of immigration.

Instead of seeing the current form of national identity as no longer suitable for new global realities, as I will eventually show, Buchanan gives biological and tribal shapes to nations, unwittingly taking us back to medieval and early modern Spain, for it was there that national identities, made possible by the persecution of Jewish and Muslim minorities, were imagined in such terms for the first time. It's hard to remember that much (but not all) of what applies Muslim minorities today once applied to the Jews as well. To its credit, when reviewing Fallaci's *The Force of Reason,* the conservative *New York Sun* (now a defunct publication) thought it prudent to make a connection that is ultimately the problem with this sort of nationalism:

> The more serious problem is the sweeping nature of [Fallaci's] condemna-
> tion of Islam and Muslims. She faults them for the fact that "they breed like
> rats"; for requiring their meat to be slaughtered in a "barbaric" manner she
> says is similar to kosher butchery; for having their own schools, hospitals, and
> cemeteries; for immigrating; and for wanting accommodation of their reli-
> gious holidays and Sabbath in schools and workplaces.
>
> Much of her complaint about Islam, in other words, might as well be
> directed at Orthodox Jews, and a good deal of it at American Catholics.[36]

The attack on Muslim and Hispanic immigrants is not merely an academic matter. I will discuss the case of the two communities more extensively later in the book, but it's worth noting here that political and legislative debates in Europe and the United States are very much attuned to such "warnings." Although both Moroccans and Mexicans have strong historical attachments to the nations they are now trying to immigrate to, the Spanish scholar Ana Maria Manzanas Calvo has argued, Spain (and, by extension, Europe) and the United States imagine their southern borders as the last defense against the dissolution of their national identities.[37]

Not long after Fallaci, Steyn, and Buchanan issued their apocalyptic ser-mons, an extreme right-wing Swiss political party, eager to warn Swiss cit-izens about the perils of unchecked immigration from darker nations, including Muslim ones, published a picture of three white sheep standing on the Swiss flag while kicking a black one out. The Swiss People's Party, or SVP, claimed that its anti-immigrant policies, including the deportation of the innocent relatives of immigrants who committed crimes (a com-mon practice in Nazi Germany), were simply a security measure designed to protect the purity of the Swiss nation.[38] Around the same time, French- and Dutch-speaking Belgians, caught in a heated argument over the iden-tity of a nation divided between Wallonia and Flanders, abruptly suspended their squabbles and united over the threat immigrants posed to their coun-try.[39] A few months before the Belgians and the Swiss publicly wrestled over what to with their Muslim immigrants, the U.S. Congress and the White House had come to a virtual standstill over the issue of illegal, particularly Hispanic and Mexican, immigration. For many U.S. politicians and scholars, the matter was not to be taken lightly: as Buchanan suggested, the bedraggled, Spanish-speaking border crosser or settler has become the ultimate security threat to the American nation. According to this logic, the Mexican state, which actively encourages immigration and promotes the rights of its citizens in the United States, might as well be blacklisted as a sponsor of terrorism.

It's hard to find the right place to start when talking about the swirling debate over Hispanic immigration in the United States, but one place as good as any is an April 2006 speech by President George W. Bush, who came into office promising some sort of entente with President Vicente Fox of Mexico on the contentious subject. Bush, addressing an audience in Orange County, California (one of the most anti-Hispanic enclaves in that state, as we shall see), acknowledged to business leaders that the topic of immigration is "emotional" and that, regardless of what position one might take on it, "massive deportation of the people here is unrealistic. It's just not going to work. You can hear people out there hollering it's going to work. It's not going to work."[40] What is remarkable about President Bush's statement, repeated when he spoke directly to the nation from the Oval Office on May 15 of that same year, is that deporting an estimated 12 million illegal immigrants must have been a serious option—or else why would he plead with his audience to realize the impossibility of the task?[41] Relieved that mass deportation was not an option, one man wrote to the *New York Times* and described what such an operation might entail:

> First, each arrest would require probable cause. (A bullhorn and a police wagon will not suffice.) And if the arrestee declined to speak and had no papers, an investigation would have to be conducted to determine where he hailed from. Scores of lockups and courts would have to be built, and thousands of police officers and judges would have to be hired. Many, many vehicles for transporting the deportees would need to be procured. . . . Some illegal immigrants would die trying to escape apprehension, and others would die on the journey home. Some would lose their possessions; others, their loved ones. Not pretty. Not pretty at all.[42]

Reading this, I couldn't help but hear a disturbing echo of sixteenth-century Spain's high-level deliberations on what to do with the Moors and Moriscos, as chapter 1 will show. The *Times* reader's picture of the logistics involved and the impact on the deportees and the society at large is eerily reminiscent of the periodic persecutions visited on the Moors after 1492. The more I listened to the acrimonious dispute over the fate of illegal aliens in the United States, the more I realized the extent to which modern Western nations are still operating by the principles of Spanish conquistadors and inquisitors in their war against Islam. Spain's crusade for religious purity was not a blessing to that nation, but the delusion that a nation could regain its strength by excluding those who are different, the minorities who don't belong to the common stock, continues to drive states to the brink of folly.

The controversy over immigration reform emerged when the House of Representatives passed the Border Protection, Antiterrorism, and Illegal Immigration Control Act of 2005—better known as HR 4437—sponsored by the Republican representatives F. James Sensenbrenner, from Wisconsin, and Peter King, from New York, and passed (233 to 189) on December 16, 2005, making illegal aliens and those who harbor or assist them felons, tightening up the Mexico-U.S. border, and screening inbound airline passengers to the United States, among many other tough, security-minded provisions.[43] Interfaith organizations quickly signed a statement to denounce this scheme and highlight the obligation, stated in the Bible and Qur'an, to honor the stranger as one's own.[44] Cardinal Roger Mahony openly declared his dissent in the pages of the *New York Times* and led marches in Los Angeles, the largest archdiocese in the nation, which is also "75 percent Latino."[45] Such Las Casas–like figures and dozens of similarly minded organizations soon inspired some of the largest mass protests in American history.[46] On March 25, 2006, tens of thousands of Hispanics and their allies protested in cities across the nation; in Los Angeles alone, between 500,000 and 1 million people, including thousands of students waving Mexican flags and chanting "Viva Mexico!" marched to denounce this draconian bill. "Attendance at the demonstration," wrote the *Los Angeles Times,* "far surpassed the number of people who protested against the Vietnam War."[47] A few weeks later, even bigger rallies were staged around the nation. In Dallas, more than 350,000 people came out in support of immigrants' rights. One granddaughter of Jewish immigrants who had fled czarist

Russia joined the crowds in New York to register her solidarity.[48] More powerfully, the bill reminded Andrew S. Grove, a Jewish survivor of Nazi Germany and former chairman of Intel Corporation, of his own childhood experience hiding from the Nazis in Hungary. "I saw," Grove wrote in the *Wall Street Journal*, "how the persecution of non-Jewish Hungarians who hid their Jewish friends or neighbors cast a wide blanket of fear over everyone. This fear led to mistrust, and mistrust led to hostility, until neighbors turned upon neighbors in order to protect themselves. Is this what we want?"[49]

In fact, even when they came to the United States as "displaced persons" in the 1950s, Holocaust survivors were met with the same disdain and persecution reserved today for other minorities. So harsh was their treatment at times that one survivor, a father of three, told his caseworker that "he was more concerned and more disturbed now than he had ever been in the Warsaw Ghetto." These survivors turned out to be far more resilient and a more important asset to their new nation than any of the patriotic officers who harassed them. As with the Jews of that era, Pedro Biaggi, the boyish "host of the morning show on Washington's 99.1 El Zol," declared in 2006, "Never have we Latinos felt as insecure and persecuted as we do now. I'm Puerto Rican. But I'm brown, too." But Biaggi added, "I am my audience, and I feel totally committed to helping them." A Salvadoran construction worker agreed that "racism in this country has grown so much it's time to say, 'Enough!'"[50]

Of course, the strong anti-immigrant forces haven't vanished. (After all, polls often show that most Americans are against illegal immigration.) In 2006, the *Los Angeles Times* reported that Michelle Dallacroce, a Lexus SUV driver, had formed Mothers against Illegal Aliens "because she feared for the future of her two young children, who could be ignored in a United States dominated by Mexican-born people." Without a moment's hesitation, she described Mexicans' invasion of her country and their use of social services as "genocide" and "rape" (exactly how Fallaci described the Muslim takeover of Europe).[51] When flared tempers calmed down a bit and the issue began to fade from view after the HR 4437 protests, Gustavo Arellano, a "fourth-generation descendant of *naranjeros* (orange pickers)" and the author of ¡Ask a Mexican! a column in the *OC (Orange County, Calif.) Weekly*, reflected on anti-Mexicanism as a whole—particularly in Orange County, headquarters to Taco Bell yet "the Mexican-bashing capital of the

United States" and the very place where President Bush addressed business leaders, telling them that deportation was impractical. The occasion was the staging of *The Mexican OC,* a play that highlights the discrimination against Mexicans in the "county of milk and Mickey." Grim as it is, the play, in Arellano's view, nevertheless omits sentiments such as, "Illegal aliens shouldn't be deported; they should be deep-fried," a statement once made by a former Republican Immigration and Naturalization Service commissioner and Newport Beach resident, Harold Ezell, as well as the common profiling of Mexicans as criminals. Racism explains Orange County's "Mexiphobic streak," because the county's "psyche is wired to view brown-skinned folks as perpetual peons." It is that simple for Arellano.[52]

The prejudice against Latinos extended to the area of language, given that the category of Hispanic conflates race and language.[53] When "Nuestro Himno," the Spanish version of "The Star-Spangled Banner," whose chorus reads, "Tell me! Does its starry beauty still wave / Above the land of the free, / The sacred flag?" was aired in April 2006 (mostly on Spanish-language radio stations), the Anglo reaction was swift and immediate. President Bush commented that "people who want to be a citizen of this country ought to learn English and they ought to learn to sing the national anthem in English," a comment he repeated in his address to the nation on May 15, 2006.[54] (It is interesting to note that around the same time that the U.S. national hymn was produced in Spanish, Germans were debating whether to allow a Turkish version of their own.)[55]

Three days after Bush's speech, the U.S. Senate voted to accept two amendments to its own immigration bill: one, by James Inhofe, of Oklahoma, declaring English the national language of the United States and directing the government and its agencies to communicate only in English, except in authorized cases; the other, simply adding the banal statement that English unites all Americans. Both measures seem to have been founded on nativist fears, given that a university study, based on the 2000 census, had reported in 2004 that children and grandchildren of Hispanic immigrants preferred English over any other language. The *New York Times* lashed out at this insidious form of xenophobia masquerading as public policy, a policy that is, moreover, "exclusionary, potentially discriminatory and embarrassingly hostile to the rest of the world." The *Times* made a point of reminding its readers of the nativist strain that runs through American history, citing the Chinese Exclusion Act of 1882, the Know-Nothings, and the Ku Klux Klan as examples.[56] However, one can go even further, both in space and in time, to realize that the "Hispanic panic," as the great-great-grandson of a Swedish immigrant who died speaking his native tongue in Iowa put it, is a problem with deeper roots in the United States and also applies to Muslims in Europe.[57] A few months before Senator Inhofe's amendment passed, the Netherlands' conservative minister of integration and immigration, Rita Verdonk, caused an uproar in her homeland by sharing her plans to allow only Dutch to be spoken in the streets.[58] (Verdonk was the same woman who infuriated much of the Western world by trying to revoke the citizenship of the Somali-born critic of Islam and member of Parliament Ayaan Hirsi Ali because Ali had misrepresented her biography to gain asylum and, later, citizenship.)[59]

In reporting on the passage of Senator Inhofe's amendment (the vote was 63 to 34), the British *Independent* titled the news "At Last, America Has an Official Language (and Yes, It's English)." The newspaper saw fit to add the facts that the colonists attempted to defeat German for the honor of the national language; that German was the language of instruction for 6 percent of American schoolchildren before World War I (losing ground only when German Americans became suspect fifth columnists, as Marc Shell shows in his study of language politics in America);[60] and that today more than 47 million Americans "speak a language other than English at home."[61]

In fact, German was such a contender for the American colonies' primary language that, in 1732, Benjamin Franklin published the first German newspaper in North America. Perhaps because of the failure of this venture, he turned against both Germans and their ways. In "Observations concerning the Increase of Mankind" (1751), Franklin complained about German aliens—"Palatine boors," he called them—who stuck to their native ways and resisted anglicization, settlers who "will never adopt our Language or Customs, any more than they can acquire our Complexion."[62] Did we hear "complexion"? Yes, because for Franklin, most Europeans (including the French, Swedes, and Germans) were "swarthy" and only the English were truly white. "These are the arguments used against Italians, Jews, and others a hundred years ago," comments Roger Daniels, a senior historian of American immigration, "and may be heard today against 'Mexicans, Latinos, Hispanics, etc.' The targets have changed, but the complaints remain largely the same. Their gravamen is simply this: they are not like us."[63] That

immigrants often speak and write in their native tongues is, of course, a
common experience in American history. As the *Washington Post* columnist Richard Cohen reminded his readers in 2006, early in the twentieth
century Henry Adams expressed contempt for the Yiddish-speaking Jews
in the Lower East Side of New York City, yet the people "doing Kosher"
printed newspapers in their native language to participate in the democratic life of their adopted land, and their progeny grew up to be masters of
English, while their old quarters have turned into the chic East Village.[64]
Things do change.

Spanish is not considered good enough for Anglo-American democracy;
it's the language of the "brown-skinned" folks, the "peons" who should be
"deep-fried." When an article published in the *National Interest* around the
same time that HR 4437 was passing in Congress (fall 2005) sets out to
explain that Anglos are best suited to rule the world because of their innate
comfort with capitalism and long history of good governance, both of which
generate the necessary wealth to arm them adequately for their global tasks,[65]
one gets a sense that Pedro Biaggi, the radio host, and Gustavo Arellano,
the *OC Weekly* columnist, are confronting deeply ingrained nativist and racist forces that only a demographic overhaul of this self-conscious, exclusive
world could force to change.

Not long after the uproar over and the fiasco of HR 4437 (only the
border-fence provision, reintroduced as the Secure Fence Act on September 13, 2006, was rescued from the comprehensive immigration act and
passed by the Senate), Senator Harry Reid, of Nevada, introduced the Secure
Borders, Economic Opportunity, and Immigration Reform Act of 2007 to
bring an end to the escalating issue. Although President Bush supported
legalizing qualified aliens, the vitriol generated by interest groups and right-
wing organizations, such as NumbersUSA, led to the removal of the bill
from the Senate agenda on June 28, 2007. During the debate on the Senate floor, Republican senators Mel Martinez, of Florida, Richard Burr, of
North Carolina, and Lindsay Graham, of South Carolina, received threatening calls and letters urging them to oppose the "amnesty bill." Senator
Graham knew that racism was the issue. "Nobody likes to talk about it,"
he said, "but a very small percentage of people involved in this debate really
have racial and bigoted remarks. The tone that we create around these
debates, whether it be rhetoric in a union hall or rhetoric on talk radio, it
can take people who are on the fence and push them over emotionally." A

cosponsor of the bill, Edward M. Kennedy, of Massachusetts, asked about his opponents' plans: "What are they going to do with the 12 million who are undocumented here? Send them back to countries around the world? Develop a type of Gestapo here to seek out these people that are in the shadows?" Fears of globalization and anxiety over jobs and stability were definitely a significant factor in the emotional debates surrounding the bill (major U.S. businesses supported the bill), but there was also no doubt that immigrants were seen as a cultural threat to the nation. Tom Tancredo, the Republican representative of a privileged, mostly white Denver suburb in Colorado and a presidential aspirant, simply said, "I believe we are in a clash of civilizations."[66]

Thus, while nations are stumbling over one another to sign free-trade agreements, fences and boundaries, both real and digital, are being mounted on the fault lines separating poverty and wealth to maintain the fiction of national essences. The truth is that the edges of privilege are being militarized within and between nations, as gated communities and other exclusive housing schemes dot the global landscape to keep the approaching hordes of barbarians at safe distances. As I argue in the conclusion, "We Are All Moors," to think that displays of militant chauvinism are an answer to the question of legal and illegal immigration in a world marked by massive social inequities, or that nativist crusades against trespassers and those who are different could preserve the elusive identities we imagine for ourselves, is simply to delay the day of reckoning and aggravate the fallout from the clashes still lying ahead. There is reason to believe that the forced exclusion of minorities will lead to the unity and stability imagined by national purists or scheming politicians. Yet, more than five hundred years after Castile captured Granada and expelled Jews, the Iberian Peninsula's unity has never materialized in quite the way the Catholic Monarchs had dreamed. (The Catalans and Basques, for instance, continue to resist Castilian hegemony to this day.) Furthermore, globalization has turned us all into strangers desperately reaching out to dreams of wholeness, and unless we reconsider the notion of human economies that enrich lives not as specters to be exorcised from our imagination but as virtues to be eagerly embraced, chasing Moors and minorities will remain a futile pursuit and a dangerous and colossal waste of time in a world that has yet to find its way out of medieval obsessions.

If I pay attention to Spain and limit my discussion to African Americans, Jews, and immigrants in this book, it is because I was born and spent my formative years in the Moroccan city of Tangier, only a few miles away from the edges of Europe and the older realm of Christendom. This ancient, borderline city, renowned for its laissez-faire attitudes, where calls for any kind of purity keep stumbling over the imperfections of our human nature and our multiple ethnicities, has certainly shaped my approach to the charged concepts of culture, history, and community. On our side of the Mediterranean, I was on Berber, African, Arab, and Muslim land at once. I also grew up in close proximity to vibrant Jewish traditions that long preceded the arrival and institutionalization of Islam. From my experience with Jewish neighbors who shared in our joys and tragedies, and the constant support I got from my American Jewish mentors and friends, I knew instinctively that Jews and Muslims share more than they realize. Morocco's sense of kinship with its ancient Semitic heritage used to be displayed on the emblem of the nation, for the Moroccan flag, before the French colonialists brought their own prejudices, once featured the seal of Solomon (Star of David), not the five-pointed star (pentagram) we see today.

When Muslim terrorists attacked a synagogue (among other targets) in Casablanca on May 16, 2003, 1 million Moroccans, including Muslims and Jews, refused to be intimidated or divided, joined hands, and walked out in protest, a remarkable event described by the American Israel Public Affairs Committee (AIPAC) as "an amazing, and unprecedented, sight." Almost four years later, Serge Berdugo, the president of the Moroccan Jewish Community Council, wrote, "As the flames of anti-Semitism continue to be fanned across much of the Islamic world, there is a risk that today's youth will grow up believing that Arabs and Jews were simply not meant to coexist, let alone thrive together. That idea conflicts with history—and is a falsehood today."[67] As if to illustrate his point, in 2007 a Jewish author of books on Jewish life in Morocco, Maguy Kakon, a member of the newly created Parti du centre social (Party of the Social Center) who traces her family origins back to the fourteenth century, ran for a parliamentary seat in September elections and was helped and warmly received by her head-covered Muslim fellow citizens in some of the poorest districts in Casablanca. (She was one of five Jewish candidates.)[68]

In July 2008, hundreds of Jews from around the world converged on the coastal city of Safi to pray at the shrine of Abraham Ben Zmirro, "a rabbi reputed to have fled persecution in Spain in the 15th century." These pilgrims, led by Aaron Monsenego, the great rabbi of Morocco, were joined by the governor of Safi and other Muslim dignitaries, who all prayed for the health of the reigning Moroccan king and his family. Although Morocco may seem unique these days (it's the only country in the Arab world with a Jewish museum), Muslims there did, and continue to, come to the rescue of their Jewish neighbors, as Albanians did during World War II and Muslim Iraqis did in 2003 when they formed a militia to protect a synagogue.[69] The more I read on this subject, the more I realized that Jewish-Muslim ties were even stronger in the centuries leading up to the mid-twentieth century, despite genuine theological differences and the not-inconsequential episodes of Jewish persecution by Muslims.

At only nine miles from our Mediterranean shore, Spain clearly framed the daily horizons of my youthful vision. I never learned Spanish in school, but I managed to use the language by watching soccer games and music shows on television, reading magazines, and talking to friends (whether Spaniards or not) in the streets and cafés of Tangier. I was able to get a closer look at Spanish culture, with its indelible Moorish traits and strong drive for membership in the European Union. Many people in Tangier read Spain's quest for this northbound modernity as an attempt to repudiate its Moorish legacy, but we also knew that Spain was no typical European country. Spain was part of who we were; it was our rival and semblable at once.

No Christian country's fate has been more intertwined with Islam. Even as Spanish crusaders, with the help of foreign legionnaires, spent centuries trying to reclaim the lands lost to Islam in 711, the peninsula they were trying to liberate was being molded into an indelibly multicultural place. As the *Song of Roland*, composed around 1100, tells us, French foreigners such as Charlemagne (grandson of the same Charles Martel who repelled Muslims from Poitiers in 732), with little knowledge of Islam, launched crusades to defeat Muslim kings in Spain. Yet in the *Poem of El Cid*, composed a century later, Rodrigo Díaz de Vivar, the legendary Spanish man of the people known as El Cid (from the honorific title in Arabic *sayyid*, or "master"), a warrior familiar with the shifting fortunes of Iberian kingdoms, liked and disliked by Muslims and Christians alike, harbored none of the zealotry expressed by his northern neighbors, whose image of Muslims was mostly imaginary. This explains why the distant French, in their ignorance of Spain's complex social realities, saw the world in black and white, a view that, unfortunately, would over time grow into the policies of exclusion and give rise to the political structures of our own world. Even Alfonso VI, the king of Léon and Castile who conquered Toledo in 1085 and banished El Cid in 1089, proclaimed himself "Emperor of the Two Religions."[70]

It is true that memories of the Moorish invasion linger. A Spanish-Moroccan dispute over an uninhabited rock in the Mediterranean in the summer of 2002 and the terrorist attacks in Madrid on March 11, 2004, brought ancient grievances back into public view. *El Mundo,* a major Spanish newspaper, published a special report titled "Morocco: The Unfaithful Brother," on the old war with the Moors, to provide background information to what was essentially a trivial border dispute. When the conservative prime minister José María Aznar, a major ally of President Bush who would be defeated in the 2004 elections following the Madrid attacks, addressed students at Georgetown University, he told them that the battle of Islam began in 711: "Spain's problem with Al-Qaida starts in the eighth century . . . when a Spain recently invaded by the Moors refused to become just another piece in the Islamic world and began a long battle to recover its identity." So influenced was Aznar by his country's legacy of the Reconquista that he sent Spanish troops to Iraq with the cross of Santiago Matamoros (St. James the Moorslayer) on their uniforms.[71] Yet Aznar's memories, though widely shared, have not made Spain tougher on Islam; few European nations, if any, can match Spain's liberal attempt to amnesty its illegal (mostly Muslim and Moroccan) immigrants, examine openly the wounds of history, and even consider granting Spanish citizenship to the long-expelled Moriscos. Spain is constantly being reminded of its Moorish heritage, although it has become a vibrant part of the European Union. Even when Spain was engaged in a colonial war in northern Morocco in the early twentieth century, Spanish writers such as Joaquín Costa openly rejected their country's claim to a superior European heritage. "Spain and Morocco," wrote Costa, "are two halves of a single geographical unit[;] they form a watershed whose exterior limits are the parallel ranges of the Atlas mountains to the south and the Pyrenees to the north. The Straits of Gibraltar are not a wall separating one house from the other. Quite the contrary, they are a gate opened by Nature to allow communication between two rooms in the same house."[72] It is this Spanish cultural and racial ambivalence that may hold the key to a more positive rapprochement between the West and Islam, as we shall see in the conclusion of this book, even if, as the great Spanish writer Juan Goytisolo noted during the dispute over the contested island in 2002, the Moor is still the target of an undying Spanish prejudice.[73]

Tangier is in Africa, too, which makes me African, whatever tint (depending on climate and season) my skin color may assume. Because Morocco is deeply connected to its African heritage, I developed a side interest first in Muslim slaves in the Americas, then in African American Islam as a whole. The epic journey of Muslim slaves in early America, as well as the significance of their legacy to contemporary African American history, is a story that has yet to take its proper place in the canons of American culture and world history. When it does, it may help us see the tortured relations between the United States and Islam in a different light.

To be from Tangier is to have grown up watching immigrants sailing away and back—sometimes legally, sometimes not—across the Straits of Gibraltar, the mythical Pillars of Hercules. Almost every family I knew had at least one member in a European country. It was, therefore, natural for me to develop an interest in Hispanic cultures when I came to the United States and eventually to pay attention to immigration issues. My discovery of Mexico and the U.S. Southwest tripled my interest in Spain and its legacies, as I saw Mexicans and New Mexicans, from all races and walks of life, work out their own vexed relationship with the country that had chartered their destiny, for better or worse. The further I looked at the fabric of Spanish America, the closer I felt to my native country. Gradually, the Mayas, Zapotecs, Navajos, and other indigenous people, as well as pre-colonial Mexico's mestizo populations, turned into the mirror image of Moroccans with their mixed Berber-Arab heritage and its multiple layers of cultures, chief among them (especially in the north) the Spanish one. Historically, Mexico was a country fashioned by the same men who had fought Muslims and Moroccans. I could see that.

Like the unfortunate Moroccans and Africans who risk their lives to cross the treacherous waters of the straits to find a better life on Spanish farms and further beyond, in the glittery spaces of Europe, Mexicans and other Hispanics undergo perilous journeys to enter the United States. To watch culturally and spiritually rich humans risking their lives and enduring horrible travails to make economic ends meet not only saddens me deeply but also reminds me of the murderous parochialisms that still regulate our lives and limit our visions. The question of immigration is not marginal, although it seems to take place on the fringes of our lives, on the borderlines of our consciousness; quite the contrary, it is central to our sense of identity. The way we deal with or, better yet, see immigrants and all those who do not fit into our conception of the prototypical citizen will probably determine the future of our civilization. If progressive thinkers don't make an effort to educate their fellow citizens about the perils of imagined identities in the age of globalization, national purists, in the name of cultural or racial ideologies, could conceivably push us into further strife, if they don't reproduce outright the climate that led to the horrors visited upon defenseless minorities in the not-so-distant past.

But to understand how we got here, we need to start from the beginning; we have to trek our way back to the old battles of Christians and Muslims, the ones that gave shape to the modern world we live in. For our current notions of sovereignty, national identity, and minorities in the West are the outcome of the Christian crusading mind-set that was sharpened in endless wars against Islam. Like the Jews yesterday, African Americans, Hispanics, and other strangers who inhabit hostile nations precariously are, in the final analysis, reincarnations of the Moor. This, I hope, will be made clear in the pages that follow.

chapter 1

Pious Cruelty

Happy is the nation that is united in all its sentiments.

—M. DÁNVILA Y COLLADO, *La Expulsión de los moriscos españoles*

It has always surprised me that so little attention has been paid to the period at the end of the Middle Ages when Islam was in the process of being eliminated from Europe. Many of the attitudes that help generate modern misunderstandings were formed at this time.

—L. P. HARVEY, *Islamic Spain, 1250 to 1500*

On April 9, 1609, King Philip III, leader of the most powerful nation in Europe, secretly signed a decree to expel all Spaniards of Muslim descent—anywhere between 300,000 and 500,000 people, or about 5 percent of Spain's total population—from his territory. This decision was the culmination of centuries of putting into effect restrictive measures against religious minorities, first the Jews, then the Moors, and sometimes the two together. The Jews had been disposed of in 1492 with the Edict of Expulsion, promulgated on March 31, less than three months after the transfer of Muslim Granada to King Ferdinand and Queen Isabella. As in Christian provinces in the past, where Mudéjarism (the acceptance of Muslim minorities) had been barely tolerated, Jews were given the option of conversion or exile. The "crypto-Jews" who chose conversion to save their lives and stay home would become Marranos (pigs), but those who stuck to their faith—anywhere between 40,000 and 50,000, according to recent estimates by Henry Kamen—were forced to leave in dreadful conditions.[1] The Santa Hermandad, a sort of national police force established in 1476 out of a vigilante order, was charged with the logistics. One witness describing the exodus of the Jews of Segovia to Portugal wrote, "Over the fields they pass, in much travail and misfortune, some falling, others standing up, some dying, others being born, others falling sick, that there was not a Christian but felt sorrow for them." Another wrote of those leaving by sea, "Half dead mothers held dying children in their arms. . . . I can hardly say how cruelly and greedily they were treated by those who transported them. Many were drowned by the avarice of the sailors, and those who were unable to pay their passage sold their children."[2]

The Moors of Granada had been given a solemn promise of total protection and the exercise of their full rights as Muslims by King Ferdinand and Queen Isabella the previous November, even though Abu Abdullah, better known as Boabdil, Granada's last Muslim king, was warned by his general, Musa Ben Abil, that Christians didn't keep their word and that such protections were futile in a country where the Inquisition, that "burning pile of the bigot," was gaining ground.[3] To no avail: on January 2, 1492, Boabdil rode out of Granada and gave his ring of authority to León don Gutierre de Cárdenas, the Count of Tendilla, the new ruler from the Mendoza family, while the monarchs watched in splendor, Isabella wearing a Moorish caftan. Four days later, on the day of Epiphany, Ferdinand and Isabella entered Granada to the tune of *Te Deum laudamus,* performed by the royal chapel choir. In March of that year, Peter Martyr, described by James Reston Jr. as the author of "the first major work on the discoveries of the New World,"[4] wrote, "This is the end of the calamities of Spain. This is the term of the happiness of this barbarous people [the Muslims], which, as they say, came from Mauritania some 800 years ago and inflicted its cruel and arrogant oppression on conquered Spain!"[5] Juan de Padilla, a popular religious author, praised the monarchs for cleansing "weakened Spain of a thousand heresies." Three years later, Dr. Hieronymous Münzer, of Nuremberg, told the Catholic Monarchs—a title conferred on them by Pope Alexander VI, a notoriously corrupt Spaniard, in 1494—that their glory was so complete that the only thing left was to reconquer the Holy Sepulchre of Jerusalem. Without a doubt, the defeat of Muslims and the conquest of Granada were far more significant events for contemporaries than the discovery of America that ensued from such victories.[6]

The interlude of tolerance under the archbishopric of Hernando de Talavera, the Hieronymite friar of Jewish lineage who praised the Moors' integrity and industriousness and learned Arabic to better proselytize, was quickly eclipsed by the arrival of the archbishop of Toledo, the Franciscan Francisco Jiménez de Cisneros, in 1499, the same year when Granada was incorporated into the district of Córdova and subjected to the Inquisition, and Talavera was accused of being an agent of Judaism. On December 18 of that year, Jiménez de Cisneros forced three thousand Moors into baptism and burned five thousand religious books (saving only medical treatises), leading to the first Moorish uprising in the mountains of Alpujarras. It was an insurgency that was crushed with even more violent measures, as mosques harboring women and children were blown up by Catholic forces and Moors from elsewhere in the Iberian Peninsula were denied entry into Granada to shield the new faith of the converts *(conversos)* from Muslim contamination.[7] (For his assiduousness, Jiménez de Cisneros would be appointed grand inquisitor of Castile in 1507.)

In Aragon, the northern kingdom that had merged with the larger and more powerful Castile through the marriage of Ferdinand and Isabella in 1469, Moors continued to enjoy their ancient liberties, or "laws and privileges" known as *fueros*; but about a year after the ban on Lutherans in 1521, Pope Clement VII released Charles V from Ferdinand's solemn oath to protect his Muslim vassals.[8] From then on, Spain would not tolerate the presence of unconverted Moors in its territory. Bathing, cleanliness, dietary choices, the use of henna, fasting during Ramadan, and the possession of books in Arabic, as well as what was called fautorship, or the favoring or defending of heretics by Christians (butchers and midwives were considered examples of fautors), became prosecutable crimes. The list of Morisco illegal activity kept mounting, in effect making Islam a crime against the state. As *doctrineros,* or catechizers, were dispatched to convert and baptize Moriscos, the *morerías* (Moorish quarters), like the old *juderías* for Jews, were destroyed. The mingling of races and intermarriage were forbidden. No Moorish names or surnames, dress, or musical dances known as *zambras* and *leilas* were allowed. Marriage between cousins was invalidated. The Moriscos were also prevented from bearing arms, leaving them defenseless and vulnerable in a country rife with banditry. They couldn't be butchers and couldn't slaughter animals. Civil ceremonies, such as marriage, birth, and death, were scrupulously monitored for signs of deviance or heresy. Scattered throughout the country, the Moriscos, confined to their residences, endured life "under perpetual surveillance."[9] Even after they converted to Catholicism, the Moriscos were denied full membership in the community, because the *limpieza de sangre* (purity-of-blood) statute of 1449 had turned faith into a racial category. (The pope initially objected to the statute, as it contravened the evangelical mission of the Roman Catholic Church.) The Moors had no genealogical claims to Catholicism, making their conversion suspect and incomplete in the eyes of Spanish authorities.

Although they were persecuted, harassed, and discriminated against, the Moriscos soon prospered again, producing anxieties real enough for Old Christians (Christians with no Jewish or Muslim lineage) to worry about their enslavement to the Moors. Not all Catholics shared such sentiments. A few faint voices recommended more love and kindness for a people who had once been rulers and masters, but freedom of conscience was "forbidden by all the canons"; it was a "Protestant heresy" that could endanger the faith and state.[10] Moreover, by fighting back tenaciously, the Moriscos were seen as traitors, even though it was the Catholic Monarchs who had reneged on their vow to protect the Moriscos. "Taking up arms," L. P. Harvey wrote, "was the last resort of desperate men, a forlorn attempt to arrest the process whereby their religion was being suppressed."[11]

No power—European or Muslim—came to the Moors' defense, for although they asked the Mamluk ruler of Egypt, and later the Ottoman sultan, to threaten retaliation against Christian minorities in their realms, neither could do it (the Mamluks were threatened with retaliation by Peter Martyr, who was dispatched to Egypt to explain the Christian point of view; and Bayazid II, the Ottoman sultan, could not contravene his *millet* policy of coexistence). Thus, short of mass exile, the only option left to the Moors in Spain was "insincere and nominal conversion," allowed by the remarkable fatwa, or religious opinion, obtained from the grand mufti of Oran as early as 1504. Nonobservance of religious obligations and hiding one's true faith under duress *(taqiyya)* were allowed, thereby condoning a sort of Muslim *marranismo*.[12] Other local imams, like the mufti Ice de Gebir, from Segovia, produced Islamic manuals, such as the *Brevario Sunni; or, Kitab segoviano,* in the Romance language of the Moors, *aljamía*. The Young Man of Arévalo *(el Mancebo de Arévalo),* a boy rumored to be a prophet, recorded accounts of encounters with Moorish leaders such as the Mora de Ubeda in Granada and Yunes Benegas, the owner of a large farm employing more than a hundred people, a man who survived the Catholic mass murder of his family and coreligionists during the first Alpujarras uprising. Benegas's is a moving tale that testifies to the sort of coexistence (however

difficult it may have been for non-Muslims) that prevailed in Granada before
the final defeat of the Moors. After recounting to the Young Man of Arévalo
the horror of losing his wife, three sons, and two daughters, he stoically
added this:

> Son, I do not weep over the past, for there is no way back, but I do weep
> for what you have yet to see, if you are spared, and live on in this land, in
> this peninsula of Spain. May it please Allah, for the sake of the nobility of
> our Koran, that what I am saying be proved empty words. May it not turn
> out as I imagine. Even so, our religion will so decline that people will ask:
> What has become of the voice of the muezzin? What has become of the reli-
> gion of our ancestors? For anybody with feelings it will all seem bitter and
> cruel. What troubles me most is that Muslims will be indistinguishable from
> Christians, accepting their dress, and not avoiding their food. May God grant
> that at least they avoid their actions, and that they do not allow the [Chris-
> tian] religion to lodge in their hearts. . . .
>
> It must appear to you that I am saying all this because I am overwrought.
> May Allah, in His infinite love grant that what I am saying is as far from the
> mark as I would desire, for I would not wish to know anything of such
> weeping. If we say that the Children of Israel wept, is it any great matter
> that we too should weep? . . . If now after such a short space of time we
> appear to have difficulty in keeping our footing, what will those in years to
> come do? If the fathers scant the religion, how are the great-grandchildren
> to raise it up again? *If the King of the Conquest fails to keep faith, what are we
> to expect from his successors?* I tell you more, my son, that our decline will
> continue. May His Holy Goodness direct His pity towards us, and support
> us with His divine grace.[13]

Although this account poignantly illustrates a request for help sent to the
Ottoman sultan, it also testifies to the close relations Muslims had with
Jews, as there are references to the Jews' plight throughout the account: "If
we say that the Children of Israel wept, is it any great matter that we too
should weep?" About Yunes Benegas, the Young Man of Arévalo further
reported, "I never saw anybody with his facility for reading and explicat-
ing the Koran, and any Arabic or Hebrew work of commentary."[14]

The Moriscos, including women, fought valiantly when, in 1567, Philip II
renewed an edict making Arabic and the entire Moorish culture a crime.

During this second Alpujarras uprising (1568–1570), also known as the Second Granadan War, the Moriscos got some help from Turkish and Moroccan volunteers; but by the spring of 1571, they were defeated. The besieged village of Galera was razed to the ground by John of Austria (known as Don John), the illegitimate son of Charles V, after its people, including women, children, and the elderly, were massacred and their bodies sprinkled with salt. Rebels were smoked out of caves; many, including children and women, were asphyxiated.[15] Some 100,000 Moriscos from Granada were deported under very inhumane conditions (with the death rate reaching 30 percent), and Old Christians from northern Spain resettled on their lands.[16] As brutal as his actions were, Don John did not remain unmoved by the deportation of the Moriscos; it was, in his own words, "the saddest sight in the world, for at the time they set out there was so much rain, wind and snow that mothers had to abandon their children by the wayside and wives their husbands. . . . It cannot be denied that the most distressing sight one can imagine is to see the depopulation of a kingdom."[17]

According to the Granada-born Luis de Marmol y Carvajal, author of *Historia del rebellion y castigo de los moriscos del reyno de Granada,* a letter found on Aben Daúd, a Morisco captured near the coast of Almería, details the sufferings of the beleaguered Moriscos and their call for help, probably from Muslim rulers:

> You must know, our lords, that the Christians have ordered us to abandon our Arabic language. He who loses his Arabic tongue loses his faith. We must uncover our faces and we can no longer greet each other, even though such greetings are the noblest of virtues. They have forced us to open our doors so that we may suffer misery and sin. They have increased their exactions and our drudgeries, and wanted to change our attire. They settle in our homes and unveil our honor and our shame and demand that we not complain from the pain in our hearts. All of this after they had taken our property, captured our people, and expelled us from our villages. They have thrown us in despair and they separate us from our brothers and friends.[18]

Many disinterested intellectuals and caring nobles objected to the persecutions of Moriscos and their deportation. One Sancho de Cardona, admiral of Aragon, was condemned to a life sentence and to wearing the *sambenito,* the dress of shame, for having allowed his Morisco vassals to keep their traditions and honor their ancestral faith by taking care of their mosque. In 1606, Pedro de Valencia wrote a treatise on the Moriscos, trying to understand their violent reactions and calling for integration through dispersion, mixed marriages, and better living conditions. Similarly, Mateo López Bravo and Fadrique Furió Ceriol, the latter of whom wrote *Concejo y consejeros del principe* (1559), fought hard against racial discrimination and arbitrary religious divisions.[19]

But such voices were in the minority. Because the Moriscos were often suspected of being fifth columnists for the Turks or other foreign powers, a permanent solution had to be found, for, as the scholar Mary Elizabeth Perry notes, they represented a "counteridentity" that was just too risky in a nascent state and polyglot empire.[20] No option for the elimination of this "homegrown" threat was out of conceptual bounds. The castration of Morisco infants was contemplated and rejected. The Dominican Jaime Bleda, "the most hateful, the most violent detractor of the Moriscos," suggested that all Moriscos be massacred in a single day, that such an act "would be a work of great piety and edification to the faithful and a wholesome warning to heretics."[21] (Bleda would die in the midst of the expulsion, which fulfilled his last wish to see the memory of the Moriscos erased from his country.) In 1582, the inquisitors of Valencia proposed shipping their Moriscos to Newfoundland. All these measures were rejected by Philip II, but when he died, on September 13, 1598, his much weaker and less experienced son, Philip III, fell under the sway of Morisco detractors, chiefly Francisco Gómez de Sandoval y Rojas, better known in the annals of history as the Duke of Lerma, a rich, powerful, conniving landowner and the monarch's main adviser in the Royal Council.

By the first decade of the seventeenth century, Spain was no longer the rich, confident nation it had been in the late fifteenth, and, as history repeatedly shows, times of crisis and doubt always lead to the rise of intolerance and the persecution of minority groups. The defeat of the Spanish armada led to a new fundamentalist wave across the country, with talk of purification and fighting heresy. A big and constant worry during this time was the increasing number of Moriscos and therefore growing diversity within the nation, both of which threatened the interests of Old Christians. Because Moriscos were excluded from the army and the priesthood, they had no impediments to sexual reproduction, giving rise to the fear that they might someday become the majority. And the multiple and constant attempts to convert the forcibly baptized Moriscos into the true Christian faith led to frustration and despair, as the case of Juan de Ribera dramatically illustrates.

In 1568, Philip II appointed the thirty-six-year-old Ribera archbishop of Valencia (the same year Pope Pius V bestowed on the young prelate the honorary title of patriarch of Antioch, given that the ancient town of Antioch was held by Muslims), mostly to speed up the conversion of the Moriscos in that province. The energetic archbishop, however, quickly realized that the Moriscos had no intention of abandoning their ancestral faith. When Francisco Zenequi, an elderly Morisco, was tried in 1583 by the Inquisition for practicing Islam, the defendant simply bemoaned the fact that, "unlike the Turk, who recognizes the three laws of Moors, Jews, and Christians, the king of Spain does not allow each one to live by his own law." Such exhortations, however, had no effect on his accusers. For his obstinacy, Zenequi was sentenced to three years' seclusion.[22]

The Moriscos, who remained confident in their better way of life and the liberalism of their faith, thought that the king of Spain was unwise to alienate his Morisco subjects and not follow the better example of Turkish rulers. And they were not alone in holding such views. In the middle of the sixteenth century, the anonymous author of *Viaje de Turquía* implicitly chastised the rulers of his own nation for not following the Turkish model:

> Suppose . . . Turkey is not called Turkey because all of its people are Turks, because there are more Christians who . . . practice their faith than there are Turks, although they are neither subjects of the Pope nor of our Latin church but have their own patriarch who [*sic*] they consider as their pope.
>   Then why does the Turk consent to them?
>   What does it matter to him, as long as they pay him his tribute, if they are Jewish or Christian or Moslem? In Spain, weren't there once Moors and Jews?[23]

Moreover, the fair treatment of Moriscos could give the Spanish monarchs added support in their wars against Spain's enemies. As one Muslim leader commented on Philip II's attempts to add Portugal to his domains after 1578, "If His Majesty wants to win Portugal he should arm the [M]oriscos and let each live according to his own law; they would win it for him."[24]

When Ribera despaired of converting the Moriscos, he wrote a letter in 1582 to Gaspar de Quiroga, the grand inquisitor, calling the Moriscos enemies of the state and recommending their expulsion. Gradually, the Moriscos were recast as dangerous Moors and fifth columnists for the Ottoman sultan and Spain's Protestant enemies, threatening the completion of the Reconquista of 1492 and impeding the "religious unity" of the new nation. In a twenty-eight-page letter drafted in 1602, the archbishop described the Moriscos as "the sponge of all the wealth of Spain," hoarders of gold whose expulsion would allow the king to confiscate their wealth and enrich the state's coffers. Paraphrasing the Bible, Ribera argued that the only solution was "to pull them up by the roots, so they will not cause damage nor send out new shoots that quickly grow into trees." He also blamed the Moriscos for the rising wave of banditry in Valencia. And, if this were not enough to sway the monarch, he added that the Moriscos were members of a different race, therefore making them all guilty, regardless of their degree of assimilation.[25]

Thus, during his tenure in Valencia, Ribera "developed a series of arguments, economic, religious, historical, and *racial,* to depict the [M]oriscos as a diaspora community of the dreaded Moors living in the heart of Spain."[26] His views would resonate through much of modern history, as racializing religious minorities led to unimaginable horrors and the quest for assimilation continued to motivate minority groups to resist oppressive systems. Benjamin Ehlers, the author of an excellent study on Ribera, thinks that the predicament of the Moriscos "prefigured the challenges faced by Muslim societies in the modern era of Western expansion, forced to choose among accommodation, survival, and resistance."[27] This is true, but I find the situation of Muslim minorities in European societies even more poignantly relevant, as I will show in the course of this book.

In late January 1608, the Royal Council assembled to discuss the case of the Moriscos. Slaughtering all adults was, once again, proposed as an option, but expulsion was ultimately seen as the better solution.[28] Thus, on April 4, 1609, the Royal Council, led by the Duke of Lerma, reiterating the same fears about the Moriscos, decreed the expulsion of all Moriscos from Spain.[29] The cessation of hostilities with England and the United Provinces (Netherlands) "made possible the concentration of land and maritime forces indispensable for the success of the operation." And so, just as the discovery of America was considered the divine compensation for expelling Jews in

1492, so was the Twelve Years' Truce (with the United Provinces) thought to be a reward for the expulsion of the Moriscos from the holy body of Christian Spain.[30] The expulsion would be "one of the greatest events in the history of Spain and the Mediterranean,"[31] draining enormous state resources and requiring a very elaborate military preparation, including chartering hundreds of English, French, and Italian vessels.[32]

Soon after the Edict of Expulsion was first publicly announced in Valencia, in September 1609, Ribera gave a sermon explaining that the Moriscos had conspired with the Turks to invade Spain. The entire discourse of classical anti-Semitism was deployed against the Moriscos, making the two minority groups in Europe—the Jews and the Muslims—almost interchangeable in the Catholic imagination. In 1611, as the expulsion was under way, the Portuguese Dominican Damián Fonseca used the phrase "agreeable holocaust" *(el agradable holocausto)* to describe the burnt offering God expected from the king. Meanwhile, squads of Christians robbed and murdered the exiles. "Pedro Aznar Cardona, whose treatise justifying the expulsion was published in 1612, stated that between October 1609 and July 1611, over 50,000 died resisting expulsion, while over 60,000 died during their passage abroad, either by land or sea at the hands of their co-religionists [fellow Muslims] after disembarking on the North African coast"; others, such as Bleda, estimated that 75 percent of Moriscos perished during this ordeal.[33] Many Moriscos were abused in the Muslim lands they landed on, such as Oran and Tlemcen in present-day Algeria. In the Moroccan town of Tetouan, they were treated as Christians, refused entry to mosques, and even "lapidated or put to death in other ways."[34]

In his seminal study *The Moriscos of Spain* (1901), the American historian Henry Charles Lea estimated that "half a million" Moriscos, out of a general population of 8 million, were ultimately expelled in the five-year period of 1609–1614.[35] (Some remained in the country undetected, others as slaves, although the Inquisition never relaxed its vigilant eye.) On February 20, 1614, more than nine hundred years after Islam had entered Spain, the Royal Council "advised the king that the Expulsion might be deemed to be complete."[36] Philip III then declared the expulsion successful and warned "all Moriscos who have not left or have returned must leave under the pain of slavery in the galleys and confiscation of goods. If it be a woman or very old to be whipped with 200 lashes and branded."[37] The monarch didn't have to worry, for "the operation must be accounted as much as an administrative success as was the gruesome organization by the Nazis of the emptying of Europe's ghettos," commented L. P. Harvey. "Careful records were kept of those expelled, and these figures provide not just estimates but highly reliable statistics (often susceptible to checking and cross-checking)."[38]

The expulsion of the last Morisco, in 1614, was greeted with great joy. Bleda, whose book *Defensio fidei in causa neophytorum sive Morischorum regni Valenciae, totiusque Hispaniae* was described by Henry Charles Lea as a treatise "calculated to excite horror and detestation,"[39] declared it "the most glorious event for Spain since the resurrection of Christ and its conversion from paganism," announcing a new golden age of riches. Once again, the recapture of Jerusalem was seen as imminent. Unfortunately, no new golden age appeared on the horizon of an already fraying empire. Depopulation precipitated the decline of production and revenues for both nobles and churches in many areas. The Inquisition, without a major enemy and revenues, suffered. Agriculture and industry were seriously affected. Because so many Christians were in the army (foreign wars, New World conquests), busy with matters of faith (in convents), or employed by the state, they paid no taxes. With no Moriscos to fill state coffers, a "terrible atrophy . . . fell upon Spain as the seventeenth century advanced." Arabia Felix became Arabia Deserta. "History offers few examples of retribution so complete and so disastrous," commented Lea, "as that which followed on the fanatic labors of [Jiménez de Cisneros]." Although there had been no problems with Mudéjars when Christians were still fighting Moors—such as the Almoravids and Almohads from Morocco—to say that scattered and beaten Moriscos in a Christian nation posed a threat "was self-evidently the merest illusion, born of intolerance."[40] Still, Lea concluded, had Ferdinand kept his promise, Spain, and probably the world, would have known an altogether different future:

> Had these agreements been preserved inviolate the future of Spain would have been wholly different; kindly intercourse would have amalgamated the races; in time Mahometanism would have died out, and, supreme in the arts of war and peace, the prosperity and power of the Spanish kingdoms would have been enduring. This, however, was too foreign to the spirit of the age to come to pass. Fanaticism and greed led to persecution and oppression, while

Castilian pride inflicted humiliation even more galling. The estrangement of the races grew ever greater, the gulf between them more impassable, until the position became intolerable, leading to a remedy which crippled the prosperity of Spain.[41]

Despite routinely expressed fears of Morisco fertility rates, "the final expulsion was a cruel coup de grace to a community long in decline, not a measure of self-defense taken by Christian folk in any real danger of being demographically overwhelmed and outbred."[42] As Spain was forced to sign peace treaties with its European rivals, the state's muscle turned on the hapless Moriscos, leading Cardinal Richelieu (1585–1642) to write in his memoirs that the expulsion of the Moriscos was "the boldest and most barbarous [act] recorded in human annals," and the French writer Voltaire (1694–1778) to comment that "Philip III could not get the better of a few Dutchman [*sic*], and unfortunately he could drive out 700,000 Moors from his dominions."[43] But such moral preoccupations were of little interest to Castilian leaders bent on uniting a diverse peninsula with multiple traditions and allegiances. National homogeneity mattered more than *convivencia*; conformity was better than dissent. Centuries later, in 1889, the Spanish historian M. Dánvila y Collado, in his *La Expulsión de los moriscos españoles,* considered the fate meted out to the Moriscos to be "part of . . . a religious war, a war of extermination of the opposite race," one that had near-universal support among the Spaniards:

> The expulsion of the Spanish Moriscos was carried out without regard to young and old, fit or unfit, guilty or innocent. The question of political unity was a sequel to the necessity of church unity. It was initiated by the Catholic kings. Charles V and Philip II attempted to accomplish it, but it had to fall back in the face of its consequences. Philip III, exercising the power through his favorites, made it easy through the combination of religious and political power. The religious war was much alive against the Moorish race, and the sweetest sentiments of the soul came face to face with the political question. Humanity and religion fought, but religion emerged victorious. Spain lost its most industrious sons; children were separated from the lap of their mothers, and from paternal love. There was no pity or mercy for any Morisco, but religious unity appeared radiant and luminous in the sky of Spain. Happy is the nation that is united in all its sentiments.[44]

It was this quest for national unity, considered to be essential to national greatness, that made a large portion of the Spanish population expendable. Of course, the ethnic cleansing of Spain did not result in the unified nation so many Castilians dreamed of. The nation remained a patchwork of precariously connected kingdoms that would retain their cultural autonomy, more or less, to the present period. Perhaps, just as England managed to metamorphose into the United Kingdom or Great Britain, so did Castile manage to subsume other kingdoms and provinces into the grand but misleading title of Spain. It remains to be seen whether the "solvent of globalization," as Raymond Carr puts it,[45] will finally erase strong regional distinctions or exacerbate them, as Basques and Catalans, for instance, seek a total breakaway from the long stranglehold of Madrid.

As is often the case, the quest for religious unity across the land was not really about religion (as Lea himself knew) but about national ideology and political power. While King Ferdinand was engaged in stitching together a peninsula of diverse cultures and kingdoms and unifying his subjects around the Catholic faith, the Florentine diplomat, citizen, and astute student of politics Niccolò Machiavelli (1469–1527) noted the genius of the Spanish monarch but saw nothing ethical about his behavior at all. Machiavelli made it clear, in *The Prince,* that King Ferdinand's attack on Granada was "the cornerstone of his reign." By taking his time to reconquer the last Moorish citadel, he was able to marginalize and assume power over the country's nobility. "Money from the Church and the people enabled him to recruit big armies, and in the course of this long war to build a military establishment which has since won him much honor," Machiavelli wrote. Ferdinand's "great" and even "extraordinary" actions gained him the esteem of his people and made him the "the first prince of Christendom." But Machiavelli knew that religion was a means to an end, not an end in itself. Ferdinand, he wrote, "made use of the pretext of religion to prepare the way for still greater projects, and adopted *a policy of pious cruelty* in expelling the Moors from his kingdom and despoiling them; his conduct here could not have been more despicable nor more unusual."[46]

As the Spanish state, through the Inquisition and other instruments, was making life intolerable for the Moriscos, another Italian scholar, the Jesuit Giovanni Botero (ca. 1544–1617), published a book titled *Della ragion di stato* (*The Reason of State,* or, as the expression is commonly known in French, *raison d'état*) in 1589, making the case for infusing Christian ethics into the system of government by positing religious unity as the main guarantor of stability and good governance. In Botero's formula, conversion of the infidels, particularly the worst kinds—the Muslims and Calvinists—is of the essence: "These, wherever they go, carry war in place of peace announced by the angels and preached by Christ; and it is the extreme of folly to trust them in affairs of state." To grant such religious minorities rights is counterproductive, because "liberty of conscience" is only a "pretext" for them; their "business is to foster seditions, foment rebellion, offer bait to malignity, hope to the ambitious, arms to the desperate," among a multitude of mischievous and evil acts. A state has no option but to force them out of the country, as did Pharaoh with the Jews; to inflict menial tasks on them, as did the Jews with the Gibeonites; or simply to confine them in low occupations, such as agriculture and the manual trades.[47]

Although Machiavelli and Botero disagreed on the reasons driving the call for unity of faith, both knew that such a policy was instrumental in forging a strong nation. About half a century ago, the historian José Antonio Maravall argued that the structure of the modern state emerged in the last quarter of the fifteenth century and the first one of the sixteenth. The Spanish monarchy developed a new ideology of sovereignty that was inseparable from territorial unity and communal homogeneity. The old medieval order of shifting alliances and antagonisms and respect for "feudal seigneurial claims" gave way to a royal system associated with citizenship and, as Alonso Ortiz, a contemporary of the Catholic Monarchs, put it, "the rights of the republic." In this emerging nation, the vassal of old became the free subject living, rather paradoxically, in an absolutist regime. "Absolute monarchy" and "fundamental laws" were thus synthesized into a new regime of rights and obligations. Like any imperial nation, Spain relied on an efficient bureaucracy; but what really distinguished it was its ruthless pursuit of homogeneity and the "feeling of community"—which meant not only annexing the kingdom of Navarre (another act of Castilian aggression underlying the elusive unity across the peninsula) but also banning foreigners from management positions (even while it welcomed them into the country) and expelling Jews and Moors, alien elements in the body politic.[48]

This is perhaps what Charles Tilly, the expert on nationalism, meant by saying that "national revolutionary situations before 1800 resulted overwhelmingly from state attempts to subordinate, expel, or eradicate imperial

minorities, as when the conquering Spaniards began to persecute the conquered Moors, then to persecute those who had been nominally Christian-
ized, the Moriscos."[49] But Maravall didn't merely talk about national unity;
he showed us that the new regime, based on exclusion, somehow promised
liberty to the king's subjects, and thus foreshadowed contemporary Western models of liberal democracy. Whatever the case, it is clear that what
Heather Rae calls "pathological homogenization," or the elites' construction
of "the bounded political community of the modern state as an exclusive
moral community from which outsiders must be expelled," is "intimately
bound up with the development of the international system of states." The
eminent historian Joseph Pérez rightly notes that the title of Catholic Monarchs not only allowed Isabella and Ferdinand to rule as-yet-unnamed territories but also enshrined the principle of making the prince's faith the
official religion of the state, an idea that would be the main assumption of
the Treaty of Westphalia in 1648.[50] National unity under such a regime is
necessarily maintained through real or symbolic expulsion of outsiders, those
who are different, even though difference can never be eradicated. The consequences of this arrangement, as we shall see, can be bloody indeed.[51] It
is not for no reason that Aristide Zolberg, the renowned scholar on migration and exile, described the expulsion of the Jews in 1492 as a "startlingly
modern measure."[52]

Indeed, the similarities between sixteenth-century Spain and the United
States of America today are striking. The title of "the first prince of Christendom" is akin to the current notion of "leader of the free world." As I
am writing this, in 2008, the United States is undertaking a process that
is similar to Ferdinand's: waging wars in the Middle East and debating the
fate of 12 million illegal (mostly Hispanic) immigrants in the country. Just
as the European Union is frantically trying to come to terms with its Muslim population, so the United States is struggling with a growing Hispanic
presence. What is at stake is more than a question of lawful immigration;
both Europe and the United States are attempting to make sense of how
such dramatic demographic and cultural shifts will affect their long-held
position of power around the globe. In other words, as the concept of nation
that King Ferdinand inaugurated is reaching the end of its life cycle and
is coming apart in the process of globalization, politicians and rulers are
still seeking to consolidate their power by invoking foundational myths,
whether in religion, race, or culture, to justify the exclusion and expulsion

of those who don't fit the ideal profile and by waging wars against foreign countries. Yet the world has now become too mixed and complex for such purist theories to hold.

The paradox of minorities in any national unit is that their presence is practically indispensable to shaping national identity, yet their vilification inevitably escalates into calls for expulsion or deportation—measures that rarely, if ever, produce the sort of tranquillity imagined in the early phases of intolerance and persecution. To cite two of the most famous examples in history: The expulsion of Moriscos in Spain and the deportation and annihilation of Jews in Germany did not strengthen either nation; on the contrary, both nations were weakened and, in the case of Germany, even defeated by such pathological measures. Spain gained nothing at all from expelling Jews in 1492 and Moriscos in 1609, whereas Germany's extermination of millions of Jews led to the occupation and dismemberment of the state. No glorious races emerged from such cruelty and barbarism, only humiliated states and troubled nations.

Today, the mounting calls to deport illegal aliens or to force Muslims or Hispanics to assimilate better into European and American societies are indexes of anxiety over rapidly changing economic conditions that would not be ameliorated by the successful execution of both policies. Similarly, the attempt to spread American values around the globe is implicitly an ambivalent gesture, for to succeed in Americanizing the world would also be to lose the driving ideology that allows the United States to justify its hegemony. Protecting national essences and spreading American ideologies around the world are both, therefore, impossible missions, because they would lead to militarized fundamentalisms on both ends of the spectrum and would never achieve the goal for which they were deployed. Yet these hegemonic drives have been indispensable to maintaining a certain degree of liberalism in the United States and western Europe. Max Weber was well aware that, much as the closing of the American frontier required a policy of global hegemony in order for the United States to maintain its culture of freedom, the West's liberal tradition depended on the conquest of other lands and people.[53] The erosion of civil rights in Western liberal societies today—often in the name of combating terrorism or unassimilated immigrants—may very well be an outcome of this shifting global reality.

That democracy could be founded on such violent beginnings has not been lost on Anthony W. Marx, who, writing in the heat of the clash-of-civilizations environment of 2003, noted that discrimination against African Americans and apartheid policies in the United States were "central to the process of uniting whites across regional antagonism as a nation," because Spain, "forged in the white heat of conflict with the Moors," provided a "template for those countries that came later to similar experiences." Before 1492 came to an end, Queen Isabella and King Ferdinand had created the pillars of a new world order based on a strong national (religious) identity, the exclusion of difference, and imperial quests. The monarchs had captured Granada, expelled Jews, invested in Columbus's voyage to India, and taken possession of the newly discovered American colonies. They had also approved the printing of the "first vernacular grammar book in Spain [Castile]." It was out of this violent culture of absolutism and exclusion that Western liberalism eventually emerged, one of the most conveniently overlooked facts of modern history:[54]

> At the very heart of liberalism is an ugly secret: Supposedly inclusive nationalism was founded on the basis of violent exclusion, used to bound and forge the nation to whom rights would then be selectively granted. Democracy itself was so founded also on exclusions in demarcating the unit to which rights of citizenship would be granted. Founded on this basis, liberal democracy would then eventually serve as cover, with gradual enfranchisement hiding past exclusions and obfuscating that at the heart of liberalism is an illiberal determination of who is a member of the incorporated community and who is not.[55]

Indeed, such attitudes continue to prevail today, given that "the cohering effect of exclusion and intolerance is still reflected in the West's views of the rest of the world." The Moor, in other words, continues to haunt nations and drive them into violent outbursts of intolerance because "Muslims in India, Tutsis in Rwanda, or Muslims in much of southeastern or Balkan Europe are the Jews, Moors, Huguenots, or Papists of our day."[56]

Unity of faith was thus essential to this nascent form of nationalism. "Between 1478 and 1502," Joseph Pérez emphasizes in the opening lines of his history of the Inquisition, "Isabella of Castile and Ferdinand of Aragon took three complementary decisions. They persuaded the pope to create the Inquisition; they expelled the Jews; and they forced the Muslims of the kingdom of Castile to convert to Catholicism. All these measures were designed to achieve the same end: the establishment of a united faith."[57] The Catholic Monarchs, Charles V, Philip II, and Philip III all pursued this policy of ethnic cleansing as a political principle, partly because they had the support of common subjects. Under the *limpieza de sangre* statute—understandably rejected by the pope because it cancelled the possibility of sincere conversion, but sanctioned by the Spanish monarch in 1501—it was the nobility (including the Jewish *converso* Tomás de Torquemada, the grand inquisitor who pushed for the expulsion of the Jews in 1492) who were genealogically suspect, whereas the sedentary peasants, attached to their land for centuries and unmixed with the foreign blood of the Moors, were considered the racial prototype, the ideal citizens of this emerging polity. (Sancho Panza in Miguel de Cervantes's *Don Quixote* proudly declares himself to be of pure blood.)[58] In this sense, then, the eradication of cultural and, presumably, racial difference also meant the elimination of dissent and contending political centers in the realm. It is not surprising, in this context, that more than 50 percent of those targeted by the Inquisition were Old Christians, not Moriscos,[59] nor, even more remarkably, that the Inquisition displayed a reasonable attitude toward accusations of witchcraft (even going so far as to see witches as victims!) when the persecution of witches was all the rage in neighboring European countries.[60]

There is no doubt at all that political and religious unity, or national consensus, was based on exclusion: the "establishment of a durable internal peace" went hand in hand with "the imposition of religious unity, the construction of a national State, and the putting together of an imperialist policy."[61] All these measures had the effect of distancing Spain from the medieval world and giving rise to a golden age, a renaissance of sorts. Intellectual and cultural production often mirrored the new ideology. In 1492, when the Jews had been expelled and hundreds of thousands of Moors left Granada (among them Al-Hassan ben Mohammed al-Wazzan ez-Zayati, who would be educated in Fez, Morocco, and would later write as a baptized Moor named Leo Africanus),[62] the great humanist Elio Antonio de Nebrija (1444–1522) published *Gramática de la lengua castellana,* symbolically connecting the Crusades and human civilization, the defeat of the enemy through the return to pure faith and the unity and prosperity of Spain. The University of Alcalá de Henares, northeast of Madrid, was founded by Jiménez de Cisneros in 1499, the same year when he forcibly baptized Moors who rose up in revolt. When it opened its doors to students, in 1508 or 1509,[63] it became Spain's foremost center of humanism and Hellenism. Its scholars, including many Jewish *conversos*, supervised by Antonio de Nebrija, eventually produced the first Polyglot Bible, in Latin, Greek, and Hebrew, thereby transferring Jewish exegesis to Christianity. (Another Jiménez de Cisneros project was a Greek and Latin edition of Aristotle's complete works, but the project was abandoned after three books.) Charles V created the University of Granada in 1526, blessed by a papal bull in 1531, to accelerate the Christianization of Moriscos. In fact, the sixteenth century in Spain was the golden age of higher education, with a rush to establish universities across the country.[64]

Some, however, saw through the glitter of orthodoxy. In 1543, a correspondent from Alcalá wrote to the Erasmian Juan Luis Vives (1492–1540), the "greatest Spanish humanist of the century," a *converso* from Valencia who chose to live abroad: "It is true what you say, that our fatherland is envious and proud: add that it is barbaric. For it is certain for them that no one modestly imbued with letters can be free of heresies, errors, and Judaism."[65] Philip II's adviser Fadique Furió Ceriol called for moderation, arguing that "in the whole world there are only two nations: that of the good and that of the bad. All the good, whether Jews, Moors, Gentiles, Christians, or some other sect, are of the same nation, family and blood; and the bad likewise." In his *Introduction to the Creed* (1582), Luis de Granada, Philip II's "own preacher and chaplain," was so moved by the expulsion of the Jews in 1492 that he condemned all religious persecution, whether directed at the "Moors or Jews or heretics or Gentiles," for to persecute "unbelievers" was a "much graver" sin, because it only made them more stubborn. A confidential report to Philip II also condemned violence in religious matters as counterproductive.[66]

Although writers such as Lope de Vega congratulated Philip III for the expulsion of the Moriscos, and Francisco Gómez de Quevedo and Vicente Espinel despised them (Cervantes was more charitable),[67] the Moriscos were sometimes redeemed in sixteenth-century literature, as when they appear as heroes in the last days of Muslim rule. This "literary Maurophilia," the critic Francisco Márquez Villanueva explained, "is the voice of a coalition of forces and groupings engaged in a struggle against the policy of duress and violence. This coalition was made up of the nobility, the Moriscos, the bourgeoisie, the [Jewish] conversos, the 'political' intellectuals, clerics of an

irenic persuasion, 'liberals' as we would say nowadays. It is a whole opposition contingent that we would hardly expect to come across if we were to
judge solely from the bibliography available to us."[68] Sometimes, the Moriscos were given a voice, as when a corsair once expelled from Valencia explains in Vicente Espinel's *Vida del escuedro Marcos de Obregón* (1618):

> I felt hurt, like all the others, because I could not aspire to honors or to
> appointment as a magistrate or higher dignities, and because I realized that
> such deprivation of honor *(infamia)* would be everlasting, and that being
> a Christian, whether in outer appearance or inner truth, would never be
> enough. Some fellow who, whether by birth, inheritance or acquired qual-
> ities did not stick up above ground level more than two fingers' breadth
> could still dare to call a very Christian man and a true gentleman by insult-
> ing names. Above all, I saw how far distant was the hope of any remedy to
> all this. What have you got to say to me about all this[?][69]

As I indicated earlier, despite the terror inflicted on the Moriscos, Castile has never succeeded in rallying the rest of the Iberian Peninsula to its
imperial banner. No matter how extreme and even genocidal the measures
perpetuated against the Moors and Moriscos were, the unity Castile sought
has eluded kings and presidents to this day. Spain's 1978 constitution, the
most "decentralized" in Europe, still maintains the autonomy of the Basque
and Catalan regions. "The Catholic Kings, Ferdinand and Isabella, did not
create, as we used to learn at school, a modern nation state," Raymond Carr
argues. "The union of the crowns of Castile and Aragon was a personal
union created by their marriage in 1469."[70] This is not to deny that religious unity has been a major leitmotif of Spanish history, at least since the
conversion of the Visigoth king Recared to Catholicism in 589. As Eva Borreguero has shown, by 754, the expression *pérdida de Hispania* appeared to
denote the "dispossession of a geographical and cultural unity," thereby,
for all intents and purposes, establishing the idea of a unified nation that
had already started reclaiming its lost lands in the Battle of Covadogna,
only seven years after the Muslims landed.[71] But whether the notion of a
lost Hispania served to rally Christians against the invading Muslims as
early as the eighth century (Iberian Jews were already being treated as fifth
columnists)[72] or the Reconquista consolidated a sense of nationhood that
simply did not exist before 1492 (at least not in its modern sense), Spain

never became as unified as its Castilian rulers hoped. After traveling two thousand miles in Spain, Richard Ford, the noted author of *Handbook for Travellers in Spain* (1844), concluded that Spain was "a bundle of local units tied together by a rope of sand." This view was echoed a century later by Gerald Brennan, in *The Spanish Labyrinth*: "In what we may call its normal condition Spain is a collection of small, mutually hostile or indifferent republics held together in a loose federation. At certain great periods (the Caliphate, the Reconquista, the Siglo de Oro) these small centres have been infected by a common feeling or idea and have moved in unison: then when the impetus given by this idea declined, they have fallen apart and resumed their separate and egoistic existence."[73] In fact, in 1640, not long after the Moriscos were expelled, the Catalans revolted and tried to secede when Castile tried to increase their tax burden to sustain an already flailing empire.[74]

Castile, in short, may have devised "a political framework which worked for a while," as the eminent historian Felipe Fernández-Armesto argues, but it did not create a "unified nation-state." It may well be that Spain's unity was elusive not because of the presence of Judaism and Islam but because of "the infinite variety of Catholic tradition itself" and the country's "pervasive localism." The saints of the *patria chica* (little country) were the real "demons" that thwarted any attempt at religious homogenization by the established universal church.[75] It was probably for this reason that Spain, even after 1492, was not considered sufficiently Christian. According to Borreguero, when "Cardinal Cisneros invited the famous scholar Erasmus of Rotterdam to the Iberian Peninsula, Erasmus rejected the offer, saying 'Non placet Hispania.'" Borreguero goes so far as to claim that the Inquisition was a response to the widespread view that Spain was barely a Christian society.[76]

By the eighteenth century, even Spaniards themselves could note that the unity of their nation was more myth than reality. For Olivares, a civil servant, Spain was "a body composed of other smaller bodies separated, and in opposition to one another, which oppress and despise each other and are in a continuous state of civil war. Each province, each religious house, each profession, is separated from the rest of the nation and concentrated in itself. . . . Modern Spain can be considered as a body without energy . . . a monstrous Republic formed of little republics which confront each other because the particular interest of each is in contradiction with the general interest."[77] That so many human lives were wasted and a vibrant multicultural society was brutally amputated for an idea that was never realized is tragic enough, but when the same impulse for unity continues to drive nations, including our own, in the modern age, we must wonder whether the very idea of "nation," at least in the modern sense bequeathed to us by the Catholic Monarchs and their heirs in the fifteenth and sixteenth centuries, is not one whose time has long passed. We now know that the ultimate horror of the Holocaust would not have been conceived without the tradition of racism initiated by Spain in the late Middle Ages and early modern period. Of course, Spain did not invent the Christian persecution of non-Christians, but it did give Christian intolerance added power by infusing it with the toxic notion of race.

The expulsion of Moriscos in 1609 may have been used by Spanish detractors as part of the Black Legend (the widely circulated notion in sixteenth-century Europe that Spain was a despotic, bloodthirsty, and intolerant nation),[78] but there is no doubt that other European powers had either practiced or learned from Spain's politics of exclusion—what Rodrigo de Zayas called "state racism." Pope Paul IV eventually relented and sanctioned the purity-of-blood statute, in 1555, thereby adding further tools to the power of the Inquisition, for the Inquisition as Zayas saw it was "not an isolated phenomenon but an essential part of the grand European state between 1481 and 1820." This is, in fact, Spain's contribution to universal, particularly modern, history. The Spanish Inquisition (born on September 27, 1480) survived long after the Moriscos were deported and would be abolished only on March 9, 1820, in the reign of Ferdinand VII (although aspects survived until 1834). The purity-of-blood doctrine was eliminated in Article V of the constitution of 1845, which opened state employment to all qualified people. A May 16, 1865, law would finally suppress any requirement to prove purity of blood for marriage or to have a political career. Meanwhile, the Catholic Church would officially distance itself from this bloody past only on October 28, 1965, during Vatican II (although the Vatican declaration *Nostra aetate: De ecclesiae habitudine ad religiones non-Christianas* remained quiet about certain aspects of Islam).[79]

As Zayas looked back at the Morisco question in Spain, he saw striking similarities between Adolf Hitler's state racism and that of Philip III. More interesting, however, is the case of Vichy France, which, in close collaboration with the Catholic establishment, resurrected another purity-of-blood doctrine, applied this time to "unassimilable" immigrants, most particularly Jews. In 1938, France was no longer willing to take in Jewish refugees because, as the president of the Foreign Affairs Commission of the Senate, Henry Béranger, indicated, France's capacity to welcome strangers was long saturated. After Maréchal Pétain assumed power, on July 10, 1940, French anti-Semitism was encoded in a series of laws restricting government employment and access to the liberal professions to French nationals whose fathers were also French, gradually revoking those privileges to Jews. The "status of Jews" *(statut des Juifs)* became an official concern, complete with an office named the Commissariat général aux questions juives (General Commissariat for Jewish Issues), headed by one Xavier Vallat, who at a 1942 conference wondered about the solution to this intractable problem. For Vallat, baptism was not sufficient to take Judaism out of a Jew and France was in direct conflict with an unassimilable Jewish tradition. He even thought that the government ought to confiscate Jewish property in order to eliminate "any Jewish influence on the national economy." Of course, it would be left to Germany to devise a "final solution."[80]

In fact, by racializing faith though *limpieza de sangre* statutes and thereby turning the genealogically multicultural Moors and Moriscos into a darker, irredeemable race—even though the immense majority, as the illustrious Spanish historian Claudio Sánchez Albornoz noted, in *La España musulmana,* were descendants of Spanish converts and had been living in the Iberian peninsula for nine hundred years or so—Spain gave birth to "the first racist State in history."[81] Not to be forgotten, too, is the fact that the term *race* is of Spanish origin. As defined in Sebastian de Covarrubias's dictionary, *Tesoro de la lengua castellana o española* (1611), *race* had negative connotations associated with the lesser human groups of Jews and Moors, because both were defiled by the *mancha* (taint). Although the term had not yet acquired the strict nineteenth-century biological meaning that gave rise to modern racism, its meaning extended beyond classic religious differences, because it grounded faith in an unchanging human essence. This is why the pope opposed the purity-of-blood statute in the first place, for to conflate faith with ethnicity was to negate the very raison d'être of the evangelical mission. Neither an expression of age-old forms of discrimination nor the sharpened biological concept of later centuries, Spain's notion of race nevertheless didn't preclude a natural connection, however tortuous, with the new etymology that arose in modern Europe. L. P. Harvey, the prominent historian of Muslim Spain, gives us a sense of the itinerary of this concept from its medieval Iberian context to the modern one:

> The word "race" (Spanish *raza*) first came into existence in Spain, and wherever it is used in the modern world it is in origin a Hispanism. It is not only in Nazi and Fascist terminology that it can have a positive connotation (as witness French *chien de race,* "pedigree dog"), but in Spain in the later Middle Ages, where it started out, it certainly carried a *negative* charge. *Raza* (*raça* in medieval spelling) meant a "defect" or "blemish" in the weaving of a piece of cloth. A bolt of cloth *sin raça* ("without any defect," "with no snags") was naturally worth more, and so by extension the ethnically pure were, for the purpose of the Inquisition, "sin raza de judíos/moros": "with no Jewish/Moorish blemish on their pedigree." The transition of this word from being an objectively negative commercial term in the late Middle Ages to its shamefully positive sense in the twentieth and twenty-first centuries, is one of the most curious semantic migrations.[82]

Associating the Moors and Moriscos with the Arab and Berber conquerors of 711, many Christian Spaniards claimed direct descent from the Visigoths, thereby cleansing their blood lineage of some nine hundred years (711–1614) of shared existence on the peninsula. Of course, such distinctions were nearly impossible to make, which is why the Inquisition had to resort to examining men's foreskins, looking for the indelible circumcision that would identify men as non-Christians (Jews or Muslims) or recent converts. Yet this view of the Moriscos persisted until our time, for, as late as 1973, *Vox,* the Spanish-language illustrated dictionary, related the term *Morisco* to "a descendant of a mulatto man and a European woman, or a mulatto woman and a European man."[83]

Scholars such as Rodrigo de Zayas, L. P. Harvey, and Joseph Pérez, who have studied the Moriscos and the Inquisition, often compare the situation in the centuries following the fall of Granada to the policies of Nazi Germany or the secret police of the twentieth-century Communist regimes in Europe. Moreover, this *passion génocidaire* (passion for genocide), a phrase with which Georges Bensoussan, the historian and chief editor at the Holocaust museum in Paris, titled his 2006 book, is a uniquely European phenomenon, born of the amalgamation of religion and politics (a fact shrewdly noted by Machiavelli, as indicated earlier). Bensoussan refuses to accept the dismissals of the Holocaust as a mere aberration, a dark, inexplicable moment in European history, and shows it to be part of an enduring culture of Christian anti-Judaism and conspiracy theories attributing evil and the quest for world domination to all Jews. "It is the Church that has taught us that Jews are a terrible danger," said the chief Italian Fascist, Roberto Farinacci, in 1938. For how can one understand the Nuremberg laws of 1935 without knowledge of Spain's fifteenth-century *limpieza de sangre* statutes or the fact that the Nazis relied on the Protestant Martin Luther's anti-Semitic ideology? The Holocaust may have shocked only because, as Aimé Césaire put it in his *Discourse on Colonialism* (1955), what had long applied to colonized natives came back to haunt Europe itself. The British, for instance, had annihilated the entire native population of the island of Tasmania in the nineteenth century.[84] Because of such wanton European atrocities against non-European people, the humanist European bourgeois, in Césaire's opinion, shared more of Hitler's traits than he dared to admit:

> Yes, it would be worthwhile to study clinically, in detail, the steps taken by Hitler and Hitlerism and to reveal to the very distinguished, very humanistic, very Christian bourgeois of the twentieth century that without being aware of it, he has a Hitler inside him, that Hitler *inhabits* him, that Hitler is his *demon,* that if he rails against him, he is being inconsistent and that, at bottom, what he cannot forgive Hitler for is not *the crime* in itself, *the crime against man,* it is not *the humiliation of man as such,* it is the crime against the white man, the humiliation of the white man, and the fact he applied to Europe colonialist procedures which until then had been reserved exclusively for the Arabs of Algeria, the "coolies" of India, and the "niggers" of Africa.[85]

It is this long, archaic genealogy of violence at the heart of European culture that explains the phenomenon of the Holocaust, so to say that the event is a parenthetical one in Europe's culture of reason is to preempt the acknowledgment of its genealogy and roots, which might possibly be the only way to prevent it from happening again, although "cultural and political regressions are an integral part of our possibilities."[86]

Given that the contempt, vilification, demonization, and dehumanization of Jews were an inextricable part of Christian Europe's history, and that Jews had been treated as the enemy within—associated since the Middle Ages with the plague, ritual murders, nauseating odors (eliminated only through baptism, and even then, as the case of Spain shows, not really), and the anti-Christ—one might consider the Holocaust to be "the violent resurgence of the most archaic part of Christian Europe's repressed."[87] The Jew, in fact, is at the heart of the eschatology of Christian apocalyptic messianism, because her conversion is essential to the coming of Christ's reign on earth. Here, as has happened throughout European history, Muslims are connected to Jews, as seventeenth-century English millenarianism shows. In his *Revelations of the Apocalypse,* Thomas Brightman (1562–1607) explained that the collapse of the papacy, the defeat of the Ottoman Empire, and the conversion of Jews were essential to the heralding of the new millennial order. In fact, the London Society of Promoting Christianity among the Jews was created in 1809 in this spirit, advocating the return of the Jews to the Holy Land (a view shared by Isaac Newton), as expressed in the Balfour Declaration of November 2, 1917. Jews were either vilified or idealized, and rarely treated as mere human beings. "In this universe," concludes Bensoussan, "the image of the Jew remains ambivalent. He has killed the Savior, but his redemption (his disappearance as a Jew) heralds the end of misfortune for the whole of humanity."[88]

With the exception of making these brief connections, Bensoussan's study doesn't address the long history of European violence against the Moors, for it was often in the larger context of the Muslim-Christian clash that the Jews got labeled allies of the Muslim enemy. Moreover, it is quite conceivable to consider the expulsion of Spanish Moriscos from their native land a genocidal act.[89] One might understand the hesitation to highlight Muslim suffering in light of recent Muslim Judeophobia fueled by the Israeli-Palestinian conflict and the wider West-versus-Islam conflict—a tragic development, as we shall see, in the common suffering of Jew and Muslim in Europe's exclusivist traditions. For, at least in the case of Spain, the Jew and Muslim suffered equally. "Whose situation was the most abominable, that of the Jew or of the Moor?" asked Henry Méchoulan in his lyrical study *Le Sang de l'autre; ou, L'Honneur de Dieu* (1979). There were differences, to be sure, but these differences were a matter of degree within a common consensus that the treatment of both, unlike that of Indians and blacks (for whom the purity-of-blood statutes didn't apply), was equally despicable. The Old Testament Jew was a theological challenge to the Bible-believing

Christian, despised and accused but part of the church's corpus neverthe-less. The Jew's conversion could be (and evidently was) sincere, if one were to count the number of *conversos* who denounced Judaism. The Moriscos, who had no one like the Dominican Bartolomé de Las Casas to defend their cause, were merely a barbaric people in comparison to Indians. Their faith made them aggravated Jews, so to speak. They were suspect members of a heretical religion with threatening military powers in the region. They en-gaged in pleasures of the flesh, practiced sodomy and bestiality, and prolif-erated. Salvatierra, the bishop of Ségovia, like many others we encountered earlier, considered Moriscos to be "far worse than the Jews and proposed a solution for them that the Nazis would try to apply": he proposed deporta-tion accompanied by the castration of men and the sterilization of women.[90] To Joseph Pérez, the Moriscos were the victims of a "strikingly modern racism, one that is aimed at a population that everyone knows is indispens-able to the country's economic life and yet is hated not because of its reli-gious difference but because it represents a different, and therefore suspect, kind of civilization."[91]

In a later article, Méchoulan listed the many ways in which Jews and Moors or Moriscos suffered the same fate. They both tried to maintain their faith, and both were subjected to the Inquisition. Purity-of-blood statutes excluded both communities from public service, branding them with the permanent taint of impurity. Like the Jews who converted to Christianity, the Moriscos were not accorded the privileges of conversion, as baptismal waters were not enough to remove the taint of infidelity. Just as Jews were associated with bad odors, suffering from permanent cases of hemorrhoids and anal bleeding, the Moriscos were accused of being shameless sex mani-acs who copulated even with animals.[92]

Today, the status of the Jew has improved considerably within European culture. Old Christian and racial condemnations, still espoused only a few decades ago by conservative and nationalist parties, have been discarded. The Jew, in fact, has become the ideal prototype for the new European cit-izen, one who can live comfortably with at least two major identities. As Matti Bunzl argues in what is certainly one of the most insightful and artic-ulate examinations of the differences between Jews and Muslims in modern European history, if anti-Semitism defined Europe's culture of exclusion prior to the mid-twentieth century, "Islamophobia is a phenomenon of the current age."[93]

Thus, Islamophobia can be included in the genocidal impulse that Bensoussan alludes to. By asserting that Muslims, including the nation of Turkey, cannot fit into European civilization, the European Right (traditionally
the hotbed of anti-Semitism) and other detractors of Islam are in fact re-
peating an old tenet of anti-Semitism: that no matter how successfully a Jew
might be integrated into European culture, he or she will always remain
an outsider. Such views have been so widely held that even progressive intellectuals have taken them for granted. The nineteenth-century French
utopian socialist Pierre-Joseph Proudhon, for instance, had no problem declaring the Jews enemies of humanity and wanted them sent back to Asia
or exterminated.[94] The following statement by the English writer Joseph
Banister, in his 1901 book, *England under the Jews,* is also a good indica-
tion of the very long road Muslims have had to travel to be treated as an
integral part of Europe's population: "It is only when [the Jew] insists upon
posing as a European, and being judged as a European, that one realizes
what an obnoxious creature he is, and how utterly out of place in a European country and in European society."[95]

Despite political differences that separate many Jews and Muslims today,
the Jew, as we shall see in more detail in chapter 3, was long the Moor
within European civilization—the dark, anti-Christian menace that threatened the unity of pure nations, a notion, as Bensoussan noted, that was
reactivated in modern Germany but was widely shared across the continent.
For most of modern history, Jews and Muslims have been cultural allies and
fellow victims of the European social order. Indeed, when given the opportunity, many Jews proudly embraced their kinship with their fellow Semites and Orientals. This brings us to a surprising twist in the Moors' journey,
one in which Jews, like African Americans in the New World, proudly (re)-
claimed their Moorish identity as a token of cultural superiority over barbarous Europe, even as they paid a horrible price for doing so. I will return
to this intriguing moment in Semitic bonding after I trace the survival of
Moors and Moorishness in the New World that Spain created across the
Atlantic.

chapter 2

New World Moors

It may be said unequivocally that the image of al-Andalūs engraved on the
retina of the *reconquistador* once again appeared in the eyes of the conquistador
of the New World.

> —RAFAEL A. GUEVARA BAZÁN, "Muslim Immigration to
> Spanish America"

From Columbus's day through the thirteen colonies' declaration of independence
on July 4, 1776, and into the early days of U.S. history, the struggle against
Muslims was one of the most significant issues in Christendom.

> —ALLAN D. AUSTIN, *African Muslims in Antebellum America*

In October 2005, more than five hundred years after Granada fell and America
was conquered, and almost four hundred years since the order was given
to expel the Moriscos from Spain, the *New York Times* published an intriguing article about the number of Chicanos who undergo DNA testing
to find out whether they might have Jewish ancestry. It turns out that 10
percent of those who take the test show "Semitic ancestry strongly suggesting a Jewish background."[1] These would be the crypto-Jews (commonly
known, as we saw in chapter 1, by the originally pejorative label Marranos),
living in disguise in the relative safety of the outer edges of the Spanish
Empire for centuries. Upon unearthing their buried roots, many Marranos
revert—not convert—to their ancestors' faith. Leaving alone the astound-
ing powers of DNA testing and what it can do to bring down nefarious
myths about race[2] or to help people seek membership privileges (such as
benefits to people of Native American descent, or citizenship in Israel on

the basis of a Jewish gene),[3] what particularly struck me was a passing note in the article that the results of some people tested turn out to "suggest North African Muslim ancestry." For a Hispanic to rediscover his or her Jewish heritage would make some sense, given that the Jews are now successfully assimilated in the United States and most Western societies, and it might be a matter of pride to associate oneself with this once-marginalized community. Many Hispanics in the United States are, in some ways, what the Jews used to be, and reclaiming one's Jewish heritage might strike a blow at the essentialist ideologies of Anglo-Saxon supremacists.[4] So imagine the surprise that must hit those who find out that they are not Jews but North African Muslims, the Moors of old! The year 2005 was certainly not a good time to find out that one is Muslim—at least not in post-9/11 America.

Yet, despite this prevailing anti-Muslim climate, Hispanics—and not just Chicanos—have been discovering Islam and, like their peers in the African American community, converting, or reverting, in the last few years. Indeed, the conversion story of Malcolm X has almost become a parable or template for all minorities not just in the United States but also, increasingly, in Europe, where, in a remarkable historical twist, Arab prisoners are inspired by Malcolm X's redemption saga. Quite a few African Americans and Latinos have been influenced by Islam to change their ways and find a higher calling in the message of social justice that Islam conveys. Less than six weeks after 9/11, the *New York Times* reported an expert's opinion that around 25,000 people in America convert to Islam every single year, the vast majority of whom are African American.[5] Latinos convert in fewer numbers, but many, the paper reported in another article, "are drawn to Islam as a way of reaching back to what they consider their true culture, the world of Islamic Spain that existed for more than 700 years after the first Muslim conquests in the eighth century."[6]

Hispanics' identification with Islam and Arab culture is not a recent phenomenon. As far back as 1959, Fidel Castro commented that Latin Americans "have lighter or darker skin. Lighter skin implies descent from Spaniards who themselves were colonized by the Moors that came from Africa. Those who are more or less dark-skinned came directly from Africa. Moreover, nobody can consider himself as being of pure, much less superior race."[7] Not only that, but, according to Hisham Aidi, one of the most astute observers of the dynamic cultural exchanges between the West's minorities, Arab and Islamic cultures, and the African American tradition, José

Padilla (found guilty in 2007 of conspiracy to commit acts of terrorism, after a Kafkaesque judicial process); Hiram Torres, a bright Yale student who dropped college for Pakistan; and other Latinos were part of a large contingent of African American and Latino Muslims volunteering to fight for Muslim causes in Bosnia, Chechnya, Lebanon, and Afghanistan. Even the firebrand leader of Venezuela, Hugo Chávez, started urging his fellow Venezuelans to "return to their Arab roots."[8] Such statements not only prove that Spain's methodical attempts to cleanse its newly acquired territories from Moorish presence have failed, but they also reveal that the cultural heirs to Spain in the New World are embracing their Moorish heritage as a badge of honor.

It may be tempting, and to some extent not untrue, to say that the reasons for such identifications and conversions are the solid sense of belonging, meaningful social solidarities, and the fulfilling rituals of faith that Islam provides to alienated people from all races and backgrounds. There is also the element of reconnecting with one's origins in the Old World, whether such origins are real or imagined. All this is fairly obvious, but what interested me as I read about Hispanics' DNA testing and reverting/ converting is their attempt to resist the dominant Anglo-Protestant ideology that has kept them in the margins, much as Muslims and Arabs in Europe resist their confinement in social ghettos. For Chicanos or Hispanics to find out that they are Jewish or even Muslim is to connect with more than a race, for such vital affiliations make them part of glorious legacies, ones that included both a great degree of cultural achievement and a history of heroic resistance to disenfranchisement, systematic marginalization, and the constant threat of expulsion. Connecting with one's Moorish or Jewish heritage is to be united with kindred spirits who endured and survived discriminations of the worst sort because they found themselves in a world not of their making. For Jews and Muslims share more than common religious rituals or mutual hatred born of struggles over land and politics; they also share the history of being second-class citizens in Europe.

The post-Andalusian condition that emerged out of the Reconquista— the long process whereby the Iberian Peninsula was gradually reconquered from Muslims, was shaped and defined by the Catholic Monarchs of Spain, and then mutated over time into a variety of ideologies and idioms—has been adept at both producing Otherness and, paradoxically, punishing the Other for not being the Same. As I suggested earlier, this almost-willed ambivalence that defines the West's liberal project is worth contemplating, if only in passing, because one might argue that this unresolved ambiguity—the call to be the same and different at the same time—is at the heart of the global crisis today. Minorities serve the vital political function of uniting nations, but to identify a minority group is also to launch a crusade to assimilate it into the mainstream, to make it an undifferentiated mass. As imperfect and unfinished as the project was, Spain depended on its war against Islam, on the conversion of the defeated Moors, and finally on the expulsion of Jews and Moriscos to create and consolidate a sense of its identity, an element that was crucial in its early expansionist ventures.

I suggest that Hispanics today are the Anglos' Moors, just as the Jews were Europe's Muslims for much of that continent's history. I am not in any way suggesting that these situations are exact mirrors of each other or that the situation of the Moors in late-medieval and early-modern Spain is similar to that of minorities in other places and later centuries. Not only are the historical conditions vastly different, but also history, in its details, never repeats itself. The criteria for national membership in sixteenth-century Spain are not those of people living in twenty-first-century secular Western states. By drawing the analogy between Moors and non-Muslim minorities in modern history, I am mostly interested in the paradigm: the categories that determine the main culture and its outsiders, and how social groups are placed in relation to dominant national ideologies. It is the political, social, and above all symbolic function of the Moor—Europe's quintessential Other and its perennial outsider—in the modern West that I find consistent throughout modern history. If, as John V. Tolan concludes in his study of the image of Islam in medieval Europe, the "Saracen (and more generally the non-Christian, be he Jew or Cathar or, in the centuries that followed, an African animist or an Inca priest) was different, was inferior, precisely because he refused the universal message of Christianity,"[9] the Moor is now anyone who remains outside the Western economic, cultural, and political consensus. The Moors are those not sufficiently assimilated into Western societies, those who still cling tenaciously to their ancestral ways and languages.

Christianity may have been transmuted into more secular conceptions of national identity, and the Saracens, or Moors, may have acquired new characteristics over the centuries, but the paradigm defining proper membership in a community has remained remarkably consistent. Resistance to national languages, racially coded concepts of nationalism, and immigration policies that do not take into account unfair global economic policies turn Muslim and Hispanic immigrants and other minorities into vulnerable communities in Western liberal societies. The criteria for exclusion are vastly different in our era of globalization and multicultural tensions than they were for Moors and Moriscos under Spanish rule in earlier centuries, but the value of minority groups as sacrificial elements in a nation's quest for national unity has retained much of its power. A nation's unifying principles may change, thereby shifting the status of minority to any entity that remains outside of the new mainstream consensus, but the vital function of minorities in creating a sense of identity and solidifying the dominant regime has remained essentially unchanged since Queen Isabella and King Ferdinand consciously tied their hold on power and the strength of their emerging nation to the unity of faith.

It may be well to recall that the Moor was not the only scapegoat against whom Castile tried to unify a number of independent kingdoms in the Iberian Peninsula and thereby to create the sense of national identity crucial to empire building and the conquest of the newly discovered continent of North America. Moorishness, as Renaissance Europe and *Othello* make clear, remained an indeterminate category, one defined solely by its difference from the nascent concept of European identity. Emily Bartels explains:

> While blackness and Mohammedism were stereotyped as evil, Renaissance representations of the Moor were vague, varied, inconsistent, and contradictory. As critics have established, the term "Moor" was used interchangeably with such similarly ambiguous terms as "African," "Ethiopian," "Negro," and even "Indian" to designate a figure from different parts or the whole of Africa (or beyond) who was either black or Moslem, neither, or both. To complicate the vision further, the Moor was characterized alternately and sometimes simultaneously in contradictory extremes, as noble or monstrous, civil or savage.[10]

Michael Neill, echoing Bartels's description, elaborates by saying that

> insofar as [the term *Moor*] was a term of racial description it could refer quite specifically to the Berber-Arab people of the part of North Africa then rather

vaguely denominated as "Morocco," "Mauritania," or "Barbary"; or it could
be used to embrace the inhabitants of the whole North African littoral; or
it might be extended to refer to Africans generally (whether "white," "black,"
or tawny Moors); or by an even more promiscuous extension, it might be
applied (like "Indian") to almost any darker-skinned peoples—even, on occasion, those of the New World. Consequently when Marlowe's Valdes refers
to the supine obedience of "Indian *Moores*" to "their Spanish Lords" (*Faus-
tus*, 1.1.148), it is usually assumed that the two terms are simply mutually
intensifying synonyms, and that the magician means something like "dusky
New World natives." But *Moor* could often be deployed (in a fashion perhaps inflected, even for the English, by memories of the Spanish *Reconquista*)
as a religious category. Thus Muslims on the Indian subcontinent were habit-
ually called "Moors," and the same term is used in East India Company literature to describe the Muslim inhabitants of Southeast Asia, whether they be
Arab or Indian traders, or indigenous Malays. So Valdes's "Indian Moores"
could equally well be Muslims from the Spanish-controlled Portuguese East
Indies. In such contexts it is simply impossible to be sure whether *Moor* is a
description of color or religion or some vague amalgam of the two, and in
the intoxicated exoticism of Marlovian geography, such discriminations hardly
matter.[11]

Both Bartels and Neill note that the Moor category extended to Asians.
In his *The Principal Navigations, Voyages, Traffiques, & Discoveries of the English Nation* (1589), Richard Hakluyt reported the account of an anonymous Portuguese adventurer who had gone to China and found Moors so
far removed from their origins that they had only a rudimentary notion of
their belief: "They could say nothing else but Mahomet, my father was a
Moore, and I am a Moore, with some other wordes of their Alcoran, where-
withal, in abstinence from swines flesh, they live until the divel take them
all."[12] Describing the people he had met in China, the Dutch traveler Jan
Huyghen van Linschoten wrote, in his *Discours of Voyages into ye Easte &
West Indies* (1598), that "those that dwell on the Sea side . . . are a people
of a *brownish* colour, like the *white* Moores in Africa and Barbaria, and part
of the Spaniards, but those that dwell within the land, *are for color like
Netherlanders & high Dutches*."[13] Because of the interaction between Muslims from the Philippines (later called Moros by Spanish colonialists) and
the Hui Chinese in the Shandong Province in the fifteenth century, the

contemporary scholar Mansur Xu Xianiong was told by a Chinese Communist official in 1989 that he was a Moor![14]

As is obvious in chapter 1, and indeed through much of this book, the Moor served as a foil for an emerging European consciousness. Patricia Seed has noted that the term *Europe* was rarely used before the fifteenth century, proving that the impetus for a European identity, traversed as it was by growing national singularities, was expansionism and colonialism.[15] Around the time the Moriscos were being expelled from Spain, Europeans were beginning to define themselves as white. For example, Samuel Purchas, author of *Hakluytus Posthumus; or, Purchas His Pilgrimes* (1625), used whiteness as a distinguishing feature of the nascent settlement as early as 1613 and so excluded darker-skinned people from membership.[16] If the First Crusade against Islam united Europe around a Christian identity, the defeat of the Moors in Spain and the expulsion of the Moriscos in the early seventeenth century created a new European consciousness, one that gave more depth to the eighth-century Andalusian priest Isidore Pacensis's term *Europenses,* which itself was forged out of the defeat of Muslims in France. Thus, Europe would grow to believe in its cultural and racial distinctiveness and would use such exceptionalism to shape its relations with non-Europeans.

But let's focus on New Mexico for a moment. The more I think about this culturally intriguing southwestern state, the better I can decipher the ghostly presence of the Moor in its history and traditions. The capital of the state was named after the fortress of faith, the *castrum* founded in 1491 and built by the army on the edge of Muslim Granada before its surrender to King Ferdinand and Queen Isabella in 1492. Santa Fe's "name, design, and general aspects," writes Mercedes García-Arenal, would later become the model for a new architecture blending the styles of holy war and modernity, including in the Americas. (The city of Santa Fe, whose patron saint and protector, the Virgin of the Rosary, is also known as the Conquistadora, obviously stands as the triumph of the Spanish over the Indians-as-Moors.) The people's hospitals *(hospitales-pueblo),* founded by Vasco de Quiroga, would be named Santa Fe, just as numerous towns and cities would be designed on the model of the provisional city built next to Granada. In fact, in 1541, Quiroga and the viceroy Antonio de Mendoza tried to change the name Valladolid de Michoacán to Santa Cruz de Granada.[17]

The conquest of the Indians was simply an extension of the Crusades launched against Muslims in earlier centuries, culminating in the surrender of Granada in 1492 and the forced conversion of Muslims, and then, as was shown in chapter 1, the persecution of the converted, whether the converted were sincere in their conversion or not. In his book *La Herencia medieval de México*, Luis Weckmann makes the connection between Moor and Indian, in the eye of the conquistador, unambiguous:

> The Hieronymite friars referred to the inhabitants of Hispaniola as "these Moors." In the initial years in New Spain the term "mosque" was used to name the indigenous places of worship and the term "alfaqui" to refer to the indigenous priests. . . . Martín Vázquez calls Cholula a "Moorish pueblo." . . . Castilblanco had fourteen "mosques," or places of worship, and many more existed in Tlaxcala and Tenochtitlán, whose largest temple "with exquisite stonework and wood (has) 'zaquizamíes,' meaning 'alfarjes.'" The conquistadors were not surprised at finding in New Galicia—as mentioned in the second Anonymous Report—"women branded (that is, marked with a branding iron) on the chin like Moorish women," nor at finding "mosques" in Florida and Chícora (Hernando Soto) or in New Mexico (Castaño de Sosa).[18]

The defeat of the Moors in Granada and the Aztecs in Mexico set in motion an assimilationist ideology, using conversion and education as vehicles to sever the ties of Moriscos and indigenous peoples of New Spain from their past. Language and grammar books were deployed for this specific purpose. Some, such as Hernando de Talavera, the liberal and first archbishop of Granada, and founder of the first seminary in Europe, allowed for the coexistence of local customs; others, such as Cardinal Francisco Jiménez de Cisneros, preferred a policy of conversion through outright coercion. The University of Granada, for instance, was established with the aim of converting the Moriscos at home and educating the missionaries among the indigenous populations.[19] With the Christianization of the state, the provincial council of Seville (1512), convened in a city with a heavy Muslim and Jewish population, would become the model for later American councils; but the *modelo granadino* is even closer to our purposes, for it was in this old Nasrid territory that state-church relations in the New World would be worked out, especially in the 1554 synod of Guadix, which outlined new norms for the newly converted Old Christians and ecclesiastical reforms. The Guadix provisions inspired the first provincial council of Mexico, in 1555, presided over by Alonso de Montúfar, second archbishop of Mexico, who had been born and raised in Granada and had taught in Seville and at the newly established University of Granada. Both the Guadix and Mexico conferences emphasized the teaching (indoctrination) of Morisco and Indian children and adults, paying special attention to religious education; the practice of sacraments; and vigilance against the temptation of the natives to slide back into their old beliefs.[20] Antonio Domínguez Ortiz and Bernard Vincent have explained that the evangelical efforts of Jesuits focused primarily on the children of Moriscos and Indians, for as a 1525 policy by King Charles V cynically put it, if children were made Christian, it would be easier for their parents to follow suit, because parents would otherwise have to lose their children.[21]

The formal annexation of the "kingdoms and provinces of New Mexico" into the Spanish Empire, on April 30, 1598, by Juan de Oñate, was described by Gaspar Pérez de Villagrá, Oñate's captain, as an act of "baptism" for the province's "barbarians" in the epic poem *Historia de la Nueva Mexico* (1610). The Pueblo Indians of New Mexico are compared to the Moors, discovering the error of their ways and miraculously seeing the light of Christian truth. The poem is also a propaganda piece. The new conquistadors are compared to the brave Spaniards "who hurl themselves, / Into the famous land of Barbary, / To capture the dispersed Moors." The Moor was ever present, as noisy plays making use of harquebuses were staged during the Oñate expedition to terrify the natives:

A solemn feast that did endure
For a whole week, in which there were
Tilts with cane-spears, bullfights, tilts at the ring,
A jolly drama, well-composed,
Playing at Moors and Christians,
With much artillery, whose roar
Did cause notable fear and marveling
To many bold barbarians who had
Come there as spies to spy on us,
To see the strength and arms possessed
By the Spaniards. . . .[22]

The staged defeat of the Moor was thus a warning to natives; it was a dramatic preemptive strike.

The specter of the Moor haunted the Iberian New World. As in the home country, the Moor—like the Jew, the heretic, and even the Lutheran—was a disruptive element that had to be kept away from Spain's overseas bonanza. As I noted in the introduction, Spain's policy toward Muslim immigrants to the New World amounted to a form of Islamophobia, although the meaning may have been slightly different in the sixteenth century than it is now, for however fierce Spain's fear of Islam may have been, it was more doctrinal than racial, closer to classical anti-Semitism than to newer forms of racism.[23] In 1501, Muslims, Jews, heretics, and recent *conversos* were forbidden entry to America; only "Negro slaves or other Negro slaves who have been born in the possession of our native Christian subjects" were granted an exception, which is how African converts to Catholicism (known at that time as Ladinos) arrived in the New World. Muslims first arrived as "slaves, merchants or sailors." By 1517, Muslims and Jews were practicing their faith so openly in the Caribbean that, on July 22 of that year, Cardinal Jiménez de Cisneros "delegated his powers as general Apostolic Inquisitor to the Bishops of Santa María of the islands of Santo Domingo and Conception," because the practices of Muslims and Jews were "offensive to our Christian religion and evangelical law, and a grave scandal to Christian believers." On September 15, 1522, the Spanish king Charles V published a law decreeing that "no recent convert to our holy faith, be he Moor or Jew, or children of such, may go to the Indies without our special license." On February 25, 1530, another law was issued to punish, primarily through a fine of one thousand pesos, those who transported slaves to America without obtaining a license, particularly if such slaves were Berbers, Moors, Jews, or mulattoes. The same caution against transporting "white Berber" slaves was reiterated the following year, on December 19, 1531. In 1539, the Spanish king issued a decree strongly prohibiting "the transfer to the West Indies of sons and grandsons of persons burned at the stake *(quemados)*, Jewish or Moorish abjurers *(reconciliados),*" Jewish *conversos,* and Moriscos. Five years later, in 1543, Charles V went further and decreed the expulsion of Muslims already settled in America, "impos[ing] a new penalty of 10,000 *maravedíes* upon those who disregarded the law."[24] On July 13, 1556, yet another law, issued to the Spanish rulers of the New World (Indies) to repatriate to Spain all Muslims—including converts and their children—began by expressing frustration over the failed attempts to rid America of Muslims: "Be it known to you that we are informed that Berber slaves and other free persons, recently converted Moors and their sons, have gone, and each day continue to go, to those parts, [though] we have decreed that under no condition should they go, on account of the many annoyances which seem, from practical experience, to follow those who have gone."[25]

As more restrictions were placed on Muslim slaves, especially those from the eastern Mediterranean, the price of non-Muslim slaves from Africa understandably went up. By 1559, the tone of desperation was becoming palpable, as the Lutherans were added to the list of people denied entry. On July 13 of that year, a decree issued in Valladolid by order of His Majesty appealed for increased vigilance:

> It is fitting that wherever our Catholic faith has recently been established great vigilance be observed that no heresy be sown or found. And if such be found, it should be exterminated, destroyed and punished with vigor. Thus I beg of you, each and every one in our dioceses, archbishoprics and bishoprics, to be on the alert to inform us and let us know if any Lutherans, Moors, Jews or those who may follow any heresies have gone there, and finding such, to punish them. We send the same warning to our viceroys, presidents, judges of our royal courts in these parts, and to any of our governors there, that they give you all the support and help that you request and need.[26]

By 1570, the Spanish king was recommending tolerance toward Indians who had "embraced the faith (secta) of Muhammad," although the policy of excluding "Berber slaves" and Moriscos from Spanish dominions kept being reaffirmed until at least 1578.[27] Spain wanted docile subjects, not troublesome Muslims. As Rafael A. Guevara Bazán noted in a 1971 essay, Islam was such a powerful vehicle of contest that the first European to spot American land, Rodrigo de Tríana (or Rodrigo de Lepe) converted to Islam upon his return to Spain "because Columbus did not give him credit, nor the King any recompense, for having seen—before any other man in the crew—light in the Indies" (spotting light and land were considered two different matters).[28] In fact, reports (no doubt exaggerated) had it that, to object to Cardinal Jiménez de Cisneros's reforms in the 1490s, "more than a thousand friars quitted the country and passed over to Barbary, preferring rather to live with the infidel than conform." Later, under the reign of Philip II in the sixteenth century, "unpaid garrison soldiers in the African ports were reported to be deserting to the Muslims."[29] The New World, if one were

to believe the procession of royal decrees and restrictive immigration policies crafted in the sixteenth century, was crawling with Muslims and Morisco
illegal immigrants.

Although I had visited several times before, my new appreciation of New
Mexico's history made my trip there in 2005 feel like a sort of homecom-
ing, particularly given that Esteban the Moor, the first non-Indian to enter
that territory, a fellow native of Morocco, is proudly reclaimed by Moroccan scholars not only as a long-lost compatriot and brave explorer but also
as a martyr. Abdelhamid Lotfi, author of a study on Islam in America,
dedicates his book to Mustafa Zemmouri, the Arabic name for Esteban,
thus: "To the memory of my countryman, Mustafa Zemmouri, martyred
in Hawikuh, New Mexico, in 1539, who opened the vast territories of the
American Southwest."[30] Esteban made famous the Moroccan coastal town
of Azemmour, occupied by the Portuguese in 1513. It was from there that
he was shipped to Portugal and sold in the slave market, before ending
up in the New World and joining Pánfilo de Narváez's expedition to the
"island" of Florida, in 1527–1528. This "black Arab" *(negro alárabe)* belonged
to Andrés Dorantes, who was also part of the expedition. Both, together
with Alvar Núñez Cabeza de Vaca and Alonso del Castillo Maldonado,
survived the harrowing adventure, ending up, in 1536, in San Miguel Culiacan, on the Pacific coast of New Spain. So impressed was New Spain's
first viceroy, Granada-born Antonio de Mendoza, with Esteban's intelligence
and enterprising spirit that he purchased him from Dorantes and sent him
back to explore the northern region with the Franciscan Marcos de Niza
in 1539. It was then that Esteban sent back word that he had found Cibola,
one of the seven fabled cities—the biggest and wealthiest in the world. By
having diffused this myth, probably learned in the Iberian Peninsula, he
contributed to the later expedition financed by Francisco Vázquez Coronado, which led to the discovery of the Grand Canyon of Colorado.[31]

Moorish connections keep unfolding. The seven fabled cities that Esteban was supposed to have found grew out of the myth of the Seven Cities
on the island of Antilia, the place on the western horizon where the Portuguese, led by seven bishops, had fled upon the conquest of the Iberian Peninsula by the Moors in 711. Eventually, the geography shifted, though the
Seven Cities remained across the Atlantic; but by the end of the sixteenth
century the name disappeared from the maps, and survives only as the name
of a village (Sete Cidades) on the island of San Miguel in the Azores.

(Culiacan itself, the Pacific town from which the Cibola expedition started, had been founded by Nuño de Guzmán in 1531, during a failed quest for the Seven Cities triggered by information from his Indian slave Tejo.)[32] It was thus that the bearded Esteban, leading 300 men and many women, entered the Zuni pueblo of Hawikuh in 1539, where he was arrested and killed for reasons that are not quite clear. He would have been "martyred," to use Lotfi's expression, if he had been the victim of a possible misunderstanding, as a Ladino or Morisco slave leading a reconnaissance mission on behalf of white Christians being caught in the crossfire of colonial wars. How ironic it would have been if Esteban had lived to see Francisco Vasquez de Coronado (1510–1554), the military leader of the failed expedition, rename Hawikuh Granada the following year because the Zuni pueblo reminded him of the Moorish quarter of the Albaicín (near the Alhambra) in that Spanish city![33] This is yet another example of how Spaniards, in fashioning the New World and waging war on Native Americans, treated the latter as embodiments of the Moor.

By being a Morisco, a convert to Christianity, Esteban not only bridged the Muslim and Catholic worlds, the worlds of the conquistadors and the Moors, but also, with his black skin color, blurred the color lines that sometimes separated North and sub-Saharan Africans. Even more fascinating, and surely confusing to the natives dealing with their own shock of discovery, Esteban the Moor was considered part of the white culture, since a Pueblo saying has it that "the first *white* man our people saw was a *black* man."[34] Of course, Esteban's skin color was not white, but he certainly expands the category of Moorishness to West Africa, the main source of slaves in the New World. In 1940, on the occasion of the Coronado Cuarto Centennial, the scholar Rayford Logan made the case, against those who wanted to highlight Esteban's Moorish or Arab identity, that the Moor was in fact a Negro in the North American sense of the word. It's not as if such fine skin-color distinctions would have mattered much in 1940: "Even if the Cuarto Centennial officials had made Estevancio [Esteban] a Moor rather than a Negro," Logan wryly reflected, "he might have suffered in Texas in 1940 the fate that he met in New Mexico in 1539."[35]

If this were the case, then, why did Logan write an essay arguing for the blackness of Esteban? What does it matter if Esteban were black, Arab, or *negro,* in the Spanish sense of being dark skinned, not necessarily black? Such fine racial distinctions, when viewed in the larger history of Africans in America, appear rather trivial, for to be Moorish meant being Muslim, whether one was black, white, or any color in between. As the historian Michael Gomez explains, "The long and extensive interaction between North and West Africans, bond and free, both in Africa and al-Andalus, was such that the distinction between 'black' and 'white' Africans was often devoid of biological meaning, though it was maintained as part of very real social conventions." Still, slave traders and holders could distinguish between *sarracenos negros* (black Muslims), *azenagues* (Tuaregs), "blackmoor" captives, *negros de jalof* (commonly known as Wolofs, an ethnic group found in today's Senegal, Gambia, and Mauritania), and particularly the infamous *mandingas,* Mande-speaking slaves (from the Senegambian and Sierra Leonean regions) whose enterprising spirit and rebelliousness across Spanish America got them associated with the "black devil" in Mexico, Venezuela, and Rio de la Plata.[36]

Actually, an exotic system of racial classifications, well documented by G. Aguirre Beltran, emerged in Latin America to somehow make sense of the multiple racial mixings. Profiles of individuals "subjected to prosecution by the Sacred Tribunal of the Inquisition" in Mexico included "differences of tegumentary hue" and "certain other anatomical characteristics," such as "the form and color of the hair of the head and beard; thinness, thickness, and prominence of the lips; form of the nose; color of the iris; and, on occasion, bodily morphology and facial breadth." America had its own Moriscos, often the outcome of white and mulatto mixings. There were, for instance, two types of Moriscos in Mexico: *mulatos moriscos* and the typical, Spanish-looking whites classified as *bermejo moriscos.* And to make sure that certain *mulatos moriscos* in servitude didn't pass for white, they were sometimes branded "with hot irons in places where the insignia of servitude could not for a moment be hidden."[37]

Rayford Logan's concern about the politics of color may have been influenced by peculiar U.S. race politics of the period, but I have never heard of a Moroccan interested in Esteban's pigmentation. Lotfi, whom I quoted earlier, follows his tribute to Esteban with an appreciation for African American Muslims: "To the memory of the thousands of African Muslims who made Islam the second revealed religion in the New World." Those black Muslims, particularly ones who left an impression or who deliberately challenged slavery, racism, or discrimination, would often be called Moors because of their faith, or because of the assumption that Islam conferred on such Africans a higher degree of cultural achievement. By Allan Austin's estimate, "there may have been about forty thousand African Muslims in the colonial and pre–Civil War territory making up the United States before 1860."[38]

Such Muslims, or Moors, would leave a significant imprint on American culture, although the contribution of Muslim slaves has remained somehow obscure in the larger annals of African American history. *Some Memoirs of the Life of Job Ben Solomon* (1734), the account of a runaway slave who found his way back to Africa (present-day Senegal), is the "oldest text in African American literature." Solomon's memoirs, which included his trip to England and encounters with prominent people, including members of the royal family, were written by his English friend and amanuensis Thomas Bluett, but that should not explain why, as Austin put it, they "do not appear in any collection of African American literature." Many Muslim slaves were educated or, at least, literate in Arabic and left a major impression on their contemporaries. In 1768, an unidentified slave in South Carolina wrote two pages of verses from the Qur'an.[39] During a trip to New Orleans in 1822, Thomas Tea met a Moorish slave from Timbuktu in Natchez, Mississippi, who "lamented in terms of bitter regret, that his situation as a slave in America, prevents him from obeying the dictates of his religion. He is under the necessity of eating pork, but denies ever tasting any kind of spirits. He has one wife. He will not allow that the Americans are a polite and hospitable society as the Moors—not that they enjoy a tenth part of the comfort they do—and that for learning and talents they are far behind them."[40]

Umar ibn Said's autobiographical account, "Life," composed in 1831 in a sixteen-page manuscript, is "one of two known autobiographies written in Arabic in the New World" (the other was by Abu Bakr as-Siddiq, in Jamaica). So impressive and famous was Ibn Said (ca. 1765–1864) that he received a letter in Arabic from a Chinese fellow Muslim in 1858. As if such racial differences mattered, white Christians tried to associate him with Moors and Arabs, not his black Senegalese ancestors. They also proclaimed him a proud Christian who had renounced his native faith of Islam (Francis Scott Key, author of the U.S. national anthem, even sent him a Bible in Arabic). But, as if to register his true Muslim beliefs, Ibn Said resisted the attempts to remake his identity by writing Islamic messages on Christian documents.[41]

Abu Bakr as-Siddiq, in Jamaica, was equally impressive. In 1837, Richard
Robert Madden, an Irish magistrate and abolitionist who met with him,
noted that "his attainments, as an Arabic scholar, were the least of his merits. I found him a person of excellent conduct, of great discernment and
discretion. I think if I wanted advice, on any important matter, in which
it required extreme prudence, and a high sense of moral rectitude to qual-
ify the possessor to give counsel, I would as soon have recourse to the advice
of this poor negro as any person I know."[42]

In 1828, the six-foot-tall Abd al-Rahman Ibrahima (ca. 1762–1829) was
"the most famous African in America." Manumitted thanks to the inter-
vention of the U.S. president and secretary of state, Ibrahima was outfitted
with a "white turban topped with a crescent, blue cloth coat with yellow
buttons, white pantaloons gathered at the ankles, yellow boots," and "sometimes a scimitar" and sent on a tour of the country with his American-
born wife, Isabella, raising money for his children and lending himself to
abolitionist causes. From Cincinnati, where he arrived on April 19, 1828, to
"the time he left for Liberia on February 7, 1829," Ibrahima raised $3,500 in
the Northeast to buy freedom and passage to Africa for eight of his descendants, who duly arrived the following year. So determined was the "sometime lawyer Cyrus Griffin" (who wrote a series about Ibrahima's misfortune
titled "The Unfortunate Moor") that the freedman was a Moor that he
argued that Ibrahima "had been lighter skinned when he came to America and that his hair had grown woolly only as it had grown whiter." (Ibrahima was sixty-five when he was manumitted.) Like many a Morisco,
Ibrahima promised the American Colonization Society to spread Christianity in Africa, but reverted to Islam as soon as he reached his ancestral
land. Why, one might ask, did the U.S. president intervene on Ibrahima's
behalf? The man had been wrongly assumed to be Moroccan, and the
administration wanted to extend a token of friendship to Morocco because,
Austin says, it was "the only African Muslim nation with which the [state]
department was familiar."[43]

The struggle of African Muslims, amply documented in the work of Allan
Austin, Michael Gomez, Sylvanie Diouf, Richard Brent Turner, Robert Dannin, and Sherman A. Jackson, shows that their resistance to slavery and oppression was a crucial link to the twentieth-century African American fight
for justice and civil rights.[44] Just as the Spanish monarchs had predicted,

Muslims in the New World never ceased resisting their enslavement and subjugation. The Moor remained the quintessential Other among Europeans in the New World, as Richard Brent Turner explains: "Although Europeans had finally surpassed global Islam in terms of technology and military power by the time of the antebellum period in America, the image of the 'Moor' or the Muslim enemy was still a powerful signification for people of European descent everywhere. It explained the awe and respect that some African Muslim slaves received from some white Americans, as well as the repeated attempts on the part of whites to facilitate their return back to Africa, in order to rid America of Islam."[45]

The fear of the Moor was not without justification. In 1522, machete-wielding sugar slaves, mostly from Senegambia (the northern arc of Islam in West Africa), revolted in Santo Domingo (Hispaniola); five years later, they did the same in Puerto Rico, forcing the Spanish king, Charles V, to issue more—but futile—decrees supplementing those of 1501, 1506, and 1509, banning Moors (black and white alike), together with Jews and others, from the Americas.[46] Michael Gomez has traced the Moors' presence in New York as far back as 1624, when New Netherland was established. A controversial figure, Anthony Jansen Van Salee, a freeman commonly known as "Anthony the Turk," assumed to have been born in the Moroccan seaport town of Salé to the Dutch renegade Jan Jansen (Morat Rais) and a Muslim African woman, became "one of the largest landowners in Manhattan." Van Salee and his wife, Gietje Reyniers, reputed to have been a "tavern girl" in Amsterdam, were branded "troublesome persons" and expelled from New Netherland in 1639, which led them to settle on a two-hundred-acre tract on Long Island (known as the "Turk's land" in property records) and to pioneer the towns of Utrecht and Gravesend, while buying a house on Bridge Street in New Amsterdam, the capital of New Netherland. One of Anthony's descendants later sold "a beautiful copy of the Koran," leading one to believe that some of his troubles may have been caused by nonconformist attitudes, not atypical of slaves of Muslim origin. Anthony's brother Abraham Van Salee was also known as "the Turk" or "the mulatto" in New York. Elsewhere, in 1753, men named Abel Conder and Mahamut, both claiming to be from "Sali on the Barbary coast" (the same Salee, or Salé, Anthony Jansen Van Salee hailed from), "petitioned South Carolina's royal council in 'Arabick'" for their release from illegal enslavement. Other "free Moors" claiming to be Moroccan filed a petition with the South Carolina General Assembly in 1790 for equal rights with whites. Many enslaved Muslims simply escaped and probably sought refuge among the Indians, as in the case of a man named Homady in the late eighteenth century. Finally, records show that Muslims were also involved in the *Amistad* insurrection of 1838.[47]

The Muslim sense of superiority over fellow African slaves (a view shared by many slave owners across the Americas) and sometimes white masters was not uncommon; it reflected their cultural, religious, and even biological differences.[48] In Brazil, according to Gilberto Freyre, the Portuguese, who were heavily influenced by Moorish arts and sciences, were well aware that "a brown people" like the Moors in the Iberian Peninsula could be superior to white Europeans.[49] The Muslims who wanted to go back to their native lands believed that the quality of life in their homelands was better than the life they found in America. In Trinidad, for instance, prominent and industrious Muslims sought help with repatriation to their native lands in West Africa, writing three letters (dated 1831, 1833, and 1838) to the king of England and other high officials, expressing their attachment to Islam and their unwillingness to stay in "postemancipation Trinidad."[50] All three requests were denied. Still, as Gomez comments, "the Trinidadian African Muslim community registered a definitive rejection of western civilization in that they wanted neither western religion nor life under western authority. Having achieved positions of advantage in Trinidadian society, they nevertheless preferred the culture and civilization of their West African homelands. Perhaps the refusal of assimilation into a European cultural mode represents the ultimate revolt against colonialism."[51] Everywhere, Muslims represented resistance and, on occasion, contempt for the slaveholding society, earning the respect of fellow blacks, whether slave or free. The Moorish connection of slaves like Abd al-Rahman Ibrahima remained a strong motif well into the twentieth century. It was through this Moorish heritage that Muslim slaves maintained their Pan-Africanist outlook, connecting globally with fellow Muslims and keeping the memory of an increasingly distant past alive in the habits of everyday life. And it was this Pan-Africanist spirit that would connect a generation of "old Muslims" to adherents of a "new American Islam" that emerged by the turn of the nineteenth century.[52]

Pan-Africanist leaders such as Edward Wilmot Blyden (1832–1912), the Presbyterian missionary in Liberia and Sierra Leone, and Henry McNeal

Turner (1834–1925), bishop of the African Methodist Episcopal (AME) Church, acknowledged the vital role Islam played in medieval West African civilization, whose salutary effects upon Africans stood in sharp contrast to the injurious legacy of Christianity among people of African descent in the Americas. These sharp differences were noted by David Walker in his *Appeal to the Colored Citizens of the World, but in Particular, and Very Expressly, to Those of the United States of America* (1829): "I believe if any candid person would take the trouble to go through the Southern and Western sections of this country, and could have the heart to see the cruelties inflicted by these *Christians* on us, he would say, that the Algerines, Turks and Arabs treat their dogs a thousand times better than we are treated by the *Christians*."[53]

The 1850 Fugitive Slave Law, the 1857 *Dred Scott v. Sandford* decision by the Supreme Court, and later the *Plessy v. Ferguson* case terrorized African Americans (1,240 African Americans were lynched between 1889 and 1899) and encouraged them to contrast the policies of their Christian society with those of Africans in Muslim ones. In 1895, a former U.S. consul in Liberia, John Henry Smyth (1844–1908), addressed the Congress of Africa in Atlanta and repeated what Blyden and Turner had noticed, namely that blacks in West Africa "represent a very high and unique type of Mohammedanism and Arabic training. They have adopted the religion of the Prophet and made it conform to themselves. . . . They are not controlled by the Arab, the Persian, or the Turk, as to their conception of the Koran."[54] This echoes what Blyden had written in his book *Christianity, Islam, and the Negro Race* (1888): "In all thriving Mohammedan communities in the West and Central Africa, it may be noticed that the Arab superstructure has been superimposed on a permanent indigenous substructure; so that what really took place, when the Arab met the Negro in his home was a healthy amalgamation, and not an absorption or an undue repression."[55] In his book *The Lost-Found Nation of Islam in America,* Clifton E. Marsh writes that "the assertion of a distinct life-style and world view in such ways as assuming African or Arabic names, wearing African clothes, and speaking African languages is essential to becoming free." Malcolm X told much the same thing to Alex Haley in a 1963 interview.[56] At the 1893 World's Columbian Exposition, with its World's Parliament of Religions, organized in Chicago to celebrate the four hundredth anniversary of Christopher Columbus's "discovery" of America, persecuted African Americans had the rare opportunity to see and hear the world's Muslims, including a white convert, Mohammed Alexander Russell Webb, a former U.S. consul in the Philippines, who denounced the misrepresentation of Islam and embraced a "jihad of words" to effect change. Black leaders, such as Frederick Douglass, who attended the exposition must have paid notice.[57]

Islam was everywhere in the black nationalist movement. The Jamaican-born Marcus Garvey (jailed and deported from the United States in 1927 for mail fraud), a convert to Catholicism and founder of the Universal Negro Improvement Association (UNIA), was influenced by Duse Mohammed Ali, the Sudanese-Egyptian author of *In the Land of the Pharaohs* (1911), which made the case for Islam as a basis for self-government in nineteenth-century Egypt. Garvey's followers, particularly writers for the *Negro World*, and Garvey himself made analogies between the struggles of Muslims in Africa against European colonialist powers and their own struggle for equality in the United States, as well as between Garvey's mission and that of Mohammed, the Prophet of Islam. At one point, Garvey compared his work and that of his followers to the Prophet. "As Mohammed did in the religious world," he said, "so in the political arena we have had men who have paid the price for leading the people toward the great light of liberty." In 1923, the Garveyite columnist for the *Negro World* gave a speech in Boston titled "Islam and the Redemption of Africa."[58]

Islam and identification with Moors was especially clear in the case of the Moorish Science Temple of America, established by the enigmatic American Muslim Noble Drew Ali during the epoch of the Great Migration of blacks from the South to the North and Midwest between 1913 and 1930. Noble Drew Ali, born Timothy Drew on January 8, 1886, in North Carolina (died July 20, 1929), shaped the New Negro ideology into a unique combination of homegrown Islamic doctrines and elements of Freemasonry, particularly from the Shriners, known officially as the Ancient Arabic Order of Nobles of the Mystic Shrine. Drew Ali claimed Moroccan ancestry and issued "nationality cards" with a Moroccan flag. Blacks, in his ideology, were from Amexem (instead of from Africa) and were part of the galaxy of Asiatic races, extending from Asia to Native and Hispanic America, and all these races were Muslim. Of course, Drew Ali's brand of Islam was bound to be attacked by orthodox and Sunni Muslims, as happened when the al-Azhar-educated Sudanese Sātti Majid Muhammad al-Qadi Suwar al-Dhahab sued Drew Ali in court for defaming Islam and agitating for the issuing of three fatwas against him in Egypt and Sudan. (The fatwas were issued around 1930, after Drew Ali's death.) As Richard Brent Turner explains, echoing Clifton Marsh's observation, naming was crucial for Noble Drew Ali: "Noble Drew Ali chose to connect his movement to Morocco, connecting it to the first African Muslim slaves in America. Abdal-Rahman Ibrahima—the extraordinary 'Moorish Prince' from Futa Jalon . . . had used a pretended connection to Morocco to gain his freedom. If this strategy for liberation worked in the nineteenth century, Drew Ali probably reasoned that it might also work for black people in the twentieth century."[59] No doubt, these "Moors" were problematic, as is evident in one Detroit police officer's complaint: "Those fellows! he cried out. What a terrible gang. Thieves and cutthroats! Wouldn't answer anything. Wouldn't sit down when you told them. Wouldn't stand up when you told them. Pretending they didn't understand you, that they were Moors from Morocco. They never saw Morocco! Those Moors never saw anything before they came to Detroit except Florida and Alabama!"[60]

Peter Lamborn Wilson has postulated that Drew Ali and his family may have met with and studied under the great Muslim reformer Jamal ad-Din al-Afghani (1838–1897) in Newark, New Jersey, when al-Afghani visited the United States in 1882–1883, an idea which, if true, "would obviously radically alter what we know about Noble Drew Ali"—and, one might add, about the legacy of the Salafiyya (nineteenth-century reform movement in the Arab world) in general. (It was from Newark, in 1912 or 1913, that Drew Ali received his prophetic calling to found a religion "for the uplifting of mankind.")[61] But Drew Ali's movement was not without its controversies. The Bible of the Moorish Science Temple of America, a long title abridged as the *Circle Seven Koran* (1927), was heavily plagiarized from the Rosicrucian text *Unto Thee I Grant* (1925) and Eva S. and Levi Dowling's *The Aquarian Gospel of Jesus the Christ* (1909). Furthermore, Drew Ali's personal life turned out not to be as exemplary as one might expect of a prophetic figure who demanded a high degree of moral rectitude from his disciples and members of the temple. But his new religion, which sponsored, according to Turner, "the first mass religious movement in the history of Islam in America," filled a psychological and social vacuum for people who had been uprooted and were rejected by a slave society that continued to hold them in bondage.[62] Despite rivalries, infighting, and harassment by the FBI during World War II (because of their kinship with the Asiatic and dark races, Muslims were suspected of being allies of the Japanese and, therefore, a national-security threat), Drew Ali and his followers persevered and survived. So convinced were they of their Moroccan heritage and so persistent were they in getting such recognition that, in 1986, the Moroccan ambassador to the United States acknowledged the movement's "special" relationship with Morocco.[63]

Also around 1920, the India-originated Ahmadiyya, a heterodox and heretical movement within Islam (centered on a belief in "continuous prophecy" and in Jesus's migration to India) founded by the self-proclaimed messiah Ghulam Ahmad (1835?–1908), was brought to the United States by Mufti Muhammad Sadiq, who preached and converted first in prison (where he had been detained by immigration authorities), then outside in a climate of open hostility to Asiatic races. In 1921, he started a magazine, *The Moslem Sunrise,* to give a voice to this missionary movement, whose goal, in the words of its leader Mahmud Ahmad, was "the spiritual colonization of the western world." Although fears of Islam were rife in the popular media and imagination, Sadiq worked tirelessly to preach the color blindness of Islam. "In Islam," he said when addressing the race problem in the United States, "no church [sic] has ever had seats reserved for anybody and if a Negro enters first and takes the front seat even the Sultan if he happens to come after him never thinks of removing him from the seat." In the United States of the early 1920s, Sadiq noted, Jesus himself would be denied entry to the country on several legal grounds. In 1923, Sadiq returned to India after having converted "over seven hundred Americans to Islam" and established a movement that would attract accomplished jazz players Art Blakey, Talib Daoud, Yusef Lateef, Ahmad Jamal, Sahib Shihab, and others.[64]

On the eve of Noble Drew Ali's death, in 1929, W. D. Fard Muhammad, probably born to a man from East India (what would later become Pakistan) and a white Englishwoman on February 25, 1891, in New Zealand, appeared in Chicago, after having entered the United States (via Canada) illegally in 1913 with an anglicized name and having joined the Theosophical Society of San Francisco, Garvey's UNIA, and, once in Chicago, the Moorish Science Temple, "while attending the Ahmadiyya mosque on the city's South Side." When Fard Muhammad moved to Detroit in 1930, with its estimated 120,000 black people, to peddle exotic clothes and such, Noble Drew Ali had passed away and Fard Muhammad soon started preaching to Drew Ali's working-class customers, establishing a movement of "Muslims" as opposed to Drew Ali's "Moslems."[65] Officially, the Lost-Found Nation of Islam, stressing consumer discipline, education, strict dietary laws, and pride in one's origins, was founded on July 4, 1930, but it would be Elijah Poole from Georgia, down on his luck in the cold, forbidding North, who would designate the mysterious Fard Muhammad as God incarnate after meeting him in 1931. The following year, Fard Muhammad was arrested on strange charges pertaining to a follower's alleged sacrifice of another man, then again in 1933 for disturbing the peace. In June 1934, Fard left as abruptly as he had appeared in 1929, leaving behind Elijah Muhammad (as Elijah Poole was now known) to lead a fractious movement caught up in internecine conflict and division.

Elijah Muhammad began an odyssey south, using the assumed names of Muhammad Rassoull and Gulam Bogans, the latter being the name under which he was arrested and jailed in 1934 in Washington, D.C., for failing to register for the draft. When he was released from prison, in August 1946, he took the reins of his organization and turned it into a successful business enterprise, uplifting the status of his working-class followers considerably and attracting middle-class African Americans. By 1960, the man called the Messenger was firmly in control of an organization whose members carried identity cards similar to those issued by the Moorish Science Temple.

Like that of most minority movements, the Nation of Islam's theology was centered on self-affirmation and reversing the dehumanizing regime of oppression that black Muslims had been subjected to for hundreds of years. If the Moors of Moorish Science were Moabites or Canaanites from Morocco who founded Mecca, the Nation's ancestors—the lost tribe of Shabazz, creatures of a black god called Allah—were directly from Mecca. Blacks were thus the norm, whereas the "blue-eyed devils," or white Caucasians, were invented by a "big head scientist" called Yakub, a genius who was relocated from Mecca to "the island of Pelan, or Patmos of the Aegean," where after a six-hundred-year experiment the white race emerged to become "gods of this world" and to wreak havoc on the black races.

This narrative of racial differences was part of a long African American speculation and conversation about the nature of whites, one that is perhaps best exemplified in David Walker's *Appeal to the Colored Citizens of the World*. In Walker's account, whites are essentialized as "natural enemies," perhaps because of their grim record:

The whites have always been an unjust, jealous, unmerciful, avaricious and blood thirsty set of beings, always seeking after power and authority. We view them all over the confederacy of Greece, where they were first known to be any thing, (in consequence of education) we see them there, cutting each other's throats—trying to subject each other to wretchedness and misery, to effect which they used all kinds of deceitful, unfair and unmerciful means. We view them next in Rome, where the spirit of tyranny and deceit raged still higher.—We view them in Gaul, Spain and in Britain—in fine, we view them all over Europe, together with what were scattered about in Asia and Africa, as heathens, and we see them acting more like the *devils* than account-able men. But some may ask, did not the blacks of Africa, and the mulattoes of Asia, go on in the same way as did the whites of Europe. I answer no— they were never half as avaricious deceitful and unmerciful as the whites, according to their knowledge.[66]

Walker's views were echoed by W. E. B. Du Bois and Aimé Césaire. For Du Bois, who saw through the duplicity and cruelty of European bourgeois civilization, "there was no Nazi atrocity—concentration camps, wholesale maiming and murder, defilement of women or ghastly blasphemy of child-hood—which the Christian civilization of Europe had not long been prac-ticing against colored folk in all parts of the world in the name of and for the defense of a Superior Race born to rule the world."[67] We have already noted that Césaire, in his *Discourse on Colonialism,* also wondered about the inability to connect Nazi atrocities with white European civilization:

People are surprised, they become indignant. They say: "How strange! But never mind—it's Nazism, it will pass!" And they wait, and they hope; and they hide the truth from themselves, that it is barbarism, but the supreme barbarism, the crowning barbarism that sums up all the daily barbarisms; that it is Nazism, yes, but that before they were its victims, they were its accomplices; that they tolerated that Nazism before it was inflicted on them, that they absolved it, shut their eyes to it, legitimized it, because, until then, it had been applied only to non-European peoples; that they have cul-tivated that Nazism, that they are responsible for it, and that before engulf-ing the whole edifice of Western, Christian civilization in its reddened waters, it oozes, seeps, and trickles from every crack.[68]

To be sure, the Nation of Islam's view of whites was shot with contradic-
tions, but it did provide a framework through which mostly illiterate and
working-class African Americans could make sense of their subjugation, of
the "spooky" religion of Christianity (the Nation of Islam rejects the notion
of abstract deities, heaven, and hell), of the white man's "tricknology," and
even of the apocalyptic future which would see the burning of America (and
white civilization) in a period of 390 years, followed by a cooling period of
610 years, before the continent would be resettled by 144,000 black people,
all looking sixteen years old and living to the ripe age of one thousand.[69]

Both in his personal life and in the ideologies he espoused while a minister for the Nation of Islam and after leaving it, in 1964, Malcolm X (1925–
1965) embodied the tight connection between African American nationalist, Pan-African consciousness, and Islam as a global faith. He ultimately
understood that the struggle of African Americans was part of the African,
Arab, Asian, and, indeed, third-world struggle against Western imperialism.
In a 1960 speech at the Harvard Law School Forum, Malcolm X affirmed
this global community by saying, "We here in America who are under the
Divine Leadership of the Honorable Elijah Muhammad are an integral part
of the world of Islam that stretches from the China Seas to the sunny shores
of Africa."[70] Malcolm X made the African American struggle global once
he broke ranks with Elijah Muhammad and the Nation of Islam by founding the Organization of Afro-American Unity (OAAU) in Ghana to represent Afro-Americans in the Western Hemisphere, correcting the provincial
misconception that U.S. black struggle was confined to the United States.
As he explained in a June 28, 1964, talk at the Audubon Ballroom, "Many
of us fool ourselves into thinking of Afro-Americans as those only who are
in the United States. America is North America, Central America, and South
America. Anybody of African ancestry in South America is an Afro-American.
Anybody in Central America of African blood is an Afro-American. Anybody here in North America, including Canada, is an Afro-American if he has
African ancestry—even down in the Caribbean, he's an Afro-American."[71]
Malcolm X was well aware that the term *Moor* meant "black" and that "the
red, the brown and the yellow are indeed all part of the black nation" and,
therefore, broadly speaking, Muslims. It was probably this inclusive philosophy of race that unsettled U.S. government officials. Indeed, so worrisome
was his Pan-Africanist, anticolonial, internationalist stand "that officials
within the American government seriously contemplated charging him with

violating the Logan Act, which makes it illegal for American citizens to seek to influence foreign governments' policies toward the United States."[72]

In addition to broadening the definition of Afro-Americans, and possibly of blackness itself, Malcolm X, in a meeting in Paris in 1964, dismissed the philosophy of nonviolence as a "trick" put upon blacks by white people to dissuade them from rebelling and seeking their freedom and rights. Thus, in his short life, and through his global experience, Malcolm X brought the "African-derived community" of Muslims closer to the religious mainstream (while holding onto a few Nation of Islam myths, such as his last name). The quintessential "trickster" had managed, with his "jihad of words," to address several constituencies at once, too, by achieving "a multivalent discourse, a multifaceted glossolalia that, having taken into account the history, struggles, fears, and aspirations of his people, responded with entreaties and behavior targeting specific communities of interest."[73] His assassination, on February 21, 1965, was a traumatic event that, over time, has turned him into a sacrificial prophet. For no sooner had Elijah Muhammad died, on February 25, 1975, than his son, Warith Deen Mohammed, went orthodox and founded the American Muslim Society, leaving Louis Farrakhan to oversee the old order. (Imam Mohammed passed away in 2008, and Farrakhan is seriously ill at the time of this writing.) Both organizations, connected by family and historical ties, were closer to mainstream Islam at this time than had even been possible under the reign of Elijah Muhammad and Noble Drew Ali before him. Remarkably, as the twentieth century wore on, American Islam gradually returned to its Afro-Moorish roots.[74]

Despite enormous hurdles, the struggle of America's Muslims for inclusion and dignity continues in earnest. In November 2006, more than five years after 9/11, when Islam had become associated with all things un-American, Keith Ellison, a progressive African American Muslim from Minneapolis, was elected to represent that mostly white city and its suburbs in the House of Representatives. For the first time in American history, a Muslim (of African descent, it must be noted) had been elected to the U.S. Congress. This historic event was not lost on Muslims around the world—it was a shining example of the possibilities of U.S. democracy when allowed to take its course.[75] Rather predictably, however, Ellison was soon accused of being un-American simply for being Muslim and for choosing to take the oath of office on Thomas Jefferson's copy of the first English translation of the Qur'an;[76] but he remained steadfast in promoting his progressive agenda in the areas of health care, immigration, and civil rights in general, including condemning anti-Semitism by joining the Congressional Anti-Semitism Task Force and visiting Israel.

This brief aperçu of the pervasive Moorish presence—physical, cultural, symbolic, and of course spectral—in America indicates that the newly "discovered" continent is, in many ways, merely a new front on which old antagonisms and religious hatreds were worked out with an almost astonishing consistency. "The great and overpowering river of anti-Islamic feelings overflowed the European boundaries and flooded the American lands," wrote Rafael Guevara Bazán. "The conquerors were men moving to the New World in order to complete the catholicity, or ecumenicity, of the Christian faith, according to medieval theological ideas."[77] But what must be noted here, at least in regard to the clash of Islam and Christendom that sets the background to the unfolding of modern history, is that Islam worked *both against and for* the Moorish minority; the religion and culture that made the African, for instance, an outsider also made him a model, a rebel leader in Brazilian uprisings and the Haitian revolution, a mutineer on the *Amistad,* and, paradoxically, a cultural snob vis-à-vis the white master. Moorish identity, whether innate or acquired, turned out to be a powerful tool of resistance to the depredations of slavery, racism, and social exclusion.

Berbers, Moriscos (black and white), and West African slaves were not the only ones who found strength in their Moorish identity, however; Jews in Europe, and by extension in America, did so, too, thereby shedding light on a most remarkable legacy that could reduce unfounded suspicions and alleviate the escalating hatreds between Muslims and Jews in the contemporary Middle East and in the world at large. It is this close affinity between Muslims and all those deemed exterior to Christian or European purity that explains the Moorish identity of European Jews during the Enlightenment and, later, the troubling issue of nonwhite immigrants in the contemporary West.

chapter 3

Muslim Jews

A Jew is not a Jew until he converts to Islam.

—PETER THE VENERABLE (1094–1156)

In 2005, around the time I was thinking about the Moorish legacy in New Mexico, and indeed all of the Americas, Tom Reiss, an American writer of Jewish heritage, published the story of an enigmatic Jew with the Muslim name of Kurban Said, considered to be the Shiite nation of Azerbaijan's national writer and author of *Ali and Nino* (first published in Germany, in 1937), a love story between a Christian girl and a Muslim boy set during the early twentieth-century oil boom in the wildly cosmopolitan atmosphere of Baku. When Reiss later came across a book titled *Blood and Oil in the Orient,* he found out that Kurban Said was another name for Essad-Bey, both pseudonyms of Lev Nussimbaum, known throughout the world as a Muslim writer. Nussimbaum published sixteen books, "most of them international bestsellers and one enduring masterpiece, all by the age of thirty," but he "refused to be branded or categorized from the outside" and was therefore "an ideological Houdini, becoming a racial and religious cross-dresser in a decade when race and religion were as fixed as a death sentence." He was born on a train between Zurich and Baku to Abraham Nussimbaum, an Ashkenazi Jew and oil-rich millionaire, one of the wealthiest men in the city, and a revolutionary mother, also an Ashkenazi Jew, probably from a shtetl in the Pale of Settlement (the geographical area to which Jews of the Russian Empire were confined after 1791), who apparently plotted with Stalin against her own bourgeois husband and committed suicide (by drinking acid) in 1911 or 1912, when Lev was six or seven and she was in her twenties. Lev grew up amid the tolerance, multiculturalism, and

cosmopolitanism of Muslim rule in the Caucasus, not in the virulent anti-
Semitic culture of Russia.[1]

From a very early age, Nussimbaum was drawn to the Muslim section
of Baku; it was a place of relief and escape, where he had inexplicable feelings of kinship to Muslim culture. "To this day," he later wrote, "I still do
not know whence this feeling came, nor how to explain it. Perhaps it, too,
was inherited from an unknown ancestor? I do know that throughout my
entire childhood, I dreamed of the Arabic edifices every night. [And] I do
know that it was the most powerful, most formative feeling of my life." Such
feelings had a big hold on his imagination: "Things I had read, heard, and
thought mixed themselves into these dreams. I saw the broad expanse of
the sandy Arabian desert, I saw the horsemen, their snow-white burnooses
billowing in the wind, I saw the flocks of prophets praying toward Mecca
and I wanted to be one with this wall, one with this desert, one with this
incomprehensible, intricate script, one with the entire Islamic Orient, which
in our Baku had been so ceremoniously carried to the grave, to the victo-
rious drumbeats of European culture."[2] When he discovered the "Kipta,
or Bani Israel—the mountain Jews of Azerbaijan" speaking a medieval dia-
lect of Persian, he found them to be indistinguishable from their Muslim
neighbors. He even believed that the two were sworn allies against the West.
No wonder, then, that Nussimbaum reinvented his father as a descendant
of Turkic and Persian aristocrats.[3]

In the summer of 1918, Nussimbaum and his father fled Bolshevik-
occupied Baku to Turkistan, then to Bukhara, and from there to Persia (the
country would become Iran in 1935, "land of the Aryans," partly because
of German influence), whose civilization with its many sects and ancient
traditions mesmerized him. It was a land whose mostly Shiite people, despite
their celebration of passion plays commemorating the deaths of Ali and his
children, "did not like to fight" and "where poetry and art mattered more
than ideology and weapons." In fact, "Shiism's encouragement of the under-
dog nurtured Lev's view of Islam as a bastion of heroic resistance in a world
of brute force and injustice." After a few misadventures and refuge in a
mosque, father and son eventually returned to their house in Baku, now
guarded and occupied by German and Turkish officers.[4]

It didn't take long for the Bolsheviks to come back with their dreadful
cheka, the police unit that would inspire Hitler's gestapo, and whose autos-
da-fé were reminiscent of the Spanish Inquisition (a point that wasn't lost

on Joseph Pérez, the historian of the Inquisition);[5] so they escaped through Georgia to Constantinople, the same city that had once welcomed Spain's expelled Jews but now, in 1921, was so caught up in its own political re-making that the good times for refugees couldn't last. Yet, here, Nussimbaum was in heaven. "I think I went mad for days," he wrote before he died. "Walking among the palaces, the viziers and court officials . . . I was reeling with ecstasy, walking through the streets of the Caliph city. . . . Was that even I? A stranger with different feelings, different thoughts. . . . I believe that my life began in Istanbul. I was 15 then. I saw the life of the Orient and I knew that as much as I yearned for Europe, I would be forever captivated by this life."[6]

Soon, father and son boarded a ship to Italy, leaving behind, as the younger Nussimbaum saw it, the Muslim culture of Constantinople that had given him purpose in life. "As he traveled west, dressed in his Euro-pean suit, he was increasingly sure that no matter how he might appear to people on the outside or what it said in his Georgian passport, inwardly he was a Man from the East, a realm of lost glory and mystery. He began to fantasize about a pan-Islamic spirit that would preserve everything from revolutionary upheaval." A monarchist by necessity, he thought that the "end of the imperial system in Europe and the Near East [such as the Haps-burg monarchy and the Ottoman Empire] unleashed a string of little geno-cides all across the continent" and that, like the Gypsies, the Jews, without a single Jewish nation in the world, "couldn't claim a patch of ground as their ancestral land." It was around this time that he decided to "adopt an Ottoman identity."[7]

After a brief stay in Italy in 1921, where the anti-Bolshevik movement of fascism was being born and Mussolini was highly praised by European and American leaders, the Nussimbaums went to Paris, the center of White Russian exiles and home to Lev's mother's relatives. Ironically, the White Russian exodus was the first of its kind in twentieth-century Europe, and only the expulsion of the Jews in 1492, in Reiss's view, can be compared to it (Reiss doesn't seem to be aware of the case of the Moriscos in 1609): "Of course, there was a historic irony in that the Russians now found them-selves in a position mirroring that of the Jews throughout the millennia, for entering the twentieth century, Russia had been the capital of world anti-Semitism." After much thought, it was decided that the by-now-rather-odd, sixteen-year-old Nussimbaum would be educated in Germany.

While attending a Russian gymnasium in Berlin, with mostly Russian Jewish and other White Russian students, Nussimbaum was challenged to rethink his sense of separateness. By this time, too, German nationalists had been influenced by Russian anti-Semitism and the widespread circulation of *The Protocols of the Learned Elders of Zion,* first "published as a series of newspaper articles in St. Petersburg in 1903." The White Russians had come to see bolshevism "as a mask for a vast Asiatic devil plot led by Jews, Freemasons, Muslims, and a host of other 'Eastern' bogeymen." This diabolical synthesis of German and Russian nationalisms turned Germany into a menacing and foreboding place.[8] Lying about his citizenship status (as he always did), Nussimbaum discovered that he could indulge in his love for the Orient at the Seminar for Oriental Languages at the Friedrich-Wilhelms-Universität in Berlin and promptly signed up as Essad Bey Nousimbaoum, despite not having finished his gymnasium curriculum (a fact he hid from both schools): "There was no holding me back. I went to the rector, I went to the dean, I went to the director of the institute, begged for them to let me study there and I was successful. . . . I tore my way into the discipline like a starved dog who'd suddenly come on a piece of meat."[9]

Nussimbaum realized that the Orient was a profession to his professors, not "a mysterious compulsion" as it was for him. Still, he was now an orientalist. In fact, it was his knowledge of the Orient that helped him graduate from the Russian gymnasium, where he had been considered "a very poor candidate." Not only did he relish studying the Orient but, in August 1922, he walked into the Turkish embassy in Berlin and converted to Islam, assuming the aristocratic name of Essad Bey. (His first attempt at conversion in Constantinople, when he was fifteen, had gotten muddled by the ignorance of a mullah.) The following year, he joined a group of Muslims in founding the Islamic community of Berlin and, though he had no attraction for politics, started speaking out "about the wretched situation of Muslims in the colonial world." He also became a prolific writer, writing for one of the leading publications in Germany, *Die Literarische Welt* (The Literary World), eventually outpacing Walter Benjamin, another contributor, in publishing "an average of one book every ten months" before he died, at age thirty-six. So prolific was he that his business manager begged him in 1934 to publish less.[10]

The "turbaned, dagger-toting Azeri *literato* named Essad Bey" was at home in the world of the German Jewish poet Else Lasker-Schüler, who wore "harem pants, a turban, and with long black hair, with a cigarette in a holder," claimed to speak the "Asiatic" of the "Wild Jews." (She would later win the Kleist Prize, Germany's highest literary honor, in 1932.)[11] To be sure, as Reiss puts it, "many Jewish journalists and scholars were writing books on the Middle East at the time, often out of a deep and sympathetic knowledge of the Muslim world, but they did not tramp around Berlin dressed in turbans, speak of their filial ties to warrior chieftains, and call themselves by fancy Turkish names." Nussimbaum's biographies of Mohammed and Stalin were best sellers, whereas *Blood and Oil in the Orient* turned the German army, right-wing groups, and certain Muslim nationalists who misread his sympathies for the Orient against him, and they outed him as an impostor who had forged his Muslim identity.

Nussimbaum, however, remained undaunted. After marrying a newly hired, dark-eyed secretary at *Die Literarische Welt*, the Jewish Erika Loewendahl, daughter of the wealthy Walter ("Daddy") Loewendahl who owned the Czech-based shoe brand Bata in Germany, he lectured in Turkey, where his command of the language was appreciated. When the couple moved to the United States in 1933 and settled in a lavish residence in Manhattan, Nussimbaum was described by the *New York Herald Tribune* as "a true descendant of the race of Scheherazade," a proud Muslim, monarchist, and orientalist who was a "tough morsel for the [U.S.] melting pot." But Nussimbaum didn't like U.S. commercial culture, with its postlecture receptions and Manhattan's lonely skyscrapers. By 1938, he was back in Europe without his wife, who left him for a friend. His membership in the Third Reich's German Writers Union was canceled, leaving him no serious publishing outlets in the German-speaking world. By this time, he had made the decision not to return to the United States (a mysterious, inexplicable decision that he would ponder on his deathbed). He published novellas in Polish, took a new agent, and eventually coauthored, with Wolfgang von Weisl, a Zionist who tried to convert Arabs to Zionism, *Allah Is Great: The Decline and Rise of the Islamic World*, about which *Die Jüdische Rundschau* (The Jewish Review) wrote that the authors "predict the loss of European colonial empires in Asia and the corresponding fear of an alliance of Islam with the yellow and brown races."[12]

Thus banned, Nussimbaum sought the help of a fellow orientalist, the Austrian convert to Islam Baron Omar-Rolf von Ehrenfels, who wrote about the potential of "interfaith healing between Muslims and Jews," among many other topics. It was under the name of Kurban Said (presumably the pseudonym of Elfriede Ehrenfels von Bodmershof, Omar-Rolf's second wife, to whom the work was legally copyrighted) that Nussimbaum managed to publish *Ali and Nino,* in 1937. Meanwhile, although his father remained in Vienna, Nussimbaum ended up in Italy, where he hoped to write Mussolini's biography but was denied access to him. Denounced by his enemies to the Fascist authorities, he moved into Casa Pattison, a house in the coastal town of Positano, where, with Raynaud's syndrome suddenly plaguing his feet, he scribbled furiously in his notebooks and on whatever paper he could find, eventually producing *The Man Who Knew Nothing about Love.* Poor, starving, and dying, the "unfortunate Muslim," as he was known, received the community's help. A mysterious Algerian, Dr. Ahmed Giamil Vacca-Mazzara, probably a native of Tripoli named Bello Vacca, a drug dealer, smuggler, and convert to Islam, helped Nussimbaum during his last days and built his gravestone in the village cemetery overlooking the Tyrrhenian Sea, next to a medieval tower that "had been erected to warn of approaching Saracen raiders."[13] The tombstone was capped with a stone turban and inscribed in Arabic. Nussimbaum's remains may have later been rearranged to face Mecca more properly, as John Steinbeck wrote in a 1935 article for *Harper's Bazaar,* describing the strange fate of Positano's "Muslim," unaware that the man he was writing about had also been a prominent author.

Nussimbaum died in late August 1942, more than a year after his father had been deported to Poland and most likely had died in Treblinka. Had Nussimbaum's father been sent to the death camp Auschwitz and meekly accepted his fate, he would, ironically, have been called Muslim—*Muselmann*—by the camp's Nazi guards, because that is how the category of doomed Jew was designated in the made-up Nazi idiom.[14] In the Nazi artificial language, Lingua Tertii Imperii (LTI), Muslims were the Jews who had given up all hope of struggle and survival, the "men and women reduced to staring," in the words of Inga Clendinnen, "listless creatures, no longer responding even to beatings, who for a few weeks existed barely—and who then collapsed and were sent out to the gas."[15] The label designated, in the words of Elie Wiesel, "those resigned, extinguished souls who had suffered so much evil as to drift to a waking death," those "who were dead but didn't know it."[16] Primo Levi remembered the *Muselmänner* as the "backbone of the camp, an anonymous mass, continually renewed and always identical, of non-men, who march and labor in silence, the divine spark dead in them, already too empty to really suffer. One hesitates to call them living; one hesitates to call their death death, in the face of which they have no fear, as they are too tired to understand." The *Muselmänner* crowded Levi's "memory with their faceless presence" because they were the very embodiment of humanity's evil to humanity. "If I could enclose all the evil of our time in one image," wrote Levi, "I would choose this image which is familiar to me: an emaciated man, with head dropped and shoulders curved, on whose face and in whose eyes not a trace of thought is to be seen."[17] So horrific was the case of the "Muslims" among the internees that one writer, Emil Fackenheim, described them as "the most truly original contribution of the Third Reich to civilization."[18] "It is for [the *Muselmann*] that Auschwitz was created," wrote the Hebrew novelist Yehiel Feiner (also known as Yehiel De-Nur or, better still, as Ka-Tzetnik 135633) in *Moni: A Novel of Auschwitz.*[19]

The term *Muslims* was chosen to designate Jews in their most helpless state because, Inga Clendinnen and Giorgio Agamben postulate, it connects the docility of the victims and the widespread view of Islam as a religion of fatalism. "The term," though, "like the condition, was current in many camps among prisoners and guards: a small linguistic indicator of the coherence of the *univers concentrationnaire.*" In Buchenwald and Ravensbrück, for instance, the *Muselmänner* were known as "tired sheikhs" and *Muselweiber* (female Muslims). Yet, probably because of the code name, the *Muselmänner* vanished from studies and encyclopedias of the Holocaust, ceding their place to the Nazi-sympathizing mufti of Jerusalem, thereby reordering priorities and effacing the pain of the original victims because of the politics of the moment. "It is a striking fact," wrote Agamben, in *Remnants of Auschwitz,* "that although all witnesses speak of him as a central experience, the *Muselmann* is barely named in the historical studies on the destruction of European Jewry."[20] Whatever the origin of the choice of this word for this category of Jews, we know that a popular German song of the time, which associated coffee (a Turkish, and therefore Muslim, drink) with weak nerves, paleness, and sickness, concluded with these lines: "Sei doch kein Muselmann, / der ihn nicht lassen kann!" (Don't be a Muslim / who can't help it!)[21]

The Muslim, then, took the place of the Jew at the very end of Europe's genocidal impulse as conceived by Georges Bensoussan. Just as Jew and Muslim started out as Christianity's Other in the Middle Ages, and just as the Jew embraced the Moorish heritage to better resist European barbarism in the high age of the Enlightenment, the Jew reached the end of the genocidal rope, or gas chamber, as a Muslim. In a "ferocious irony," commented Agamben, "the Jews knew that they would not die at Auschwitz as Jews."[22] It is this remarkable fate, this overlapping of Jewish and Muslim identities in the European imagination, that has been largely unexplored, in the opinion of Gil Anidjar. As Anidjar emphasizes, "The Jewish question has never been anything but the Arab question," because, in truth, one doesn't exist without the other: "From the Crusades to accusations of ritual murder, from Shylock and Othello to the perverse distinctions that the French colonial regime established between Jews and Arabs in Algeria and in France, the Jew, the Arab [a phrase that Anidjar borrows from Jacques Derrida] has been in turns the theological or political enemy, but also the military, religious and ethnic enemy against whom the West fails." Hence, "holy wars and expulsion, colonialism and genocide, *mission civilisatrice* and secularization, Islamophobia and Judeophobia have always been the two faces of the same and only question, the same strategy."[23]

One needs to remember, too, that much of the Jewish heritage (language, theology, philosophy) is coterminous with the Islamic one, both happening within the same culture or sphere.[24] In any case, Judaism would appear to be a quintessentially oriental religion, at least in the geographical and cultural sense, one that emerged and later developed in what are today the lands of Islam. It is Judaism's embeddedness in the Middle East, regardless of its theological proximity to Islam, that has made the Jew the oriental Other in Christian Europe, for one can assume (at least in the primordial sense that religions are stamped by their birthplaces as much as by their historical evolution, not to mention genes)[25] that, of the three Abrahamic religions, Christianity is the most European, having been established as an imperial faith in the early centuries after Jesus's death.

That Judaism is deeply intertwined with the Middle East and that Middle Eastern Jews have played a major role in the making of the Jewish religion are facts at the center of Raymond Scheindlin's history of the Jewish people. Through trials, migrations, triumphs, defeats, and diasporas, early Jewish history was staged in what is today the larger Middle East. A Jewish identity, with its god (Yahweh) and the Jews' "messianic dream" of someday returning to their glorious kingdom,[26] was forged in the wake of the Diaspora following the fall and leveling of Jerusalem and its Temple by

Babylonian forces in 587 BC. Though Jews survived the second loss of Jerusalem, to the Romans in AD 70, through the adoption of a rabbinical system and its scriptures (particularly the Babylonian Talmud), and then endured Greek and Roman anti-Semitic persecutions, the rise of Islam may very well have given the Jews a new lease on life, as they were for the first time united, with minor exceptions, by a common language across Muslim lands and protected by law from random persecution. "Aramaic-speaking Jews and Hellenized Jews" were brought together by the Islamic expanse and the lingua franca of Arabic. Thus, noted the eminent historian Bernard Lewis, Arabic "became the language of science and philosophy, of government and commerce, even the language of Jewish theology when such a discipline began to develop under Islamic influence." While living in Cairo in 1190, the celebrated rabbi-philosopher Moses ben Maimon, better known as Maimonides (1135–1204), wrote his famous treatise, *Guide to the Perplexed,* in Arabic before it was translated into Hebrew. So close were the two religions that one could talk about a Judeo-Islamic culture or tradition, one that parallels "the Judaeo-Christian tradition of which we are accustomed to speak in the modern world."[27]

Major intellectual centers flourished in Baghdad, where Greek philosophy and sciences were studied by Muslims and Jews alike, and where the *geonim* (spiritual leaders) became the undisputed authority on religious law. One of these, the *gaon* of the Academy of Sura, Saadia ben Joseph (882–942), wrote in both Arabic and Hebrew, introduced philosophy to the study of religion, and founded a Judeo-Arabic literature. "Saadia may be said to have Arabized rabbinic Judaism not merely through his choice of the Arabic language, but by adapting the rabbinic tradition to the best of contemporary intellectual life." According to Lucien Gubbay, the *geonim* of Baghdad "continued to uphold the unchallenged primacy of Babylonian Jewry, which lasted for close on seven hundred years." The Karaites, "the people of Scripture," a movement founded by Anan ben David, also emerged in Iraq, preaching *sola scriptura* and rejecting rabbinic law as "a fraudulent distortion of the principles of the Jewish religion," instead paying close attention to Hebrew grammar and the commentaries. "It was in the tenth century that the Hebrew text of the Bible was authoritatively fixed, if not by Karaites, at least as a result of the impetus lent to this kind of work by their influence."[28]

In fact, "the emergence of a Jewish theology took place entirely in Islamic lands," and the use of Arabic had a significant impact on Hebrew philology:

"Jews, studying Hebrew to achieve a better understanding of the Hebrew Bible, followed many of the procedures devised by Muslims examining Arabic for the parallel purpose of studying the sacred text of the Qur'ān." Forms of worship, not to mention literature and the arts, were influenced by Islam. In many ways, the training and appointment of the Muslim ulema is comparable to the practice of the Orthodox rabbinate. The halakha and the shari'a, meaning "path" or "way," "are surely closely related." Both religions have dietary restrictions, although the Jewish ones are more extensive. The Muslim *fatwa* resembles the Jewish *teshwot,* and the Muslim notion of *jihad* has parallels with the Jewish doctrine of *milhemet mitsva* or *milhemet hova,* the only difference being that *jihad* can be global whereas the Jewish doctrine is "limited to one country."

Unlike in Spain and Portugal after the Jews' expulsion, *marranismo* was easier to tolerate in Islamic lands, perhaps because of the two religions' strict monotheism, for, as Bernard Lewis argued, it was easier for Jews to live with the prophecy of Mohammed than with the Son of God. Despite hardships, conversion to Islam granted unequivocally equal status. In Muslim Spain, the Jew Samuel ha-Nagid, or Samuel ibn Nagrela (993–1056), "enjoyed a remarkably successful career as a statesman and general in the service of a Muslim ruler, and as a scholar, poet, and communal leader among the Jews."[29] Although Maimonides fled Muslim zealots in Spain, he prospered in Egypt, writing seminal works, as we have seen, in Hebrew and Arabic. But the combined attacks on Islam by crusaders and Mongols in Palestine, Spain, and Iraq compromised the status of *dhimmis* (religious minorities, mostly Christians and Jews) and gave occasional rise to public persecutions, leading rulers (as in Morocco) to give Jews special protection.[30] Negative stereotypes of Jews certainly existed in Muslim lands, but the greatest Arab historian of all time, Ibn Khaldun (1332–1406), attributed such depictions to the hardships of discrimination, not to some essential, unchanging quality: "[Injury has been done] to every nation that has been dominated by others and treated harshly. The same thing can be seen clearly in all those persons who are subject to the will of others, and who do not enjoy full control of their lives. Consider, for instance, the Jews, whose characters owing to such treatment had degenerated so that they are renowned, in every age and climate, for their wickedness and their slyness."[31]

After their expulsion from Spain, the Sephardim (Jews of Spain) were welcomed with open arms by Ottoman sultans and experienced, for about a century and a half, yet another golden age under the auspices of Islam. Over time, the Sephardim's Spanish language was mixed with Turkish and Greek terms and evolved into Ladino or Judezmo. Unlike the Ashkenazim, who had focused almost exclusively on the study of the Talmud, the Sephardim in multiethnic and cosmopolitan Constantinople and Salonika recreated the vibrant cultural life of their ancestors in Muslim Spain. Safed, in Upper Galilee, became a major center of Jewish mysticism, home to Rabbi Isaac Luria. The impact of the Smyrna-born messianic kabbalist Shabbetai Zevi was widely felt—the Dönmeh, a sect of Muslim crypto-Jews, is his legacy—and an attempt by the Polish Jewish leader Jacob Frank to revive Zevi's movement in the eighteenth century failed (Frank converted to Islam).[32] Clearly, up to the fifteenth century, Jews in Muslim lands fared far better than their brethren in Christendom. A French Jew writing in the fifteenth century was so impressed by the status of Jews in Turkey that he called on his coreligionists to leave Christian lands and join him there:

I have heard of the afflictions, more bitter than death, that have befallen our brethren in Germany—of the tyrannical laws, the compulsory baptisms and the banishments, which are of daily occurrence. I am told that when they flee from one place a yet harder fate befalls them in another. . . . On all sides I learn of anguish of soul and torment of body; of daily exactions levied by merciless oppressors. The clergy and the monks, false priests that they are, rise up against the unhappy people of God. . . . For this reason they have made a law that every Jew found upon a Christian ship bound for the East shall be flung into the sea. Alas! How evil are the people of God in Germany entreated; how sad is their strength departed! They are driven hither and thither, and they are pursued even unto death. . . . Brothers and teachers, friends and acquaintances! I, Isaac Zarfati, though I spring from a French stock, yet I was born in Germany, and sat there at the feet of my esteemed teachers. I proclaim to you that Turkey is a land wherein nothing is lacking, and where, if you will, all shall yet be well with you. The way to the Holy Land lies open to you through Turkey. Is it not better for you to live under Muslims than under Christians? Here every man may dwell at peace under his own vine and fig tree. Here you are allowed to wear the most precious garments. In Christendom, on the contrary, you dare not even venture to clothe your children in red or in blue, according to our taste, without exposing them to the insult of beaten black and blue, or kicked green and red,

and therefore are ye condemned to go about meanly clad in sad colored rai-
ment. . . . And now, seeing all these things, O Israel, wherefore sleepest thou?
Arise! And leave this accursed land forever![33]

As Muslim power waned in relation to an aggressively ascending Europe,
the status of Jews stagnated and deteriorated, especially as classical Christian anti-Semitism found its way into Arab lands (through Christian clients
of France). Zionist nationalism also clashed with the Arab variety. Soon
after Israel was created, in 1948, Jews in Arab and Muslim lands left for
good, bringing an end to what was once the largest, most successful community of Jews in the world.

Before this dramatic turning point in relations between Jews and Muslims,
many European Jews, like Africans in the United States, had adopted the
Moorish or Arabian Islamic heritage as their own, using it to resist Europe's
assimilationist pressures. They proudly proclaimed themselves Orientals,
not in the sense popularized by Edward Said in his classic study *Orientalism*
(1978)[34] but in a process of coming out, so to speak, after a long history in
which the Jew stood for the Muslim at home and was thereby a target for
domestic crusaders. We have seen that the two religions have much in
common, but one must also remember that Islam is the younger partner
in this marriage of faiths—a proud, jealous one, for that matter, because
although aspects of Jewish theology were influenced by Islamic thinking,
Islam consciously developed as an alternative or rival to Judaism following
early disputes with the Jews in Medina and elsewhere in Arabia, after the
migration of the Prophet, Mohammed, in 622.

   The anxiety of Jewish influence led to what Bernard Lewis called Muslims' "intentional distancing" from Jews and Christians, such as practicing
the Sabbath on Friday.[35] Mohammed, it must be recalled, was a prophet
from a nation without writing, and thus without scripture. In the early
phase of his settlement in Medina, which housed the three Arabized and
relatively educated Jewish tribes of Qaynuqa, Nadir, and Qurayza, the practices of praying toward Jerusalem and fasting during Ashura (the tenth day
of Muharram, the first month in the Islamic calendar) seem to have been
inspired by Jewish tradition; but, following disputes with the Jews, prayers
were ordered toward Mecca in 624, and soon Ramadan was established to
eclipse Ashura. Because Jews did not acknowledge Mohammed's prophecy,

Islam developed the theological theme of Abrahamism, that is, privileging the time before the prophets, and regarded itself as the "restoration of the original message." The Torah and Psalms were not incorporated into Muslim scripture as they were in Christianity, a fact that led to the ignorance of Jewish tradition. Given this history, it is faith, and faith alone, not genealogy, that counts in Islam. In 628, Muslims conquered the mostly Jewish oasis of Khaybar, ninety-nine miles from Medina, and Jews were forced to accept the terms of surrender. The defeat and agreement with the Jews of Khaybar would become a model, "a *locus classicus* for later legal discussions of the status of conquered non-Muslim subjects of the Muslim state." Early on, Muslims imposed restrictions and a dress code on *dhimmis,* including wearing a special emblem, which later turned into the yellow badge, "introduced by a caliph in Baghdad in the ninth century and spread into Western lands in later medieval times." Caliph 'Umar I (634–644) expelled Jews and Christians from the whole of Arabia. As we have seen in the case of the Crusades and European encroachments on the Ottoman Empire, relations between *dhimmis* and Muslims would be affected by Muslims' relations with the outside world.[36]

Though relatively better sheltered in Islamic lands, Jews were nevertheless persecuted and routinely humiliated for their faith. As a kid growing up in the cosmopolitan city of Tangier, in Morocco, a place that still boasts today an active synagogue, I witnessed firsthand the plight of Jewish minorities in our midst. Because the *lihud* (Jews) symbolized treachery and greed, to call someone a Jew was an insult. Muslims talk a lot about their respect for *ahl al-kitab* (People of the Book), but this is merely a ready-made excuse for not examining the fabric of our social patterns critically. *Dhimmitude,* the second-class status conferred on Christians and Jews in Islamic regimes—which is often presented by Muslim apologists as a testament to the tolerance of minorities in Islam—does not meet the minimum human rights expectations in nation-states. Under this theological legal code, Jews have lived precariously among Muslims throughout history, relying, at best, on the ruler's protection against the ever-lurking violence of the mob. That an occasional courtier would rise to a position of prominence and power in no way meant that the collective rights of the Jewish community were secure. Without royal protection, Jews and Christians in Muslim societies were but one sermon away from catastrophe.

On the whole, Muslim violence is largely born out of ignorance. But it is, in some ways, a willed ignorance—the persistent refusal to measure Muslims' complicity in the systematic discrimination against those who don't share their faith. The ongoing conflict between Israel and Palestine should not erase the precarious status of the Jew in Muslim societies. Organizing colloquiums centered on the Holocaust in order to downplay the horrors visited upon European Jews is both a futile and pernicious attempt to soften centuries-old realities that cannot be ignored. Even if the goal is to shed light on the victimization of the Palestinians—the collateral damage of what Georges Bensoussan has termed Europe's "genocidal passion"[37]— this approach makes sense only within the callous logic of a monstrous calculus.

One needs to keep in mind, then, this history of sharing, borrowing, rivalry, dispute, and persecution even as we focus on Muslims and Jews as substitutes for one another in Christian Europe's imaginary, and on modern Jews embracing their Moorish heritage. Islam's "intentional distancing" that Lewis mentions has not been entirely successful. Not only did the Semites originate from Arabia, but Moses is also by far the most cited biblical figure in the Qur'an. Islam may be the younger progeny of the Jewish monotheistic cosmogony, but if Arabic is the youngest of the Semitic languages, it is also the most archaic one, "probably the nearest to the ancestral Semitic language" and the "most widely spoken and written of all the Semitic languages." Hebrew, revived as a common language for Zionists, is the second most widely spoken. (In fact, before the term *Semitic* was coined, in 1781, the German Gottfried Wilhelm Leibniz classified Hebrew as a member of the "Arabic" languages.)[38] It is therefore as quarreling Semites that Jew and Moor stood on the stage of European history to face the long arm of persecution. Before the birth of Israel, such quarrels were minor enough to inspire prominent Jews to boast of their Muslim or Arab descent.

In their massive historical study *The Jew as Ally of the Muslim* (1986), using an exhaustive comparativist approach (193 pages of tightly packed notes, bibliographical resources in several languages, and a 40-page index), Allan Harris Cutler and Helen Elmquist Cutler set out to change our understanding of anti-Semitism by showing that classical anti-Semitism, rooted in Christian medieval charges of deicide and in social rivalries, was given new life by anti-Muslimism born out of the ongoing clash between the two world religions since, basically, the birth of Islam. Christian anti-Semitism, which had been dormant during the three centuries prior to the year 1000, emerged as a corollary of the Crusades, as the Jews came to be seen as the natural allies of the Muslims. At the end of their first campaign, Christian crusaders ruthlessly slaughtered Muslims and Jews alike in Jerusalem, seeing them both as "the shadow-self of Christendom," in the words of the noted interfaith historian Karen Armstrong.[39] Indeed, the Cutlers go so far as to assert that, "had there been no such outburst of Christian hatred against the Muslims, anti-Semitism might well have died out altogether in Western society."[40] The edict of the Fourth Lateran Council of 1215 imposing distinctive clothing and a "badge of shame" on Jews (and Muslims) was part of a messianic policy whose final aims were the reconquest of Jerusalem and the degrading of its Muslim inhabitants. The fate of Jews in Spain, their persecution by the Inquisition after their sincere conversion in the late fourteenth and early fifteenth centuries, and the Jewish *conversos*' reaction by going back to their ancestral faith were the result of the clash between Christians and Muslims. Moreover, "the Iberian Inquisition and its demonic attack upon thousands of innocent people in Europe and the New World circa 1480–1825 must ultimately be traced to the Islamic conquest of Spain in 711."

Major scholars who have studied the medieval roots of modern anti-Semitism, such as Joshua Trachtenberg, author of *The Devil and the Jews* (1943), and Norman Cohn, author of, among other important works, *The Pursuit of the Millennium* (1957), "acknowledge the importance of the association of Jew with Muslim by medieval Christians as a factor in the history of anti-Semitism." Pope John XXIII's conciliatory attitude toward Islam in the mid-twentieth century may have prepared the ground for the church's new attitude toward the Jews in Vatican II and subsequent changes in Catholic theology, but the problem of anti-Semitism cannot be truly solved without addressing, and coming to terms with, anti-Muslimism. This is a particularly daunting challenge, for "racial, ethnic, and political passions and enmities [including anti-Muslimism] remain very powerful forces." Conceived during the cold war, the Cutlers' argument may appear dated, now that anti-Semitism seems to surface mostly in its Islamic guise, typically triggered by political disputes and armed conflict over land in the Middle East. Still, "this approach to the history of anti-Semitism via anti-Muslim and ethnopolitical tensions makes a far greater contribution to modern efforts to fight and cure the chronic and pernicious social disease which is anti-Semitism than the approach via Christian theology and the deicide charge!"[41]

Peter the Venerable (1094–1156), the abbot of the highly influential monastic movement at Cluny who supported the Reconquista against the Moors, sponsored the translation of texts known collectively as the *Collectio toletana,* or the Toletano-Clunaic corpus, consisting of Arabic and original Latin texts translated for the main purpose of refuting Islam. This was a watershed event in medieval Christian-Islamic relations, coinciding with the Second Crusade (1145–1150). Yet, as important as this corpus was, even more significant was the earlier work of Petrus Alfonsi, born Moses of Huesca, a Jewish convert to Christianity (baptized in 1106) who mastered Arabic and was thus able to join the refutation of Jews and Muslims in his anti-Jewish polemic *Dialogues against the Jews* (ca. 1100). (His later work included, according to the Cutler thesis, translations [under the name of Peter of Toledo] and annotations for the Toletano-Clunaic corpus.) Alfonsi was also instrumental in translating Islamic medieval science into Latin, which, along with the Toletano-Clunaic corpus, enabled the nascent movement of the Renaissance. "Indeed, the major thrust of Alfonsi's life and work taken as a whole was the attempt to solve the problem of Christian-*Islamic,* not Christian-Jewish relations," for translating the intellectual traditions of Muslims would enable Christians to defeat Muslims intellectually as well as militarily. Whatever Alfonsi's primary target, John Tolan shows that the medieval polemicist's work marks a major turning point in the move to link Muslim and Jew in the Christian imaginary. Alfonsi's influence cannot be overstated. His "attack on Islam found its way into the encyclopedic *Speculum historiale* of Vincent de Beauvais; thirteenth-century Dominican master general Humbert of Romans recommended it as required reading for those who preached the Crusades, and numerous fourteenth- and fifteenth-century authors reused it."[42]

In this way, the birth of the Renaissance (if such an expression may be used) was also the (re)birth of anti-Semitism (an interesting phenomenon to ponder, given that the pattern was repeated in nineteenth- and twentieth-century Europe), for both were inextricably linked to the all-consuming purpose of conquering Islam. This is not surprising, because Jews had always been treated as the Muslims' allies. "Was it mere coincidence that neither blood nor desecration-of-the-host libels were known in Western Europe before the Crusades?" the Cutlers asked. "Was it sheer coincidence that the first known instance of the blood libel in Western Europe, at Norwich, England, 1144, occurred during the decade of the Second Crusade, while the first known instance of the desecration-of-the-host libel, at Belitz, near Berlin, 1243, occurred the year before the Christians lost Jerusalem to the Muslims[?]" The first "major international persecution of the Jews," following on the heels of scattered accusations in Spain, France, and Italy, "is clearly and unequivocally attributed by the Christian primary sources to the charge that the Jews were in league with the Muslims (specifically, in league with al-Hakim, the Fatimid Caliph of Egypt, who destroyed the Holy Sepulchre in Jerusalem circa 1010)," thereby setting the tone for the persecutions of 1096 (the First Crusade). The Jews seemed to be natural allies of the caliph, or of Muslims, because of their similar theological and ritual practices and because the Jews of western Europe had come, directly or indirectly, from Muslim lands, where many still maintained contact.

The Crusades themselves were the outcome of a dynamic, imperialistic European civilization, driven by the messianic goal of taking back Jerusalem and converting Muslims. They also engendered the stock motifs of classical anti-Semitism. When, during the First Crusade, Jerusalem was literally submerged in its dwellers' blood, crusader chroniclers, such as Raymond d'Aguilers, justified Christian massacres with the charge that Muslims "torture and mutilate crucifixes, icons, and the Eucharist, or even Christian children," accusations that would later justify "many a pogrom, from the thirteenth century to the twentieth."[43] Equating Mohammed with the beast of the Apocalypse, the millenarian Pope Innocent III's call for a new (Fifth) Crusade, on April 19, 1213, foresaw the ending of Islam by 1284. Such a momentous event would be initiated through, first, the conquest, defeat, and degradation of Muslims (through the differentiating elements of distinctive clothing and badges), then their conversion. Jews were assumed to be part of this process. It is for this reason that canon 68 of the Fourth Lateran Council, which deals with clothing and the badge, addresses Jews and Muslims, treating them as one and the same as it collapses time and "implies that Moses imposed a distinction in clothing . . . upon both Jews and Muslims!" Clearly, Innocent III (1198–1216) was far more interested in Christian-Islamic relations than he was in Christian-Jewish differences. Yet "no one has attempted to study Pope Innocent III's Jewish policy [distinctive clothing, 'badge of shame'] in terms of his Muslim policy." For this reason, the Cutlers conclude that "the Jews were brought into the picture primarily because the Christians equated them with the Muslims and considered them Islamic fifth columnists in Christian territory. Hence, Christian-Islamic relations determined Christian-Jewish relations in one of the most crucial episodes in the history of the Jewish people in the Diaspora."[44]

Between circa AD 600 and 1100, when anti-Semitism was not a major threat, the Jews associated themselves, in some of their major writings, with Arabs and Muslims. To explain the changing image of the Jew in Christian Europe from the medieval period to the High Middle Ages (that is, from contemptuous indifference to open hostility), Jeremy Cohen proposes that it was the Jews' association with Muslims during the Crusades that accounts for this shift, this "reclassification" in Christian consciousness:

> If, during the early Middle Ages, the Jews were the only non-Christians who consistently comprised a part of the Latin Christian experience, then the crusades, conquests, scientific discovery, and intellectual vitality of the high Middle Ages introduced Western Europe to a much larger, Muslim community of monotheistic unbelievers. In the ensuing adaptations in the Christian world view, the Jew, as it were, had to move over, to make room for these others. As an infidel, he was no longer unique but now represented a small subset of a much larger class. This reclassification affected not only the substance of anti-Jewish discourse, but also the function of the Jew in Christian doctrine.[45]

As the twelfth-century rabbi Solomon bar Samson explained the violence toward Jews during the First Crusade, in 1096, if Muslims were Ishmaelites in out-of-bounds Jerusalem, Jews were now Ishmaelites at home.[46] This view was echoed by Peter the Venerable of Cluny, in 1146, when he wrote to Louis VII supporting the Second Crusade: "Why should we pursue the enemies of the Christian faith in far distant lands while vile blasphemers far worse than any Saracens, namely the Jews, who are not far away from us, but who live in our midst, blaspheme, abuse, and trample on Christ and the Christian sacraments so freely and insolently and with impunity!?"[47]

There were perceived differences between Muslims and Jews, to be sure. For Bernard of Clairvaux (1090–1153), the prominent Cistercian abbot who, according to the renowned medievalist Norman Cantor, "seems to have dominated the western church" in the middle of the twelfth century, "the Muslim exemplifies the passion for violence, conquest, and slaughter, [whereas] the Jew that for money and material profit." But such differences were merely academic, because, in Bernard's view, "the crusade expedites triumph over both."[48] The Protestant Reformation inherited the same legacy. Johannes Brenz (1499–1570), a colleague of Martin Luther and author of *How Preachers and Laymen Should Conduct Themselves If the Turk Were to Invade Germany* (1537), written after the first Ottoman siege of Vienna, in 1529, joined Luther in linking Jew and Turk.[49]

Thus, the genocidal impulse that Bensoussan traces cannot be separated from Europe's crusading spirit against Islam, because, according to Richard Southern in his *Western Views of Islam in the Middle Ages* (1962), "the existence of Islam was the most far-reaching problem in medieval Christendom."[50] Although Muslims occasionally appeared as "new Jews," making anti-Muslimism an extension of anti-Judaism,[51] it is simply impossible to disconnect the rise of medieval Christian anti-Semitism from the Christian Crusades against Islam. As the Cutlers put it,

> The climax of high medieval anti-Semitism was the Jewish badge imposed by Pope Innocent III at the Fourth Lateran Council in 1215. That badge was a key element in the ghettoization process of Central Europe (from Italy to Germany). This process began in earnest in the fourteenth century (after the Black Plague, during which frightful massacres of the Jews were perpetrated) and lasted to the time of the French Revolution/Napoleon. The badge was revived along with the ghettoization process by Hitler's Nazi movement, leading ultimately to the gas ovens and the extermination of six million Jews.[52]

It is not for no reason, then, that the Nazis called the most helpless and degraded of their Jewish victims Muslims. Although quite a few "Jewish medieval scholars" held judgment on the merits of the Cutlers' book—Gil Anidjar, for one, wondered whether "the scholars protest too much"[53]— the association of Jew with Muslim, until very recently, was not as unusual at it now appears. Some of the most prominent writers in Jewish history worked in tandem with their Muslim colleagues in Moorish Spain, despite the occasional setbacks and waves of Islamic intolerance. Even Jewish poets who were part of Christian Spain still felt closer to Muslims than to Christians. The little-known poet Todros Abulafia, who lived in thirteenth-century Christian Toledo, for instance, didn't disguise his appreciation of

high Muslim culture in contrasting sophisticated and erotically savvy Arab
women with their uncouth Spanish peers:

> There's nothing wrong in wanting a woman,
> and loving girls is hardly a sin—
> but whether or not they're pretty or pure,
> Arabia's daughters are what you should look for.
> Stay far away from the Spanish Christians,
> although they're fair and bright as the sun,
> for they'll provide neither comfort nor ease,
> even with shawls and silken sleeves:
> their dresses are always covered with mud,
> as their hems are dragged through dung and crud.
> Their minds are empty from heartless whoring—
> when it comes to seduction, they know not a thing.
> But the Arab woman's grace is her glory,
> ravishing spirits, banishing worry.
> And whether or not she's wearing her clothes,
> she looks as though she's decked out in gold.
> She'll give you pleasure when the day arrives,
> for in lewdness's ways and desire she's wise,
> her legs gripped tightly around your head,
> crying out *Lord!!*—and raising the dead.
> The lover who opts for the Christian feast
> is just like a man who'd lie with a beast.[54]

The disdain for Christian culture bound together Jew and Muslim in Christian Europe despite the differences between the two religious communities. In Christopher Marlowe's play *The Jew of Malta*, first performed in 1592,
such sentiments are clearly expressed in the exchange between Barabas and
his Muslim slave, Ithamore:

ITHAMORE:
> Once at Jerusalem, where the Pilgrims kneeled,
> I strowèd powder on the marble stones
> And therewithal their knees would rankle, so
> That I have laughed a-good to see the cripples
> Go limping home to Christendom on stilts.

BARABAS:

Why, this is something! Make account of me

As of thy fellow; we are villains both:

Both circumcisèd, we hate Christians both.

Be true and secret, thou shalt want no gold.[55]

The poet Abulafia and the character Barabas did not become Muslim, as Lev Nussimbaum did, but Nussimbaum's kinship with Islam was by no means unique. It was shared, as we shall see next, by writers and scholars throughout much of modern history.

Nineteenth- and early twentieth-century Jews, notably German-speaking ones, had an interest in promoting the positive legacies of Islam not only because they played a role in Islamic civilization but also because they wanted to prove that Semites and Orientals, long vilified in Europe or pressured into renouncing their heritage, had contributed much to European culture itself, even as they felt the sharp edge of the Christian sword. In his play *Almansor* (1823), the poet and essayist Heinrich Heine (1797–1856) highlighted the predicament of the enlightened Moors in Christian Spain to draw a parallel with that of the Jews in eighteenth- and nineteenth-century Germany:

ALMANSOR:

We heard that Ximenes the Terrible

In Granada, in the middle of the market-place

—my tongue refuses to say it!—cast the Koran

into the flames of a burning pyre!

HASSAN [his servant]:

That was only a prelude; where they burn books

They will, in the end, burn human beings too.[56]

This passage would turn out to be a terribly prophetic literary turn, for the gassing of the Jews was preceded by the burning of subversive literature, a great portion of which was written by Jewish socialists and intellectuals. As late as 1917, in the midst of war carnage in Europe, the dramatist Friedrich Wolf (1888–1953), who had renounced his Judaism and would later become a Communist, wrote his play *Mohammed* (published in 1924) to highlight Islam's egalitarianism. He has Mohammed chastising his detractor Abu Jahl for the vain pursuit of riches, which leads to violence. "One measures a people," the Muslim Prophet says, "not by how much power and how many possessions it needs, but by how little it needs to be great!"[57]

Towering nineteenth-century Jewish orientalists from Germany and the Austro-Hungarian Empire, such as Abraham Geiger (1810–1874), Heinrich Graetz (1817–1891), and Ignaz Goldziher (1850–1921), were unafraid to openly express their contempt for Christianity and the nefarious impact of Orthodox Judaism, particularly the insidious Polish variety. These proud scholars of the Jewish heritage were all convinced of "the indissoluble links that bound Judaism and Islam together in marked contrast to the breech birth that constitutes the origins of relations between Christianity and Judaism." Thus, Geiger, "an ardent defender of Jewish rights, an intellectual who repeatedly took a public stand to defend his co-religionists by asserting, like Moses Mendelssohn before him, that the attainment of German citizenship should not entail Jewish conversion to Christianity," believed that Christian Europe could never reproduce the relatively open climate in Moorish Spain that allowed Jewish thought to flourish. An implacable critic of Orthodox Judaism, he saw in Islam, with its brand of monotheism, prophecy, and divine revelation, the purest form of Judaism, particularly the Reform Judaism he favored. No wonder the highly accomplished Jews in Moorish Spain who wrote in Arabic were still, for him, the unsurpassable model, the "heroes of Wissenschaft," as he called them.[58]

Heinrich Graetz, "the greatest Jewish historian of the nineteenth century," shared the same feelings and views toward Christianity, Orthodox Judaism, and Islamic Spain. "The height of culture which the nations of modern times are striving to attain," he said, "was reached by the Jews of Spain in their most flourishing period." This was so because both Jews and Muslims had a high appreciation for intellectual inquiry. Al-Andalus was preceded by Arabia, because the latter had been a place of refuge for the Jews after the destruction of Jerusalem. Graetz saw the Arab world as a "safe haven" for "the sons of Judah" and, indeed, claimed Islamic civilization to be a "glorious page in the annals of the Jews." So contemptuous was Graetz of east European Jewry that he called Yiddish "a half-animal language."[59]

Then there is the Hungarian Ignaz Goldziher, whose work on the Middle East and Islam was considered unsurpassable by the eminent Arab historian Albert Hourani.[60] A "precocious child" who obtained a doctorate at the age of nineteen but refused to convert to obtain a professorship, Gold-ziher also rejected Orthodox Judaism, traveled through the Orient, attended lectures, and engaged Muslim scholars at the al-Azhar Mosque in Cairo. He was so impressed by what he discovered that he came to consider him-self a Muslim, particularly given that he assessed Islam, with its rational approach, closer to the essence of "prophetic Judaism" and certainly con-genial with the Reform Judaism he favored: "I termed my monotheism Islam, and I did not lie when I said I believed the prophecies of Muham-mad." While staying in Damascus in 1890, he wrote, "I truly entered in those weeks the spirit of Islam to such an extent that ultimately I became inwardly convinced that I myself was a Muslim and judiciously discovered that this was the only religion which, even in its doctrinal formulation, can satisfy philosophical minds." Goldziher was too attached to his own faith (he studied the Talmud every day) to convert, but he did want to "elevate Judaism to a similar rational level."[61] He believed that Islam and progress could be reconciled, because "classical works from the Koran to Ibn Khal-dûn's *Al-muqadimma*... even in light of Western intellectualism... were not contrary to human progress." Meanwhile, he had nothing but con-tempt for Christianity, inferior on all counts to Islam. Not only was he vehemently opposed to European imperialism[62] but he was also horrified and outraged by the Christian missionaries' activities in the Levant and minced no words when he described Christianity in his diary in 1874: "In this abominable religion, which invented the Christian blood libel, which puts its own sons to the rack, they want to entice away the believers in the one and only Jehovah—in Muslim lands. This is an insolence of which only Christianity, the most abominable of all religions, is capable. It has no forehead to become aware of the insolence that forms its historical char-acter. The forehead of a whore, that is the forehead of Christianity."[63] Not surprisingly, Goldziher condemned European colonialism, declaring that "the European in the Orient represents the class of the worst kinds of ras-cals who were spit out by European society."[64]

Britain's legendary prime minister Benjamin Disraeli (1804–1881) was also among the group of prominent Jews who saw themselves as the natural allies of Arabs. Although this British descendant of Sephardim (Marranos who fled Iberian persecution) from his father's side was baptized into the Anglican Church in 1817, at the age of twelve or thirteen,[65] he never fully identified with the European Christian heritage. Calling Jews the "Arabian tribe" and Arabs "Jews upon horseback," Disraeli could claim that "God never spoke except to an Arab," thereby expanding the category of Arabs to include all monotheistic prophets, including Jesus.[66] Even Napoleon was an Arab in Disraeli's racial view of history, for "the great Corsican . . . like most of the inhabitants of the Mediterranean isles, had probably Arab blood in his veins."[67] So triumphalist was Disraeli in his Ishmaelism, if one might call it that, that in 1877 William Gladstone (1809–1898) wrote in a private letter that "though [Disraeli] has been baptized, his Jew feelings are the most radical and the most real, and so far respectable, portion of his profoundly falsified nature."[68] Not only did Disraeli slap arrogant gentiles with the nobler Arab heritage of the Jews, but he himself, noted Lord Cromer (1841–1917), the colonial administrator of India and Egypt, in his physical appearance and manners embodied the features of the Orient.[69]

Through the character Sidonia in Disraeli's novels *Coningsby; or, The New Generation* (1844) and *Tancred; or, The New Crusade* (1847), Disraeli's alter ego, a wise and successful Sephardic Jew born to "New Christians" in Aragon, explains that Mosaic Arabs (Jews), persecuted by the Visigoths, sought the help of their brethren Mohammedan Arabs (Muslims/Arabs), therefore giving rise to al-Andalus, or Muslim Spain, which centuries later fell to the dark forces of the Reconquista. In Muslim Spain, "the children of Ishmael rewarded the children of Israel with equal rights and privileges with themselves. During these halcyon centuries, it is difficult to distinguish the followers of Moses from the votary of Mahomet. Both alike built palaces, gardens, and fountains; filled equally the highest offices of the state, competed in an extensive and enlightened commerce, and rivaled each other in renowned universities."[70] The narrator of *Coningsby* laments the loss of a culture in which "Mosaic and Mohammedan Arabs" lived and prospered together: "Where is that tribunal that summoned Medina Sidonia and Cadiz to its dark inquisition? Where is Spain? Its fall, its unparalleled and its irremediable fall, is mainly to be attributed to the expulsion of that large portion of its subjects, the most industrious and intelligent, who traced their origin to the Mosaic and Mohammedan Arabs."[71]

Sidonia is the heir to Sheikh Abraham, the son of an "unmixed race" of Mosaic and Mohammedan Arabs. In Disraeli's hands, Muslims such as Emir Fakredeen, one of Tancred's benefactors, are unimpressed by the false glories of Britain. "The country," the emir tells the young pilgrim, "produces nothing; it is an island, a mere rock, larger than Malta, but not so well fortified.

Everything they require is imported from other countries; they get their corn from Odessa, and their wine from the ports of Spain. I have been assured at Beiroot that they do not grow even their cotton, but that I can hardly believe. Even their religion is exotic; and as they are indebted for that to Syria, it is not surprising that they should import their education from Greece."[72] It is for this reason that Jerusalem, as stated in *Tancred,* will never fall into the hands of Europeans: "Jerusalem, it cannot be doubted, will ever remain the appanage either of Israel or of Ishmael; and if, in the course of those great vicissitudes which are no doubt impending for the East, there be any attempt to place upon the throne of David a prince of the House of Coburg or Deuxponts, the same fate will doubtless await him as, with all their brilliant qualities and all the sympathy of Europe, was the final doom of the Godfreys, the Baldwins, and the Lusignans."[73] Such views didn't fail to elicit this subtle rebuke from the *Times* of London: "We think better of Europe than to suppose it rotten at the core and hastening to decay. We cannot think sufficiently well of the nations of the East to suppose them now the living fountains of all that is consolatory and good in life, the pure and immaculate possessors of celestial privileges and divine prerogatives."[74] In what Russell Schweller called "Disraeli's semitic chauvinism," the north European is simply unworthy of the great treasures of human civilization. Not surprisingly, before the Congress of Berlin was held, in 1878, Disraeli tried to propose a secular Jewish state in Palestine that would accommodate Muslims and Christians without prejudice.[75]

Another fascinating figure in this regard is William Gifford Palgrave (1826–1888), whose views may have influenced the birth of Arab nationalism. The son of a baptized Jewish father who prospered after marrying into a respectable Anglican family, "the mysterious traveler, sometime-spy, sometime-Jew, sometime Jesuit" Palgrave traveled in Arabia, changed his name to Michael Suhail, was ordained as a Catholic priest in 1857, and then started calling himself Father Cohen (taking his father's original last name). Palgrave's affinity with the Arabs didn't extend to religion (he detested Wahhabi fanaticism, mostly because the Wahhabis wouldn't convert to Christianity), but his book *Narrative of a Year's Journey through Central and Eastern Arabia* was so influential on David George Hogarth (1862–1927), author of *The Penetration of Arabia* (1905) and *Arabia* (1922), who himself was influential on T. E. Lawrence, author of *Seven Pillars of Wisdom* (1922), that one could attribute much of British thinking on Arab nationalism and its compatibility with Zionism to Palgrave's influence. After all, his books sold more editions in the nineteenth century "than Burckhardt, Burton, Doughty, the Blunts, and all other Victorian travelers in Arab lands combined." He praised the town-dwelling Arabs (not the Bedouins, whom he despised) as "the Englishmen of the East."[76]

It is worth noting that proudly reclaiming one's Moorish heritage was a universal endeavor among Jews, Sephardim and Ashkenazim alike. "Moorish-style synagogues," which became the architectural rage in European Jewry as well as in the United States (reflected, for example, in the Plum Street Temple in Cincinnati, designed by the architect James Key Wilson and built between 1863 and 1868), were "not built by and for the Sephardim but for [Western-looking and often liberal] Ashkenazim," which proves that the synagogues, built at a time of Jewish confidence and ascendancy, were an affirmation of the Jews' pride in their Arab/Muslim identity. At a time when assimilation was enticing and the future of Jews looked promising, many Jews chose to assert their oriental difference through architecture, eagerly associating themselves with their Moorish heritage, a fact now obscured, according to Ivan Davidson Kalmar, "by the veil of decades of Arab-Jewish strife."[77] As late as 1884, a Jew from Turin, G. Gustalla, still made the connection:

> The most celebrated rabbis adopted into the ancestral doctrine that which was produced by the Arabs, transmitting it unaltered to [nourish] the heritage of the civilization of the late Middle Ages, and there they raised for their own religious practices temples using the same style as those famous religious and secular buildings of Córdoba, Seville, and Granada that have survived to our own day, a style that, besides, was also in harmony with their artistic genius and their temperament; seeing that it [was a style that] derived from the Orient, where their race had its origin.[78]

In fact, to build an Arab- or Muslim-style temple was to come closer to replicating the Temple of Solomon (the Temple of Jerusalem), either because Jews had always borrowed from local traditions or simply because Arab/Muslim architecture was the closet model Jews had in the absence of more information. Ludwig Förster, who designed the Vienna-Leopoldstadt synagogue (1853–1858), put the case succinctly:

It is known to be a difficult task indeed to build an Israelite Temple in a form required by the religion and suitable for its practice, and at the same time corresponding, at least in its essential features, to the hallowed ideal of all temples, the Temple of Solomon. It is doubly difficult insofar as [the building's] external architecture is concerned, for the existing records cannot nearly provide us with a reliable picture; and those Houses of God that belong to a later time either lack any distinct style or carry features that are in their inner being entirely alien to the Israelite religion.

In my humble opinion, the right way, given the circumstances, is to choose, when building an Israelite Temple, those architectural forms that have been used by Oriental ethnic groups that are related to the Israelite people, and in particular the Arabs.[79]

So strong was this belief that the Accademia delle Arti del Disegno of Florence blocked a neo-Renaissance design in 1872, explaining that, "as every nation has stamped its own history on [its] monuments, and most of all its religious monuments, so a building with the said function must manifest at first sight so effectively a marked character that it recalls the dates and the places that are of most interest for this religion, and a character such as cannot be confounded with the religious or secular monuments of other nations and religions."[80] This bold Jewish self-assertion was not without its critics. The orientalist scholar Paul de Lagarde reacted in 1881 by saying, "[Their] alien nature is stressed every day and in the most striking fashion by the Jews—who nevertheless wish to be made equal to Germans—through the style of their synagogue. What is the sense of raising claims to be called an honorary German and yet building the holiest site that one possesses in Moorish style, so as to never ever let anyone forget that one is a Semite, an Asiatic, a foreigner?"[81] But such anti-Semitic tirades had no chilling effect. As we have seen in the case of Disraeli, God revealed himself only to Arabs; therefore, it was fitting to build worship structures that reflected this divine bias.[82] In 1912, the Zionist Martin Buber stated that "the great complex of Oriental nations . . . can be shown to be one entity."[83] In fact, the great architect and urban designer Wilhelm Stiassny (1842–1910), "an ardent Zionist" who was close to both the great Ignaz Goldziher and Theodor Herzl (1860–1904), "the founder of modern political Zionism," had no problem imagining "a sort of an autonomous city-state [for Jews] under Turkish suzerainty."

It was, furthermore, Stiassny who authored a pamphlet titled *The Establishment of a Colony in the Holy Land or in One of Its Neighboring Regions* and dissuaded Herzl from seeking a homeland for the Jews outside of Palestine. In the Orient, Jews would be returning home, a fact expressed by David Ben-Gurion himself, who, posing with a fez in Istanbul, announced that Zionists were on their way back to being Orientals.[84]

Such feelings were sometimes coupled, as I have noted, with a strong contempt for the West and its values, as passages from an unpublished manuscript found in the papers of Rabbi Aladar Deutsch in Prague unequivocally indicate:

> A small fragment of the old Orient had given its old virtues, which had never decayed, a new life, in order to sweep away the Lie. The Orient is moving, it is beginning the fight with a small maneuver against the falseness of the West. . . . It is beginning to wake up, it will carry out its renaissance and reconquer what Esau of the West had snatched away from it; in order among other things to cleanse its soul of the influence of the mentally and spiritually wasted, to make "Ex oriente lux!" once more the truth. . . . The Orient as the old site of spiritually infused semitism *[Semitentum]* will, recognizing the spiritual emptiness and cowardice of the Aryan so-called culture, force back the Aryan where he belongs.[85]

Inspired by a new book on the "Teutonic-Turkish alliance jihad against the West," a writer for the German Jewish monthly journal *Jüdische Monatshefte*, edited by Rabbi Dr. P. Kohn, reflected on this profound historical connection: "It is especially us, the German Jews, who follow this wonderful spectacle of how our Fatherland and the Islamic world are connected by political threads, with particular suspense. . . . Who is Ishmael to us? What does the Islamic world mean to us? The Muslim religious doctrine, customs and laws, the Muslim science and beautiful literature contain golden seeds which seem borrowed from us and the Jewish hereditary stock and thus seem familiar and related."[86] Others, like the Zionist Eugen Hoeflich, who took on the name of Moshe Yaacov Ben-Gavriel, wanted to bond with Arabs, the Chinese, and the Indians as well as to establish a Jewish state. To him, Jews were part of the larger Asiatic fabric, and so the return to Palestine was not the return of Europeans but part of the Asiatic renaissance. Buber would have agreed, given that he condemned "the subjugation of India, the self-Europeanization of Japan, the debilitation of Persia, and lastly, the ravaging of China where the ancient Oriental spirit seemed to dwell in inviolable security."[87]

Such strong bonds between Jews and Arabs and their shared destiny in Europe didn't fail to impress the great German philosophers Immanuel Kant (1724–1804) and G. W. F. Hegel (1770–1831). Islam's strict prohibition of graven images, Kant remarked in his *Critique of Judgment,* explains the "pride which Mohammedanism inspires" among Jews. Hegel, in his *Lectures on the Philosophy of Religion,* simply stated the fact that "Arabs and Jews have only to be noticed in an external and historic way."[88]

Because of such affinities with Moors or Arabs, it was not unusual for Zionists to read their project as a reunion of Asiatic races, or, at least, a reunion of what Disraeli would have termed "Mosaic Arabs" (Jews) and their long-lost cousins, "Jews upon horseback" (Arabs). "One of the roots of Zionism . . . that has not been appropriately recognized," argues the Israeli film critic Judd Ne'eman, "was a hidden identification of the European Jew with Arab Islamic peoples." Such views, as we have seen, were not uncommon in the late nineteenth and early twentieth centuries. The conviction of one "fiery character" in M. Z. Feierberg's novella *Whither?* (1898) that it is "unnatural that we Hebrews, we Easterners, should throw in our lot with the West as we set out for the East. . . . The great East will revive from its slumber and the accursed people will march at its head, at the head of the living East" was echoed, for instance, by Martin Buber in 1912, as we have seen.[89] Even if we assume that European Jews had drunk too much from the wells of orientalism (in the sense that Europeans projected their fantasies onto the Orient) and saw themselves as the redeemers of their fallen cousins in the East, as Arthur Hertzberg insinuates in *The Fate of Zionism* (2003), that doesn't make the Jews' real affinities with Muslims and Arabs any less real.[90]

In fact, many Jews rejected the school of Zionism that adopted Europe's orientalist prejudices.[91] In the negative Jewish orientalist perspective, Israel was the land of the "new Jew," not the "exilic" or Arab one returning to an "empty" land. "By appropriating the 'nativeness' of the Arabs, these Zionists," writes Amnon Raz-Krakotzkin, "assumed the role of natives and rendered the indigenous population obsolete."[92] Initially, the Mizrahim (a category that did not exist before Israel was established), or Arab Jews, in Yehouda Shenhav's preferred expression (that is, "Arabs by culture and Jews by religion"), were not included in the European Zionist vision. Not only was Zionism a distinctly European movement (Arab Jews had no say whatsoever in its formulation),[93] but, according to Shenhav, the son of Iraqi Jews who at one time was embarrassed by his background in Israel, it was modeled on German nationalism: "Zionist thinkers adopted ideas from the German nationalist movement concerning the relationship between homeland and Diaspora, socialization into the practices of nationalization (such as national education or the establishment of national youth and sports movements), and the establishment of rural settlements as also devoted to character building. As the early Zionist thinker Hans Kohn wrote, young Zionists 'transferred Fichte's teaching into the context of our own situation.'"[94]

Israel was consciously imagined as an advanced European country bringing the light to Arab Jews who, like non-Jews in Arab societies, had yet to come out of the late Middle Ages. The Arab Jew was the Other, but she was also the same. So, because Zionism was a nationalism deeply rooted in theology, to separate Arab Jews from non-Jews, secular Arab Jews had to prove their credentials by intensifying their religiosity in Arab lands, a process of "purification" that would later work against them in Israel, with its secular, European ethos.[95]

The Mizrahim's Jewishness complicated the Zionists' "Eurocentric conception of the Jewish nation," for, like the Orientals in Europe's imagination, they represented both the origin and what had been left behind. In fact, the Mizrahim would probably not have been encouraged to migrate had the Zionists not worried about ensuring a Jewish majority in Palestine after the Holocaust. "Their mass migration was rationalized in almost purely demographic terms," says Raz-Krakotzkin. As with Palestine itself, the de-Arabization of the Mizrahim was crucial for their integration into the new polity. Although Ben-Gurion posed with a fez in Istanbul and called for a return to the Orient, he was clear about this: "We do not want the Israelis to be Arabs. It is our duty to fight against the spirit of the Levant that ruins individuals and societies." In this way, "the Mizrahim became the new Marranos," hiding from their Ashkenazi coreligionists the culture that had shaped them in the ancestral lands.[96]

The presence of the oriental Jew as Other in the fabric of modern Zionism and in Israel proper was still evident in the early 1990s, as in the following comment about Russian immigration from a prominent journalist:

"The state of Israel is about to undergo an amazing change. . . . It means a demographic earth[quake]. No, I do not speak about Arabs vs Jews. I speak about Mizrahim vs Ashkenazim. Our State, we've got to admit, that began its career as an Ashkenazi State, tilted, or if you wish, turned in the last two decades in the Mizrahi-Levantine direction. . . . I still believe that given the choice between Paris and Baghdad, [I] will choose Paris. And I still believe that the more distance there is between Baghdad and us the better off we are."[97] This point of view persisted when the Moroccan-born Amir Peretz was running for the leadership of Israel's Labor Party in 2005. Not being part of the genuine Zionist vision, Arab Jews are seen as *edot ha' mizrah,* or "oriental communities," a folk group within Israeli culture. Never mind that the hybrid status of Arab Jews was and is still mirrored in the equally hybrid ideology of Zionism, a self-identified secular vision that cannot escape its theological and biblical imaginary. Still, the orientalist motif in Israel is so strong that Yigal and Haggai Amir, the assassins of prime minister Yitzak Rabin and his brother-accomplice, were described by an Israeli secular organization as "the Muslim Brothers."[98]

Because the barely disguised contempt for Arabness put enormous pressure on the Mizrahim to prove their Israeli credentials, the Mizrahim developed a hostile attitude toward the Arabs, although, paradoxically, it was the Mizrahim who were better suited to negotiate the Zionist-Palestinian divide, because of their "in-betweenness."[99] The Sephardic scholar David Shasha sums up the tragedy of the Mizrahim and Sephardim in this eloquent passage:

> Due to the stigma against all things Arab propounded by classical Zionism and Ashkenazi modernism under a Eurocentric bias, the Sephardim have become an invisible presence in modern Jewish life. Many Arab Jews have surrendered their native Levantine perspective in favor of the ruling ideology in Israel; some Israeli Sephardim in frustration have divorced themselves from the mainstream of the traditional Jewish community; and still others have submerged their ethnic rage in a thunderous barbarity vis-à-vis the Arab Muslims. The issue of anti-Arab prejudice among Israeli and American Sephardim has made many observers question the very propriety of even raising the issue of the Levantine nativity of Arab Jews; many of whom have become among the most militant followers of the Likud and other Right Wing parties in Israel. The movement of Jews out of the Arab world and into

the orbit of the Jewish state has greatly disrupted the traditional ethos and bearings of Arab Jewry. This has translated not merely into Sephardic political intransigency, but a complete abandonment of the traditional Sephardic cultural and religious legacy. But we can indeed recall a time when Jews lived productively in the Middle East and developed a material and intellectual culture that proved amazingly durable and robust.[100]

Graetz, Goldziher, Disraeli, and others would not have accepted this state of affairs, for it went against the essence of the Jews' Arab identity they proudly promoted. One Jew who refused to subscribe to the Zionist orientalist ideology was Leopold Weiss, born in what is now Ukraine, whose condemnation of "the immoralities of Zionism" was followed by his conversion to Islam after two life-changing epiphanies.[101] After visualizing a Bedouin against the Jerusalem sky, Weiss "knew, with that clarity which sometimes bursts within us like lightning and lights up the world for the length of a heart-beat, that David and David's time, like Abraham and Abraham's time, were closer to their Arabian roots—and so to the Bedouin of today—than to the Jew of today, who claims to be their descendant."[102] Returning to Berlin after two years of travel in parts of the Islamic East, Weiss realized that Berliners looked miserable on the subway, and he found an explanation for the horrors of greed in the Qur'an. Thus, in 1926, he walked into the Berlin Islamic Society (could it be the same Islamic organization founded by Lev Nussimbaum following his conversion four years earlier?) and converted.[103]

Muhammad Asad (1900–1992) became a regular in the Arabian monarch Ibn Saud's circle (two of the four women he married were from Saudi Arabia, including Munira of the Shammar tribe, mother of the U.S.-based anthropologist Talal Asad), but later he came to see Ibn Saud as yet another Eastern despot, for he did "nothing to build up an equitable, progressive society." Asad saw possible hope in the Sanusi movement in Cyrenaica, but that also led to nothing. He then got involved with the nascent state of Pakistan, represented it at the United Nations, and married there for the fourth time. In 1934, he published a pamphlet titled *Islam at the Crossroads,* linking Western imperialism with the Crusades and thereby developing the ideology of "Crusaderism" that would influence the thought of Sayyid Qutb (1906–1966) and still influences Islamic fundamentalism today. But his constant efforts to reform Islam came to naught, although his book

The Road to Mecca, published in New York in 1954, made him famous and he was able to sway others to convert, such as Margaret Marcus (b. 1934), known as Maryam Jameelah, who became "one of the best-known ideologues of Islamic fundamentalism, famous for her methodical indictments of the West." By the mid-1960s, Asad, sponsored by King Faisal of Saudi Arabia (r. 1964–1975), settled in Tangier, Morocco, to write a new translation of the Qur'an, but it would be banned in Saudi Arabia before it was completed. Thus, Asad's view of Arabs dimmed, although he remained attached to Islamic ideals. He left Tangier in 1982 and died ten years later. He was buried in the Muslim cemetery of Granada, the last bastion of Moorish Spain.[104]

Though Zionism is often associated with the long history of European imperialism in Arab lands, and thereby recasts Jews in the Arab or Muslim imagination as allies of colonialists, there is no doubt at all that Jews and Muslims were seen as quintessentially the same: enemies to be extirpated from the holy, Christian, racially pure body of Europe. The frenetic activity of Iberian and European exploration that followed the defeat of Moorish Granada in 1492 led Europeans to define people they had never seen before as either the Lost Tribes of Israel or Moors, and sometimes both. As Tudor Parfitt explains, "To medieval Europe the two most obvious forms of the religious other were the Jews and Muslims and to some extent this binary construct continued into the twentieth century. The myth of the Moor (synonymous with Muslim in the European discourse) was one of its aspects and stood more or less for wild tribalism and a state of fairly but not irredeemable savagery [*sic*]."[105] Ivan Davidson Kalmar and Derek J. Penslar have even suggested that imperialism and anti-Semitism arose at the same time in Europe, both designed to exclude the Oriental from the main Western (white) body.[106] In the words of Adolf Wahrmund, an anti-Semitic professor in Vienna, "In Africa the nomads have been pushed back into the desert from North and South; the new Congo State and the German colonies mean cutting off the nomads and Islam from the South, [and] in Central Asia Russia has laid its fist upon the Touranian nomadic tribes . . . ; even the Turkish nomads of Asia Minor will soon have their practices stopped by the West; but among us, in the realm of Christian German statehood, the Semitic-Pharisaic nomad lays down the law."[107]

Zionism didn't necessarily mean eradicating Arab presence from Palestine, despite Ben-Gurion's remark quoted earlier. The Odessa-born militant Zionist Vladimir Jabotinsky, founder of the Jewish Legion, started out by imagining his mission as that of a superior European colonist advocating an all-out war on Palestinian Arabs and erecting an "iron wall" to protect Jewish interests in Palestine, but he eventually imagined Muslims, Christians, and Jews living side by side. In the novel *Old-New-Land (Altneuland)*, published in 1902, shortly before he died, Theodor Herzl imagined a Zionist utopia "under a kind of loose Turkish suzerainty."[108] Meanwhile, Arabs such as the celebrated Iraqi poet Ma'ruf al-Russafi denied any animosity toward the project of Zionism per se:

> We are not, as our accusers say, enemies of the Children of Israel in secret
>   or in public.
> How could we be, when they are our uncles, and the Arabs are kin to
>   them of old though Ishmael?
> The two are akin to one another, and in their languages there is proof of
>   their kinship.
> But we fear exile, and we fear a government that rules people by force.[109]

In his book *Genesis 1948: The First Arab-Israeli War*, Dan Kurzman recounted the encounter between King Abdullah of Transjordan and Golda Meir in 1948, during which the king invited Meir to consider joining his kingdom, promising that 50 percent of the seats in Parliament would be allocated to Jews, thereby creating a powerful Arab-Jewish Palestinian country. Meir refused, even as she reminded the king that "the Jews are the only friends you have." This led the king to make the following comment:

> I know that very well. I have no illusions. I know you and I believe in your
> good intentions. I believe with all my heart that divine providence has brought
> you back here [to Palestine and the Middle East], restoring you, a Semitic
> people who were exiled to Europe and shared in its progress, to the Semitic
> East which needs your knowledge and initiative. Only with your help and
> your guidance will the Semites be able to revive their ancient glory. We cannot
> expect genuine assistance from the Christian world, which looks down
> on Semitic people. We will progress only as the result of joint efforts. I know
> all this and I believe it sincerely, but conditions are difficult. One dare not
> take rash steps. Therefore, I beg you once more to be patient.[110]

King Abdullah here treated Jews as the Arabs' long-lost siblings, perhaps like a Semitic or oriental delegation bringing back European know-how to the Orient. This vision was central to many prominent Zionists and figures such as Wilhelm Stiassny and Wolfgang von Weisl, who in the 1920s published the periodical *The Nile and Palestine Gazette* in Egypt and tried hard to convert Arabs to his Zionist cause. It may sound condescending to those who are attuned to orientalist prejudices, but when the poet Uri Zvi Greenberg stated his hopes in lines such as "Believe: our race's sister, the Arab, is here / . . . we will come to instruct him, great in wisdom and experience,"[111] he seems to have simply stated the obvious fact that diasporic Jews had benefited from European knowledge and were bringing it back to their ancient lands.

But the reunion of long-separated "Mosaic Arabs" and "Mohammedan Arabs," in the terminology of Disraeli, was not destined to be in the twentieth century, and one wonders whether it will take shape in the near future. The Arab-Israeli conflict "has stifled virtually all expression of romanticized kinship or even pragmatic commonality between the children of Isaac and Ishmael. This is a tragedy," comment Kalmar and Penslar, for "although Jewish claims to propinquity with the Orient frequently masked or justified claims of cultural superiority and unfettered rights to land in Palestine, the future of Israel depends upon the formulation of a mutually acceptable conceptual framework in which the Jews' place as a sovereign collective in the Orient is assured."[112]

Looking back at the strong Jewish-Muslim bonds through the ages, there is no reason to believe that Zionism could not coexist with full Palestinian rights. In 2004, during an encounter between Arabs and Jews in France, Patrick Klugman, a member of the board of directors at the Conseil représentatif des institutions juives de France, called himself "a pro-Palestinian Zionist."[113] Even when all Muslims have become suspect in the Western imagination since the terrorist attacks of 9/11, and Jewish-Muslim relations have deteriorated even further in the wake of the conflict between the West and Islam, some Jewish leaders are still defending Muslim rights. When Muslims gathered in Rosemont, Illinois, in early September 2007 to talk about their collective plight after 9/11, the president of the Union for Reform Judaism, Rabbi Eric H. Yoffie, denounced such maltreatment in language reminiscent of nineteenth-century Jews who defended Islamic causes. "The time has come," the rabbi told the opening session, "to stand up to the opportunists, the media figures, the religious leaders and politicians who demonize Muslims and bash Islam, exploiting the fears of their fellow citizens for their own purposes."[114] A similar spirit was exhibited by Dutch Jews when they condemned the association of Qur'an-inspired violence depicted in *Fitna,* a fifteen-minute film released in early 2008 by Geert Wilders, a right-wing and pro-Israeli Dutch politician, with Muslims in general.[115] Such Jewish stances, as well as Muslims' defense of Jewish rights in Morocco and Iraq, point to a path that has yet to be fully explored in the breakdown of relations between Jews and Muslims. If both sides were to bracket off the Israeli-Palestinian conflict as a serious but, in the end, political problem and explore the history and bonds they share, perhaps enough goodwill could be generated to help Israelis and Palestinians and other aggrieved Muslims work out a solution.

Whatever the outcome of this dispiriting mistrust between Jews and Muslims today, both the triumph of the Jews in the Orient and their unprecedented acceptance and success in the diaspora after World War II[116] gradually brought an end to their proxy Moorish presence in Europe; and Mohammedan Arabs were pulled into the European economy by the dual arms of colonial control and postcolonial capitalist hegemony. Even as the Jew has morphed into a seemingly natural member of a Judeo-Christian civilization, the Moor has once again reappeared to haunt the West with her troubling presence and resistance to national assimilationist policies. The Moors were presumably expelled from Europe in the early seventeenth century for lack of assimilation into the Christian national body; now they have returned in the guise of dark-skinned immigrants seeking some form of livelihood in the nations that have played a major role in upsetting the world order in the last five centuries. Despite all appearances, it is not necessarily the resistance of Islam to Western ways that is the problem (although this plays a part and gets amplified by the media to serve nationalist agendas) but the slow unraveling of the European national order based on race that was established by King Ferdinand and Queen Isabella and culminated in the wholesale expulsion of Moriscos from Spain by 1614. However undesirable they may be, the unassimilable Moors of yesterday, the aliens against whom Spain and Europe built their identities, have come back to reclaim a seat at the global economic and political table. And from all indications, they seem intent on staying.

chapter 4

Undesirable Aliens

Hispanics in America, Muslims in Europe

The confrontation between a sanctimonious mid-nineteenth-century Anglo-
American Protestantism and a demonized Roman Catholicism strikingly
evokes the late-twentieth-century construct of a "clash of civilizations"
between the West and Islam, and more particularly European reactions
to Muslim immigrants.

—ARISTIDE R. ZOLBERG, *A Nation by Design*

The problem is that if you start counting people, they can always end up in
a stadium.

—TAHAR BEN JELLOUN, Moroccan novelist

Soon after the American Samuel Huntington, a longtime liberal hawk, set
the tone for the post–cold war period by predicting a new era of cultural and
civilizational clashes, thereby helping recast Islam as the natural enemy of
the West, he turned his attention to the problem of Hispanic immigration
in his own country and concluded that it posed an even more insidious
threat to the survival of the culture that made America great. Careful readers of his *Clash of Civilizations and the Remaking of the World Order* could
have glimpsed ideas that would later develop into a full-scale treatment of
the subject, *Who Are We?* In that earlier book, Huntington agreed with the
Mexican poet Octavio Paz that Mexico is practically an Indian nation, one
that is, moreover, insufficiently Westernized.[1] But now that Mexicans are
pouring across the border with virtual impunity, Mexico has become the

United States' Achilles' heel. It is the gateway for an unprecedented invasion of the United States, an invasion that poses a mortal threat to the American republic. It is one thing for journalists and pundits to make such claims, but when major scholars like Huntington, whose views often shape policy debates, say them, we know that this is a serious matter indeed.

In *Who Are We?* Huntington is clear that "the cement in the structure of this great nation"—what's called the "American Creed"—is the "product of the distinct Anglo-Protestant culture of the founding settlers of America in the seventeenth and eighteenth centuries," a culture whose "key elements" include "the English language; Christianity; religious commitment; English concepts of the rule of law, the responsibility of rulers, and the rights of individuals; and dissenting Protestant values of individualism, the work ethic, and the belief that humans have the ability and the duty to try to create a heaven on earth, a 'city on a hill.'"[2] It is this Anglo-Protestant culture that has separated the United States from much of the world and made it a magnet to immigrants worldwide, and it is to this cultural legacy that Americans should recommit themselves if they want to maintain what has made America an exceptional country. Huntington's book, then, is about the "continuing centrality of Anglo-Protestant culture to American national identity." To make sure that his book is not read as a racist tract, Huntington emphasizes that it is the Anglo-Protestant "culture" he is talking about, not necessarily race or ethnicity, two of the four components of American identity that have ceased to be relevant in the modern period.[3]

To Huntington, America is not the so-called nation of immigrants but "a society, or societies, of settlers," mostly from the British Isles. The settlers were what historian John Porter called the "charter group," which very deliberately wanted to put its imprint on the society it sought to found, a society whose tenets later immigrants would have to accept. It was a homogeneous and racist society, too: the American colonists and the British were basically one people, and the Revolution could be read as an argument over who was truer to the best British value of freedom. In this racially exclusivist society, Indians suffered ethnic cleansing or genocide. Slavery was abolished, but the nation remained deeply segregationist until the late 1950s and 1960s. Immigration policies kept the United States a white society until the mid-twentieth century, even though whiteness itself was a shaded category. The Immigration Restriction League, founded in 1894, deemed "Slav,

Latin and Asiatic races" inferior to the progressive and freedom-loving British, Germans, and Scandinavians. White America may have been a "melting pot," as Israel Zangwill titled his play in 1908, but everything seems to indicate that immigrants dissolved into the Anglo-Protestant cultural "soup," or were tossed in what Horace Kallen once called a "salad," adding flavor and perhaps texture to the food but not substantially changing the fundamental ingredients.[4]

America's Anglo-Protestant worldview unraveled in the later decades of the twentieth century, giving rise to what Huntington calls "deconstructionists," a movement of elites (including the courts) who read too much into and eventually subverted John F. Kennedy's 1961 Executive Order 10,925 calling on employers to take "affirmative action" not to discriminate; as well as the Civil Rights Act of 1964, by changing a protective measure into a militant policy of preferential treatment for minority groups. Because such policies, Huntington notes, go against the deeply ingrained ethos of individual merit, a reversal was to be expected. In a landmark Supreme Court case in 1989, Justice Sandra Day O'Connor worried that such preferential treatment might cause "stigmatic harm." More recently (in 2003), the Supreme Court outlawed preferential treatment for undergraduate applicants at the University of Michigan but upheld it for the university's law school, although most Americans were opposed to both. Thus, America remains "deeply divided" over race issues and policies, the debate often pitting liberal elites against the majority of citizens.

Not only race but the English language itself came under siege in the era of multiculturalism, what Huntington describes as "basically an anti-Western ideology." Courses in Western civilization were changed into courses focusing on non-Western cultures. "At the turn of the century," writes Huntington, "none of fifty top colleges and universities required a course in American history." By 1999, many "seniors at fifty-five top colleges" "could not say within a half-century *when the Civil War was fought.*" In such a multicultural moment, only a sustained terrorist attack could unite the country and weaken the deconstructionists' antinational agenda.[5]

For much of American history, assimilation through dispersion across the land (not concentrations in enclaves, as was suggested for the Moriscos by friendlier voices in early modern Spain) was encouraged and considered rather indispensable by the Founding Fathers for the better integration of immigrants into the new society. As Milton M. Gordon pointed out in his book *Assimilation in American Life,* this process was facilitated by "the numerical dominance of the Anglo-Saxon population" (a situation, as we shall see, that is now changing for the first time in American history).[6] New immigrants and immigration laws have further eroded this policy of assimilation so indispensable to successful participation in a republic. To be sure, coming to America then—as it is now—was a major choice, involving a self-selected group armed with vision and fortitude. Atlantic crossings may have claimed the lives of around 17 percent of would-be immigrants (land crossings today still claim thousands of lives), but were 15 percent of those who made it turned back at Ellis Island, as Huntington claims? If one were to take into account Roger Daniels's history of immigration to the United States, Huntington's rejection rates certainly seem too high and might more aptly apply to the "other" Ellis Island, the mythically forgotten Angel Island, established in 1910 near San Francisco, eighteen years after New York's checkpoint came into being, to process mostly Asian immigrants. It was Angel Island that had a rejection rate of 18 percent, not Ellis Island, the gateway to whiter European immigrants, whose average rejection rates were a mere 1 percent throughout its existence.[7] Still, Huntington is right to make the point that Ellis Island immigrants were ready-made Americans from the get-go. Although today's easy transport methods no longer require such fortitude and risk taking, illegal immigrants still fit the bill. "Who but the most eager and hardy can walk across forty or fifty miles of parched desert, dodge dopers, coyotes, and the feds, endure hardship and risk life and limb just to get a job at the other end of a gauntlet of discomfort and anxiety?" asks Geraldo Rivera, in his book *HisPanic.* "Don't you want these tough sons of guns on our team?"[8]

However, new immigrants are more likely to resist assimilation than their predecessors. Neither Muslims nor the new waves of immigrants from Mexico, the Caribbean, and Latin America, in general, identify fully with mainstream American culture. There is little pressure to convert to Americanism, and even business fosters separatist inclinations by catering to ethnic pride and such. Meanwhile, naturalization rates are dropping, although they peak when immigration benefits are threatened; and dual loyalties, including dual or more citizenships (by "ampersands") are rising, despite the oath of naturalization mandating one allegiance only.[9]

It is in this context of America's changing demographics that Hispanics have become the fastest-growing segment of the U.S. population. Already "more numerous than blacks," they are estimated to make up around 25 percent of the population by 2040. In 1998, José replaced Michael as the most popular name for newborn boys in both California and Texas, and "in 2003 for the first time since the 1850s a majority of newborn children in California were Hispanic" (overwhelmingly of Mexican origin).[10] With such concentrations of mostly poor Mexican and Mexican American groups having a strong sense of their separate cultural identity, contempt for Anglo-Protestant values, and a vivid memory of past wrongs by the United States against Mexico, including the conquest of Mexican lands, America's Southwest has turned into a cauldron. In fact, the sociologist Morris Janowitz has argued that "for sections of the Southwest, it is not premature to speak of a cultural and social irredenta—sectors of the United States which have in effect become Mexicanized and[,] therefore, under political pressure."[11] In 1995, the president of the National Council of La Raza was quoted saying, "The biggest problem we have is a cultural clash, a clash between our values and the values of American society."[12] Miami, meanwhile, has been thoroughly Hispanicized by middle- and upper-class Cubans and is now considered either the capital of Latin America or "an out-of-control banana republic," depending on who is evaluating Miami's remarkable transformation from a sleepy Anglo town to a dynamic financial and commercial hub.[13]

Huntington implies in more than one place that America's cohesiveness relies on the existence of an Other—whether foreign or domestic, Muslim terrorist or anti-Anglo Hispanic. John Updike's question in his 1990 novel *Rabbit at Rest,* "Without the cold war, what's the point of being American?" is a dead serious one, given that the specter of social breakdown and disunity haunts the national atmosphere. It is not race or ethnicity that worries Huntington but the threat of alien cultural traits to the Anglo-Saxon Protestant legacy, the source of all good things in life and unfailing sustainer of the American Dream. It is for this reason that he advocates a global multiculturalism based on homogeneous, well-defined national cultures. It's an interesting position, one that sounds rather isolationist: "America cannot become the world and still be America. Other peoples cannot become American and still be themselves. America is different, and that difference is defined in large part by its Anglo-Protestant culture and its religiosity. The alternative to cosmopolitanism and imperialism is nationalism devoted to the preservation and enhancement of those qualities that have defined America since its founding."[14]

As usual, Huntington's unadorned, fact-based account of American culture makes much sense; but he never wonders whether the conditions that consolidated American nationalism, which, as he readily admits, involved the dispossession of Indians, slavery, and war making, can still be tolerated in a world that has embraced the American Creed. He also doesn't consider the country's integration into the world economy, such as its reliance on oil and foreign investors; or the fact that the United States of America has found a mighty competitor in the "United States of Europe," as T. R. Reid, a *Washington Post* reporter, titled his 2004 book; or the fact that there is now, as Jeremy Rifkin puts it, a "European Dream" that is eclipsing the American one.[15] Huntington's call for nationalism all around may seem fair—protectionism and isolationism may help the United States avoid being attacked—but then he fails to take into account the violence embedded in such nationalism, for, as we have seen, there is no national project without its scapegoat(s). Moreover, as Huntington himself accepts, it is the attacks on America, whether real or imagined, that unite the people and keep the deconstructionists and multiculturalists at bay for a while. For Huntington has no illusions about the vital role of war, or at least the fear of an enemy in nation making; yet this approach is no longer a sustainable model for American civilization, particularly given the proliferation of weapons of mass destruction and the rapid flow of information. Finally, political nationalism might work only if accompanied by economic nationalism, forcing nations to rely on their resources and trade fairly in the global market.

Despite his disclaimers, there is no doubt at all that Huntington's thesis falls squarely within the long tradition of the American nativist fear and persecution of foreigners and those who are different. It is not for no reason that Aristide Zolberg, the eminent historian of immigration and refugees, comments on the "unimaginative revival of ancient nativist stereotypes such as the inanities of political scientist Samuel Huntington, for whom the latest newcomers are unpromising candidates for membership in the national body by virtue of their biological and cultural inheritance, much as the new immigrants of the turn of the twentieth century were for his intellectual ancestor Henry Cabot Lodge."[16] In fact, one might call Huntington a latter-day Lodge, the Boston Brahmin (1850–1924) who championed Anglo-Saxon supremacy and pushed for the literacy test in Congress to block U.S. entry to lower European races. In his magisterial study of nativism as a component of American nationalism, John Higham described Lodge in terms that could almost apply to Huntington as well:

When Lodge raised the banner of race against the new immigration, it acquired its most dangerous adversary. As Massachusetts' scholar-in-politics, he dominated both the intellectual and legislative phases of nativism. To this dual role, Lodge's own interests and values imperiously summoned him; he embodied in remarkable degree some of the major forces underlying late nineteenth century xenophobia. From his precise Vandyke beard to his clipped Boston accent, Lodge was the model of a patrician. He was steeped in English culture—English to the last fiber of his thought, said Henry Adams—in pride of ancestry, and in nostalgia for New England's past. During the 1870's he had plunged into a study of the Anglo-Saxons; a thesis on early Anglo-Saxon law brought him the first Ph.D. that Harvard conferred in political science. Secondly, connected with Lodge's race consciousness was a morbid sensitivity to the danger of extensive social change. He had a lively repugnance for both the rising plutocracy and the restive mob, and he felt acutely the general nativist response to class conflict. By 1888, as a fledgling Congressman, he was pointing to the diminishing supply of free land in the West and the growth of unrest in the East as reasons for restricting immigration. Finally, while attacking immigration in domestic affairs, Lodge was adopting a belligerent stance in foreign affairs. His campaign against the new immigration during the 1890's interlaced with a jingoist crusade *for* expansion. Lodge the jingo hated England as much as Lodge the Anglo-Saxon loved the English; accordingly, his diplomatic belligerence took the form of an assertion of American power, his pleas for restriction a defense of the English race. But these and other inconsistencies in the life of the cold, cultivated little Senator were merely logical. They were resolved at another level—in the emotions of nationalism which shaped and guided his career.

Although the Anglo-Saxon tradition in the mid-nineties still swayed few outside of an eastern elite, through Lodge and others around him that elite occupied a position of strategic influence. Both the ideological instrument and the political leadership necessary to bring into a single *focus* the chaotic resentments against the new immigrant were therefore at hand.[17]

Huntington's last two books make it clear that he is not a jingoist or an imperialist in the way Lodge was, but his defense of the Anglo-Saxon cultural model puts him in the company of an insidious nativist legacy of discrimination, racism, and anti-Semitism. The term *nativism* itself, coined around 1840, could be broad enough to encompass basic patterns of human behavior, but for the Know-Nothings with whom it came to be associated, and later the American Party they founded, the concern was primarily nationalistic. What the American Party stood for, a Know-Nothing publication explained in 1855, "is the principle of nationality. . . . We must do something to protect and vindicate it. If we do not it will be destroyed."[18] This is the principle that animated American nativist movements, as Higham explained:

> Here was the ideological core of nativism in every form. Whether the nativist was a workingman or a Protestant evangelist, a southern conservative or a northern reformer, he stood for a certain kind of nationalism. He believed— whether he was trembling at a Catholic menace to American liberty, fearing an invasion of pauper labor, or simply rioting against the great English actor William Macread—that some influence originating abroad threatened the very life of the nation from within. Nativism, therefore, should be defined as intense opposition to an internal minority on the ground of its foreign (i.e., "un-American") connections. Specific nativistic antagonisms may, and do, vary widely in response to the changing character of minority irritants and the shifting conditions of the day; but through each separate hostility runs the connecting, energizing force of modern nationalism. While drawing on much broader cultural antipathies and ethnocentric judgments, nativism translates them into a zeal to destroy the enemies of a distinctively American way of life.[19]

For centuries, Catholics in Protestant England, and later in the United States, were seen as potential fifth columnists; this view coalesced with the general suspicion of foreign radicals. When New York was drafting its constitution, John Jay, the prominent figure of the Revolutionary generation, wanted to build "a wall of brass around the country for the exclusion of Catholics."[20] The fear of Catholics and subversives was fanned by the widely held notion that the United States owed its great institutions to the Anglo-Saxon race, a belief that justified expansionism in Texas and California, for instance, but was opposed by people such as James Russell Lowell, who "excoriated Anglo-Saxonism as a hypocritical mask for aggression." Surely, nativists did occasionally use this argument to defend their cause, but more generally, before Anglo-Saxonism acquired the notion of a racial distinctiveness, it was conceived of more as a national character than a biological fact.[21]

The Union armies, with their 500 foreign-born soldiers, effectively brought an end to the pre–Civil War nativist strain, and postwar America launched a campaign to import European immigrants to fill its industrial and agricultural needs. Postwar America, in this age of confidence, was also an age of cosmopolitanism, one in which the nation effectively imagined itself as a "cosmic race," in the expression used in 1925 by the celebrated Mexican writer José Vasconcelos. The country portrayed itself as a beacon for the oppressed and mistreated. "Every true republican," noted an English visitor in 1866, "has in his heart the notion that his country is pointed out by God as refuge for the distressed of all the nations."[22] But with vast numbers of immigrants rising up the social ladder, a new, subdued, and positive ideology of Anglo-Saxon purity emerged to give solace to elites eager to distinguish themselves from the masses. Here, Anglo-Saxonism acted as a barrier to the vulgar arrivistes, much as the purity-of-blood statute had done for the coveted claim for undiluted Christian descent in sixteenth-century Spain.

By the 1880s, with no more lands to settle across the continent—in 1886, one writer announced in the *North American Review* that "the public domain of the United States is now exhausted"—hard economic times for U.S.-born workers (the source of all xenophobic attitudes), and businessmen's fear of radical agitators, the cheery attitude toward immigrants dimmed. Social Gospel leaders started preaching homogeneity as the basis of stability and reform. Strikes and anarchy only intensified the hysteria. Denunciations of "Europe's human and inhuman rubbish" were expressed in a publication called *Public Opinion,* and others sounded the same alarm: "Our National existence, and, as well, our National and social institutions are at stake." Darker immigrant groups, such as Russian Jews and Italians, were seen as a liability for the health of the republic. Italians were not white, a construction boss explained: "An Italian is a Dago," the lowest of the low. In his seminal study of the tenements of New York, *How the Other Half Lives: Studies among the Tenements of New York* (1890), the scholar Jacob Riis confidently said about the Jews, "Money is their God."[23] From the mid-1880s to the late 1890s, the language of nationalism grew more strident. Nativists proclaimed homogeneity as essential to a great nation; "Americanism" was spreading:

> Flag exercises, replete with special salutes and pledges, spread throughout the public schools along with agitation for inculcating patriotism. Among well-to-do, status-conscious circles, over a dozen hereditary patriotic societies sprang up in the early nineties to cultivate a keener, more exclusive sense of nationality. Beginning with the Sons of the American Revolution in 1889, these prestige organizations embarked on a round of banquets, receptions, and celebrations. Their principal theme was always the dire importance of perpetuating the pure spirit of one's ancestors.[24]

The same attitude was displayed toward foreign governments, as jingoism, "the most aggressive expression of late nineteenth century nationalism," seemingly swept the country. The slightest faux pas by a foreign national or country was treated as a casus belli:

> It is hard to doubt that these bellicose outbursts flowed from the same domestic frustrations that generated nativism. The first harbinger of both jingoism and nativism was Josiah Strong, whose attack on immigration accompanied a grandiose vision of global conquest. Not all jingoes were nativists or all nativists jingoes, but the aggressive psychology of the one and the defensive reaction of the other provided instinctive rallying points for a society dubious of its capacity to compose its conflicts.
>
> To put the matter another way, when the troubles of the late nineteenth century raised doubts of the nation's stamina, two short cuts for restoring confidence presented themselves: disunity might be rationalized as a product of foreign influence, or denied by a compensatory demonstration of national virility.[25]

So noticeable had the mood become that the leading magazine *Outlook* wrote in 1896 that newspapers "have formed the habit of talking about foreign countries as if to be a true American involved hatred of everything French, English, German, Italian, or Spanish." In 1893, fear of Catholic armed attacks on Americans, fanned by the nativist press, led to a state of siege in several places across the country. "In Toledo, the mayor, the police commissioner, and others bought Winchester rifles to repel an anticipated invasion," and "Illinois farmers feared to leave home lest Romanists burn their barns and houses." Italians were killed, hanged, and, in 1891, lynched in a major mob scene in New Orleans, leading to a "diplomatic crisis" with Italy, whereupon Italians became potential fifth columnists. The "Shylock stereotype" held firm for the Jews. No less a figure than Henry Adams opined that Jews "will completely control the finances of and Government of this country in ten years, or they will all be dead. . . . The hatred with which they are regarded . . . ought to be a warning to them. The people of this country . . . won't be starved and driven to the wall by Jews who are guilty of all the crimes, tricks and wiles that have hitherto been unknown and unthought of by civilized humanity."[26]

War with Spain and a new imperial identity, however, diminished nativist fears at home. The French ambassador in Washington shrewdly noted that Americans were hoping that war would "create a Nation out of the mass of heterogeneous populations." By this time, the Anglo-Saxon race was confident in its supremacy. "It had no need of an adversary" at home, commented Higham. "Nor could this creed permit serious doubts of America's ability to incorporate and dominate inferior races. If destiny called the Anglo-Saxon to regenerate men overseas, how could he fail to educate and discipline immigrant races at home? The newcomers, therefore, tended to figure among the lesser breeds whom the Anglo-Saxon was dedicated to uplift."

So, confidence with its cosmopolitan outlook was back. One popular journalist was sure that "the man of purest American blood is he who has the most cosmopolitan lineage." Not only that, but a concern for immigrants and their welfare led to the notion that they could keep and celebrate the best of their native traditions; these "immigrant gifts," as they were called, were the precursors of what we now call multiculturalism. The Englishman Israel Zangwill, who helped Russian Jews settle in the United States, produced *The Melting-Pot* (1908), a play in four acts enshrining the notion in the public mind and anticipating from the fusion of races a country of supermen. Franz Boas, a Jewish immigrant from Germany and "the leading anthropologist of the day," concluded in 1911 that children of immigrants were remade in America, and so one could talk about an "American type" and an "American face."[27]

Democracy had thwarted notions of racial superiority in the nineteenth century (although democratic change was of no help to blacks, Indians, and others), but a general crisis and new patterns of immigration brought such concerns to the fore, wrapped in the respectability of New England Brahmin Anglo-Saxonism. "The more anxious of the Anglo-Saxon apostles knew that the fault must lie with all the other races swarming to America. Did they not, one and all, lack the Anglo-Saxon's self-control, almost by definition? So, behind the popular image of unruly foreigners, a few caught sight of unruly races; and Anglo-Saxon nativism emerged as a corollary to anti-radical nativism—as a way of explaining why incendiary immigrants threatened the stability of the republic." There was even a fear of the "radical *races*" and socialists following the Haymarket affair of 1886.[28]

As more foreign-born people settled in New England, a sense of panic so seized its patricians that one, Barrett Wendell, "whose English accent matched his Anglophile interpretation of American literature, was settling into the conviction that his own kind had had its day, that other races had wrenched the country from its grasp for once and all." The objects of fear and loathing were southeastern Europeans, Italians, and Jews. Francis A. Walker, the president of the Massachusetts Institute of Technology, a leading economist, and the superintendent of the census in 1870, argued that older patterns of immigration no longer obtained, meaning that easy and cheap transport was bringing to America not the ablest of the natives but the worst, and that, demographically, old American stock was giving way to new, therefore surrendering to "biological defeat" or even "race suicide." Moreover, imperialism in the Philippines was exposing Americans to different shades of color, leading to a sharpened race consciousness, attacks on birth control, and warnings against "the Latin and the Hun." (The Latin here is not to be confused with the Latino of our times.) The development of eugenics in England merged with old nativist worries against the immigrant and the fear of biological reversion that was thought to derive from racial mixing. Christianity and democracy were seen as obstacles to these essential biological facts. In this way, Anglo-Saxonism seamlessly merged into white supremacy. Seminal books were published to uphold such theses, and fear of the "lesser" European races—the Alpine and Mediterranean, not to mention the Jews—became common currency.[29]

Knife-wielding Italians were either criminals or bandits, and Jews were vulgar, "acquisitive barbarians" who had to be kept out of genteel society. Many professions were closed to noncitizens and those who didn't declare their intention to become citizens (nondeclarant aliens). The State of

Michigan, for instance, "prohibited the issuance of a barber's license to any alien." So bad was the situation for Italians applying for clerical jobs that they sometimes claimed to be Turkish, among other nationalities, to avoid discrimination! On the West Coast, writers such as Homer Lea, author of *The Valor of Ignorance* (1909), and the novelist Jack London warned against the "Yellow Peril" and darker European races. Seasoned Southern whites, long exposed to the foreign, gleefully embraced this newfound nationalism and made common cause with the North.[30]

Anti-Catholic hysteria rebounded in the first decades of the twentieth century. In 1911, a weekly publication titled the *Menace* was founded in Aurora, Missouri, by one Wilbur Franklin Phelps, to deal with the Catholic threat; by April 1915, its circulation had reached an astonishing 1,507,923. Jews, too, were targeted. Tom Watson, a fiery anti-Catholic crusader, didn't see any difference in joining an anti-Semitic outburst leading to the butchery of an accused Jew, in Georgia. "From all over the world," he wrote in 1915, "the Children of Israel are flocking to this country, and plans are on foot to move them from Europe en masse . . . to empty upon our shores the very scum and dregs of the *Parasite Race*."[31]

The racial honeymoon that happily fused the liberty-loving, self-governing Teutonic (Germanic) and Anglo-Saxon races came undone during World War I, as suspicion and persecution, both populist and legal, fell on the former potential group of fifth columnists: "Through popular thinking there spread an image of the German-American community riddled with treason and conspiring under orders from Berlin." The "hyphenated-Americans" represented by German immigrants who continued to teach and publish in their ancestral or native language, and even sought U.S. neutrality in the war, came under attack as the doctrines of "preparedness" (for national defense) and "100 per cent Americanism," championed by die-hard patriots, condemned dual loyalties. Unity was demanded, required, and enforced by public vigilantism and congressional acts (such as the Espionage Act of 1917 and the Sedition Act of 1918), the internment and registration of German Americans, and even the banning of the German language in public schools. After a quarter of a century of attempts to restrict immigration to the United States to literate people, the measure became law on February 5, 1917. The Anglo-Saxon supremacist lawyer Madison Grant hastily revised his *The Passing of the Great Race; or, The Racial Basis of European History* in 1918 (the first edition had come out in 1916) and reclassified the

Germans as Alpines (they had been, together with Anglo-Saxons, Nordic); others saw them as descendants of "Asiatic barbarians."[32]

Deportation was now deployed as a "purgative" measure against foreign-born radicals. A. Mitchell Palmer, the newly appointed attorney general in 1919, swiftly launched raids, roundups, and deportations against mostly Russian and east European radicals, more for effect than with the intent of carrying out a careful legal process, but he was stopped by the assistant secretary of labor, Louis F. Post, a liberal who had read Tom Paine as a child and believed in a single-tax system and academic freedom. By 1920, the hysteria had subsided and was even denounced by newspapers. Palmer, undaunted, tried to keep the Red Scare alive in 1920 by announcing that "a gigantic bomb plot and general strike would erupt on May Day."[33] It didn't come to be.

A deliberate process of Americanization, stressing assimilation through education, seemed at this point a better response to the fear of immigrants than persecution. Yet this nationalist approach ran afoul of racial determinism, as serious periodicals such as the *Saturday Evening Post* were now asking why society would "try to make Americans out of those who will always be Americanski." (Note, again, that the language of fear was not Spanish; terms such as *Hispanics* or *Latinos* simply didn't register.) The "tribal Twenties" had arrived.[34]

The nationalist euphoria stirred by the war led inevitably to a letdown. The onset of a depression, the resumption of immigration, a crime wave (associated with immigrants during Prohibition), and seemingly compli-cated entanglements at the League of Nations joined old-style nativism with isolationism. Anglo-Saxon nativism reappeared to reassure the confused. Two more editions of Grant's *The Passing of the Great Race* came out (in 1921 and 1923), stoking the fears of Nordic "mongrelization" with the infe-rior Alpines and Mediterraneans. Books with titles such as *The Rising Tide of Color* (1920), *America: A Family Matter* (1920), and *America's Race Heritage* (1922) echoed Grant's racial philosophy. Sent to Europe to cover the issue of immigration, a writer for the *Saturday Evening Post*, Kenneth Roberts, published a book titled *Why Europe Leaves Home* (1922), concluding that more Alpine and Mediterranean immigration into the United States would produce "a hybrid race of people as worthless and futile as the good-for-nothing mongrels of Central America and Southeastern Europe." (Here, Central America makes a brief appearance as a point of comparison.)

Eugenics and psychology joined the fray by looking for an Old American type and by devising intelligence (IQ) tests to "find out" that Slavs and Latin Europeans were less intelligent than Nordics, whether native or foreign born:[35] "As scientific racism spread downward from patrician circles, it blended with the cruder Anglo-Saxon nativism that was pushing upward from the grassroots of the South and West. The two streams of racial nationalism reinforced one another: the national news magazine *Current Opinion* wrote about keeping America white with as much gusto as the Imperial Wizard of the Ku Klux Klan discussed the lessons of eugenics. No one any longer, except possibly some immigrant spokesman, claimed that America's genius derived from racial mixture." Even Christopher Columbus was recast as a Nordic![36]

The Ku Klux Klan, indeed, made a comeback, establishing roots in semi-rural America and gradually spreading through the Midwest and Texas. By 1923, the peak of its crusading success, it had a membership of "close to three million."[37] Its renewed anti-Catholic zeal reflected the rising movement of Protestant fundamentalism:

> The storm of anti-Catholic feeling, for which the Klan proved a wonderfully sensitive barometer, was closely related to the growth of fundamentalism. This militant repudiation of a liberalized gospel and a secularized culture was making itself felt in the closing years of the Progressive era, but only after the World War did it become a major force in American Protestantism. In truth, fundamentalism owed so much to the emotional aftermath of the war that one may almost define it as the characteristic response of rural Protestantism to the disillusion following America's international crusade. The wartime hope for a new and beatific world had produced nothing but crime, moral chaos, and organized selfishness on a grander scale than before. Surely here was proof that the nation had misplaced its faith, that the only true salvation for a sinful society lay in blotting out the whole spirit of innovation and returning to the theological and moral absolutism of an earlier day. Insistence on a Biblical Christianity naturally sharpened the historic lines of Protestant-Catholic cleavage, but the vigor of anti-Catholicism in the twenties could only result from the affiliations between fundamentalism and 100 per cent Americanism. The fundamentalist determination to fix and purify a Protestant orthodoxy followed the same channels and obeyed the same laws that governed the course of 100 per cent Americanism. Both epitomized

a kind of crusading conformity, reacted to a common disillusion, and represented an urge for isolation from an evil world. Who can wonder that the two movements intermingled in rural areas, or that fundamentalism energized a religious version of postwar nationalism?[38]

Thus, "anti-hyphenism, Americanization, and Palmer raids" gave way to "fundamentalism and prohibition" and eclipsed "the ideal of American nationality as an unfinished, steadily improving, cosmopolitan blend."[39]

In March 1919, Albert Johnson, who had been elected to Congress from Washington State in 1912 on a restrictionist platform, took control of the House Committee on Immigration. With a profound hatred for the Wobblies and the Japanese, and impressed by Grant's *The Passing of the Great Race* and theories of eugenics (he was elected president of the Eugenics Research Association at Cold Spring Harbor, New York, in 1923), he set the tone for an immigration system that has redefined immigration to this day. Immigration, the director of the National Industrial Conference Board conceded in 1923, was "essentially a race question." With the election of President Calvin Coolidge, who had already expressed his sympathies for Nordic theories, the stage was set for a bill that, in a compromise with the Senate, established a "national origins" quota, presumably democratically based on the stock of Americans already in the country: "In short, the national origins system offered a direct implementation of racial nationalism and an answer to all charges of discrimination. It gave expression to the tribal mood, and comfort to the democratic conscience." On April 13, 1924, more than a month before Coolidge signed the Johnson-Reed Immigration Act (which exempted Canada and Latin America from the quota system), the *Los Angeles Times* announced, "Nordic Victory Is Seen in Drastic Restrictions." In her superb study of illegal aliens in American history, the Chinese American scholar Mae M. Ngai notes not only that this new policy remapped the world along racial lines, privileging, of course, the northern European, but also that, by setting "numerical limits" on immigration (a policy that has never been fully discarded, even in the liberal Hart-Celler Immigration Act of 1965), it, in effect, created the "illegal alien" as a new legal entity, a disembodied abstraction, a specter that has haunted the American imagination ever since. The new immigration policy would institutionalize three decades of crusades for racial purity and cultural homogeneity and define the terms of both immigration and citizenship.[40]

No one who has read John Higham's *Strangers in the Land* (first published in 1955), David Bennett's *The Party of Fear* (first published in 1988), or, more recently, Roger Daniels's *Guarding the Golden Door* (2004), Mae Ngai's *Impossible Subjects* (2004), and Aristide Zolberg's *A Nation by Design* (2006) could seriously believe that the latest alarm about Latinos is a novel development in America's destiny.[41] The Irish, Asians (such as Chinese, Japanese, and Filipinos), south Europeans, Slavs, Jews, and even Germans were all treated at one point or another as lower races and the deadliest menace to the republic. The Chinese were excluded from 1882 to 1943, when the wrath of racism fell as well on loyal Japanese Americans for merely having Japanese ancestry following Japan's attack on Pearl Harbor. Huntington's expressed fears simply are—they have to be—part of a consistent strain of vilifying difference that has been essential to national unity since the fifteenth century. (Jesús Silva-Herzog Márquez, a Mexican law professor and columnist, has dubbed Huntington "the Stephen King of political scientists.")[42] This phenomenon is what Mark Fiore called in a comic video a case of "migraphobia."[43] That Mexicans cross the border on foot and don't sail or fly into the country appears to be more a minor detail in the history of American nativism than a new mortal threat. Moreover, one could argue with some justification, as Gregory Rodriguez and Rosa Brooks have argued in the pages of the *Los Angeles Times,* that not only are the hardworking poor who risk life and limb to remake their lives in the United States central to America's narrative about its pioneering days, but also such immigrants (whether legal or illegal) tend to be more law-abiding and productive than their rather lazy, native-born counterparts.[44]

If the American Dream is the product of Anglo-Protestant people, then one might not expect it to last indefinitely, particularly given that the composition of the U.S. population is now radically altered. On July 20, 2004 (the same year Huntington's book *Who Are We?* was published), the news agency Reuters reported that a survey found that "Protestants may soon account for less than half of the U.S. population for the first time since the country's founding," proving to Tom Smith, director of the National Opinion Research Center, that "the United States is on its way to being a nation of minorities." The drop may be explained by the fact that Protestants are now calling themselves Christian—which still is an important shift—or leaving religion altogether. The survey found, in 2002, that the number of Catholics remained steady, at 25 percent of the population, whereas the number of those without religion climbed to 14 percent, more than the combined numbers of all non-Christian religions (5 percent).[45] By early 2005, Spanish-language newspapers and periodicals with titles such as *¡ahora sí! La Frontera, La Voz,* and *La Vibra,* some featuring venerable Latin American writers like Mario Vargas Llosa and Carlos Fuentes, were coming out at an explosive pace in states such as Texas. Even more poignant, on February 2, 2005, Cuban-born Republican senator Mel Martinez, from Florida, facing cameras and fellow senators, "made his debut speech on the floor in both English and Spanish, telling Hispanic Americans that Alberto R. Gonzales, President George W. Bush's nominee to be attorney general, is 'one of us.'" One Senate historian noted that it was the first time in U.S. history that a speech was "made by a senator on the floor in Spanish or any language other than English." The speech was carried live by Univision and CNN en Español. On May 10, 2006, the *Washington Post* reported that a new census report showed that "nearly half of the nation's children under five are racial or ethnic minorities, and the percentage is increasing mainly because the Hispanic population is growing so rapidly." By November 2007, the U.S. Census Bureau reported that two Hispanic surnames (Garcia and Rodriguez) were among the top ten surnames in the United States, and six were among the top twenty-six. Such facts only confirmed what the renowned demographer William H. Frey had predicted, that by 2016, minorities could make up close to 40 percent of the U.S. population and will most likely be well represented in the highest echelons of the social and political order. These demographic shifts will not necessarily diminish the number of whites, however. Although most Americans will be members of minority groups by 2042, as the Census Bureau projected in 2008, the country will still add another 80 million whites, mostly because many Hispanics identify themselves as such. The country, in other words, will be both white and diverse, and today's "federally discussed racial categories" will be almost meaningless by 2026.[46]

It is not surprising at all that as soon as Muslims were contained, politicians turned their attention to Latin immigration. Influenced by Huntington's thesis, the conservative politician-cum-pundit Patrick Buchanan wrote *State of Emergency,* a book that sounds more like a Homeland Security advisory than a serious meditation on America's future in the age of diversity. Buchanan declares that the United States is now facing "an existential crisis" because the country is right now being invaded, even conquered, by third-world people with no desire whatsoever to assimilate. Just as the Moors are reinvading Europe after having been defeated in 1492 (not driven out of Granada, as Buchanan claims), states such as Texas, New Mexico, Arizona, and California (where whites have been a minority since statehood, in 1849) are bound to be practically Mexican by 2050, because those states are projected to comprise anywhere between 50 and 60 million people of Mexican ancestry. The problem with La Reconquista (as Buchanan calls it) is not only the Mexicans' different culture and the fact that they are reclaiming lands lost to Anglo imperialism in the nineteenth century (a fact breezily covered in his manifesto) but also, and equally importantly, that the Mexicans' mestizo or Amerindian race is a major handicap to assimilation. "History teaches," writes Buchanan, "that separate races take even longer to integrate." Not only that, but Mexicans and Hispanics, who are introducing crime, gangs, low academic standards, and diseases to the United States, and whose numbers might reach 102 million, or 24 percent of the population, by 2050, will render "Americans of European descent" a "minority in the nation their ancestors created and built." To espouse a multicultural agenda in the face of such imminent destruction is, in fact, to commit national suicide.[47]

Such views, though contradicted by more rigorous studies, are, in many senses, part of a chronicle long foretold, a saga that has been unfolding since the Anglo and Latin cultures met in the New World in an encounter so injurious to Hispanics that the Anglo attitude easily qualifies as Latinophobia, a term used by the *New York Times* in 2006 to condemn nativist hostility to immigrants.[48] While Europe is wrestling with its intractable Muslim minority problem, the United States is trying to come to terms with its resilient Hispanic minorities, increasingly seen as unassimilable and proudly attached to their countries of origin and mother tongues. Commenting on the positive aspects of bilingualism in American society, Cristina Rodríguez, a professor at New York University School of Law, notes that because the ancient fears of difference are now mostly voiced through the issue of language, "the Spanish language is to the United States today what the Islamic veil is to Western Europe—the potent symbol around which the assimilation debate turns." Underlying the fear of immigration in the United States is the assumption that it represents a threat to the "common national culture that sustains the unity essential to our self-government."[49]

There is absolutely no doubt in my mind that what is happening in both western Europe and the United States is the playing out of deeply embedded notions of race and the superiority of the Euro-American model disguised in the usual formulas of law and order. When I argue that Muslims and Hispanics are sometimes interchangeable (authors including Fallaci, Steyn, and Buchanan, for instance, make that abundantly clear), I mean it literally. There are at least two Hispanics—a Brazilian in London and a Colombian in Florida—who were shot dead in the wake of fears about Muslim terrorists because they behaved suspiciously.[50] No one seems to say it, but it is clear that the two had the right (or is it wrong?) profile, such as dark skin and black hair. In a series of quite revealing cartoons posted on the Web site www.HispanicMuslims.com, the conflation of Arabs and Latinos is taken for granted, so much so that Chicago, Brooklyn, and Puerto Rico were bombed in retaliation for the arrest of the suspected terrorist José Padilla.

The easiest way to show that the Anglo disdain for Hispanic immigrants is not merely a technical matter of law and order is through the United States' treatment of its Latin American neighbors, those who are both geographically and culturally "beneath," in Lars Schoultz's suggestive book title *Beneath the United States*. Covering more than two centuries of relations between the United States and its southern neighbors, Schoultz does recognize that relations are complex, often involving security issues, domestic politics, and economic interests, but one constant is the United States' entrenched conviction that Latin American culture—a medley of Spanish heritage and Indian backwardness—has made Latin Americans (the progeny of culturally and probably racially defective Spaniards) an inferior species of people. In 1779–1780, when twelve-year-old John Quincy, traveling with his father across Spain, described Spaniards as "lazy, dirty, nasty and in short I can compare them to nothing but a parcel of hogs,"[51] he was conveying a perception that would only worsen with the blending of Spanish and Indian traits in the New World mestizos. Though the Spaniards were probably brutish conquistadors, they came imbued, as the Puerto Rican writer Juan Gonzalez shows, with different notions of race, having lived in the hybrid culture of Spain, where the different races had commingled for centuries. So mongrelized was the Spanish population that, according to a historian Gonzalez quotes, "by the fifteenth century there were dark-skinned Christians, light-haired Moors, hybrids of every shape and complexion in Castile."[52] No wonder Francisco de Aguirre, the conquistador of Chile, "boasted that by fathering more than fifty *mestizo* children, his service to God had been 'greater than the sin incurred in doing so'" and that by 1800, only a fraction of the Latin American population—3 million out of 13.5 million—was considered white.[53]

Despite the Hispanics' differences with Anglo-Americans, many Latin American revolutionaries were inspired by the American Revolution and by the new nation's Founding Fathers. But U.S. leaders had no interest in Latin America's revolutionary struggle against, and liberation from, Spain. The editor of the *North America Review* commented that "We can have no well-founded political sympathy with them. We are sprung from different stocks."[54] Moreover, as a slaveholding society, the United States was wary of the Latin American revolutionary spirit. And for good reason, too: Simón Bolívar, the Liberator, as he is known in Latin America, condemned slavery as early as 1826, and by 1850 that odious institution was abolished in all liberated Latin countries.[55]

By the middle of the nineteenth century, modern racist ideologies had taken hold of the mainstream Anglo-American imagination. As the United States began to eye Spanish-occupied lands and seek their annexation or domination, it resorted to the old technique of dehumanizing their inhabitants. In the 1820s, the first U.S. envoy to Latin America, Joel Poinsett, wrote home describing Mexicans as "an ignorant and immoral race," the progeny of the foul miscegenation of Creoles and indigenous natives, a racial mixing that "contributed to render the Mexicans a more ignorant people and debauched people than their ancestors had been."[56] In the 1840s, with the imminent annexation of Texas, a proslavery senator from Mississippi, Robert Walker, considered the new territory a "godsend" that would be the blacks' gateway to Mexico and the tropics, where they would be among their own, so to speak.[57] Sam Houston, one of the founding fathers of the modern state of Texas, had no illusion that Mexicans were equal to Anglo-Saxons. "The vigor of the descendants of the sturdy north," he stated, "will never mix with the phlegm of the indolent Mexicans, no matter how long we may live among them." Stephen Austin, another icon whose name, along with Houston's, adorns a major city in that state, was even more categorical: " To be candid the majority of the whole [Mexican] nation as far as I have seen them want nothing but tails to be more brutes than the apes."[58]

It was for the same reasons that northern Whigs opposed U.S. expansion on Mexican lands and even all-out annexation of the whole of Mexico. A congressman from New York, Washington Hunt, argued that to expand would mean to change the nature of the American population: "We must prepare to receive an incongruous mass of Spaniards, Indians, and mongrel Mexicans—a medley of mixed races, who are fitted neither to enjoy nor to administer our free institutions: men of different blood and language, who cannot dwell and mingle with our people on a footing of social or political equality. They must be governed as a colonial dependency, under provincial laws, or else be incorporated into our federal system, to become an eternal source of strife, anarchy, and civil commotion."[59] "There is a moral pestilence attached to such people which is contagious," echoed the northern Whig senator from Rhode Island, John Clarke, in his argument against the annexation of Mexico, "a leprosy that will destroy." John C. Calhoun, a proslavery Democrat, repeated that "we have never dreamt of incorporating into our Union any but the Caucasian race—the free white race. To incorporate Mexico, would be the very first instance of the kind of incorporating an Indian race; for more than half the Mexicans are Indians, and the other is composed chiefly of mixed tribes. I protest against such a union as that! Ours, sir, is the Government of a white race. The greatest misfortunes of Spanish America are to be traced to the fatal error of placing these colored races on an equal footing with the white race."[60] In case one thinks that there was a distinction in American politicians' minds about the difference between Spaniard and Indian in Mexico, the Tennessee Whig John Bell summarily dispelled it. "They are Spaniards who walk the streets and highway, carrying the stiletto under their sleeve, the dagger under the folds of their cloaks, and bide their time. The race [has] deteriorated," Bell added with prophetic acumen, "but still blood will show itself, at the distance of centuries, when the cup of bitterness overflows, and when the oppressor least expects it."[61]

Science, too, lent its powers to this chorus of prejudice. One noted phrenologist, Dr. Josiah C. Nott, foresaw the withering away of dark-skinned Hispanics in the incontrovertible march of the superior white race.[62] When Col. Henry L. Kinney, founder of the Texas Rangers, tried to claim about 70 percent of Nicaragua's land, in 1854, the New York Times enthusiastically gave its full support: "Central America is destined to occupy an influential position in the family of nations, if her advantages of location, climate and soil are availed of by a race of 'Northmen' who shall supplant the tainted, mongrel and decaying race which now curses it so fearfully."[63]

Violence against such human subspecies was no great offense. The war with Mexico and the atrocities committed against Mexicans were driven by this racist spirit, leading Ulysses S. Grant to admit that it was "one of the most unjust [wars] ever waged by a stronger against a weaker nation."[64] Following the 1848 Treaty of Guadalupe, which forced Mexico to cede huge parts of its land to the United States, Mexicans, as one might have predicted, became "strangers in their own land" and, therefore, easy targets for racist assaults.[65] In 1855, the *Galveston Weekly News* of Texas described a lynching in these terms: "Eleven Mexicans, it is stated, have been found along the Nueces, in a *hung up* condition. Better so than to be left on the ground for the howling lobos to tear in pieces, and then howl the more for the red peppers that burn his insides raw [*sic*]."[66]

Latinos are victims of racial violence even today. In 1990, Leonard Cuen, a twenty-one-year-old white man, after drinking and "popping pills," killed a twelve-year-old Hispanic for fun and was sentenced to a mere two years in jail.[67] The Anti-Defamation League has recently documented shocking amounts of violence against Mexicans and Hispanics, including in video games, by white supremacist groups that sometimes combined their hatred for nonwhites with classic outbursts of anti-Semitism. In fact, the Southern Poverty Law Center (SPLC), an organization that tracks hate groups in the United States, noted a significant surge of anti-immigrant, nativist groups in the period 2005–2007, and the FBI reported increasing crimes against Latinos. Such groups' influence is so significant that by early 2008, according to SPLC, eighteen states' houses of representatives had "passed resolutions opposing the 'North American Union'—an entity [encompassing Canada, the United States, and Mexico] that does not exist and has never been planned, but nonetheless inhabits nativists' nightmares."[68]

The attacks on Latin American immigrants cannot be completely separated from the European genocidal spirit diagnosed by Georges Bensoussan and the history of racism stretching all the way back, for our purposes, to sixteenth-century Spain. By the 1920s, eastern European Jews newly arrived in the United States were described as "abnormally twisted," "unassimilable," and "filthy, un-American and often dangerous in their habits" by Albert Johnson, the Republican congressman from Hoquiam, Washington, whom we encountered earlier.[69] As the main author of the Immigration Act of 1924, one of the most racist pieces of immigration legislation in U.S. history, which established "for the first time *numerical limits* on immigration and a *global* racial and national hierarchy that favored some immigrants over others,"[70] Johnson, echoing what was to become a major tenet of Nazi ideology, explained that "our capacity to maintain our cherished institutions stands diluted by a stream of alien blood, with all its inherited misconceptions respecting the relationships of the governing power to the governed." Johnson concluded with the rather puzzling declaration that "the day of indiscriminate acceptance of all races [as if that had ever happened in the past] has definitely ended."[71] In the same vein, the Texas Democrat John C. Box thought Mexicans were "illiterate, unclean, peonized . . . a mixture of Mediterranean-blooded Spanish peasants with low-grade Indians."[72]

Interestingly enough, the 1910 and 1920 censuses classified Mexicans and their children as "foreign white stock," but this strange-sounding category was hastily revoked and the Mexicans became "non-white" in the 1930 census. For Mexicans, as for Asians, race and ethnicity were now "conjoined," turning U.S. citizens into permanently condemned aliens.[73] Most immigration laws didn't really apply to Mexicans, who were allowed to come into the country to work in agricultural fields as braceros, even to work in aircraft industries, and then were violently uprooted and "repatriated" back to their homeland when their labor or presence was no longer needed.[74] In June 1954, when the country was in recession, the Immigration and Naturalization Service commissioner, Joseph W. Swing, a former army general, launched "Operation Wetback" to stop "the hordes of aliens facing us across the border," lowly workers who threatened to invade the United States.[75] (Wetbacks were aliens who did not come through the officially sanctioned bracero program.) This episode is described by Juan Gonzalez as "one of the darkest periods in immigrant history": "Brutal dragnets were conducted in hundreds of Mexican neighborhoods as migrants were summarily thrown into jails, herded into trucks or trains, then shipped back to Mexico. Many of those abducted were American citizens of Mexican descent. The government, ignoring all due process, deported between 1 and 2 million Mexicans in a few short months."[76] To no avail. As white European immigration to the United States began drying up in the middle of the twentieth century and nonwhite immigration, particularly after the 1965 Immigration Act, increased exponentially (mostly through "chain migration," or the family reunion provisions), the lily-whiteness of the country was being irrevocably altered. (Some anti-Hispanic immigration advocates go so far as to read the 1965 act, which broadened the racial and ethnic pool of admissible immigrants, as Hitler's revenge on the United States!) Obviously, Hispanic immigrants, particularly Mexicans, constituted a major part of these new demographics.[77]

In 1980, *Time* magazine predicted that the 1980s would be the "Decade of the Hispanic," and *Foreign Affairs* (where Huntington's essay on the clash of civilizations first appeared before it grew into a book) drew attention to the fast-growing numbers of Hispanics. Five years later, Richard Lamm, then governor of Colorado, published a book called *The Immigration Time Bomb,* warning against the threat to Anglo culture from Hispanic immigration. The following year, the 1986 Immigration and Reform Control Act, making it a crime to hire illegal aliens, securing the border, and giving preferential treatment to the Irish, was passed.[78] By the 1990s, Pat Buchanan was running for president on an anti-immigrant platform, and in 1995, Peter Brimelow, a British expatriate, published his book *Alien Nation* to warn against the alien threat, unprecedented in scale, to his adopted "white nation." Just as Samuel Huntington has been compared to Henry Cabot Lodge, Brimelow was seen as "the new Madison Grant." Not surprisingly, that same year, a judge in Texas described a Mexican American mother's speaking Spanish to her five-year-old as child abuse.[79] Meanwhile, the passage of California's Proposition 187 in 1994, a "patently unconstitutional" law denying basic services to illegal immigrants, meant that Hispanic-looking citizens would be subjected to scrutiny, since how was one to tell the difference between a legal and an illegal citizen? The popular support for Proposition 187 emboldened President Bill Clinton to sign, in 1996, "a series of draconian new laws meant to sharply reduce legal and illegal immigration and speed up deportation of those the government deemed undesirable." Looking back at the rapid succession of immigration reform bills and laws in the past twenty-five years, culminating in the legislative uproar of recent years, one might add, Gonzalez marks 1980 as the start of the third major nativist backlash in U.S. history.[80]

Such (racial) views of Hispanics also explain U.S. foreign policy toward Latin America, as well as the reason that policy almost invariably results in flows of immigrants north. It is this "mind-set," as historian Schoultz put it, "that led President Monroe to announce his Doctrine, that pushed President Polk to declare war against Mexico, that inspired President Roosevelt to wield a Big Stick, that induced President Wilson to teach the Latin

Americans to elect good leaders, that prompted President Kennedy to establish the Agency for International Development, and that led President Bush to call Nicaragua's President an unwelcome dog at a garden party."[81] On the takeover of Mexican lands in 1848, Theodore Roosevelt explained that "it was inevitable, as well as in the highest degree desirable for the good of humanity at large, that the American people should ultimately crowd out the Mexicans from their sparsely populated Northern provinces."[82] As late as 1964, historian Richard Morse declared that "Latin America is subject to special imperatives as an offshoot to postmedieval, Catholic, Iberian Europe which never underwent the Protestant Reformation." Latino inferior traits included harsh and strange human laws and "the difficulty of collecting income taxes; the prevalent obligation to pay fees or bribes to officials for special or even routine services; the apathy of metropolitan police toward theft and delinquency; the thriving contraband trade at border towns; the leniency toward those who commit crimes of passion—all the way down to the nonobservance of 'no smoking' signs on buses and [in] theaters."[83] In the same year Morse's ideas were published, the academic and development specialist Lawrence Harrison traveled to Costa Rica to help Hispanic nations "get better" and came back years later convinced that Hispanic culture simply didn't lend itself to the benefits of peace and prosperity, a view he shared in books such as *Underdevelopment Is a State of Mind: The Latin American Case* (1985). After an intensive study of two hundred years of interactions between Anglos and Latin America, Lars Schoultz summed up his findings thus: "As we have sifted through nearly two centuries of dispatches from Latin America, the Alliance [for Progress] pattern has appeared with striking regularity: U.S. envoys undertake to help Latin Americans change their ways. Latin Americans resist. Envoys become frustrated. And, when their frustration becomes acute, either they call in the Marines (or create something like the Nicaraguan Contras), or they go home and write a memoir about Latin America's culture."[84] As John Perkins puts it in his *Confessions of an Economic Hit Man,* when economic hit men fail to extort extravagantly lucrative contracts for American corporations from the leaders of Latin American and other poor countries, "a more malicious form of hit man, the jackal, steps to the plate. And if the jackal fails," as happened in Iraq, for instance, "then the job falls to the military."[85]

When Oriana Fallaci thinks of Europeans as "natives," "indigenous," or even "aborigines" overtaken by Muslim fascists, and Michelle Dallacroce, the American head of Mothers against Illegal Aliens, unhesitatingly describes the Hispanic influx into the United States as "genocide" (see the introduction), we get a clear sense of how Islamophobia and Latinophobia are part and parcel of the fear of annihilation that is imperceptibly seizing the white Euro-American imagination. Fallaci's contempt for Islam is matched only by her dislike of Mexicans. She felt "disgust" for the latter's demonstrations against HR 4437 and confessed that she'd have a hard time deciding on who was worse, Muslims or Mexicans. "If you hold a gun and say, 'Choose who is worse between the Muslims and the Mexicans,'" she confessed to a journalist, "I have a moment of hesitation. Then I choose the Muslims, because they have broken my balls."[86] Mark Steyn goes even further by placing the Muslims who orchestrated the 9/11 terrorist attacks in the larger universe of undocumented (Mexican and Hispanic) aliens: "If you're looking for really deep 'root causes' for what happened that day [9/11], you could easily start with America's failure to nation-build in Mexico." Because the United States intervenes only occasionally in Mexico and other Latin American nations and doesn't stabilize them fully, the entire world literally "lives next door now."[87] When Tom Tancredo, the Republican representative from Colorado, was running for president in November 2007, he aired a television commercial in Iowa showing "a hooded terrorist in a shopping mall" to warn against the "20 million aliens who have come here to take our jobs" and against Islamic terrorism.[88]

Fear of immigrants—not just Muslims or Latinos—is now a fact of life in most of Europe, including Russia. On October 22, 2006, the London *Observer*'s main article was the government's planned move to block the immigration of Romanians and Bulgarians into Great Britain, once both nations joined the European Union in January 2007. Stories had been circulating for months about how such immigrants would "overstretch Britain's schools and hospitals, drive down wages on building sites, as well as threatening a violent crime wave and even a new HIV epidemic." On the same day the *Observer* article appeared, the *New York Times* published two reports on the growing climate of nativism in Russia and the persecution and murder of non-Russian minorities, such as the Chechens and Georgians.[89] Armed vigilantes calling themselves the Minutemen, meanwhile, kept an eye on illegal migrants crossing into the United States over the Mexican border, and the American president signed a bill to build a seven-hundred-mile fence, leading to complaints from Mexico's outgoing president, Vicente Fox, and the president-elect, Felipe Calderón, as well as from the Organization of American States.[90]

Expulsion continued to be contemplated for Muslims, in both Europe and the United States. By stating that "the central question now facing Europeans and Muslims is not whether Islam can be expelled from European soil, as during the Spanish *Reconquista* six centuries ago, or whether the Muslims can be totally assimilated in European culture," the introduction to a book titled *Islam, Europe's Second Religion* implied that expulsion is still part of the vocabulary of nationalism and an option for the intractable Muslim question in the West.[91] Although authors such as Fallaci, Steyn, and Buchanan would have us believe that the fear of Islam is the outcome of shifting demographic patterns and stubborn refusal of assimilation, the same fears were expressed earlier in the twentieth century not to defend Europe's fragile culture of secular liberalism but to denounce the culture of the Enlightenment that had dimmed the passion of Christian faith. In 1938, for instance, when Islam had virtually no presence in Europe, the Anglo-French author Hilaire Belloc wrote that

> millions of modern people of the white civilization—that is, the civilization of Europe and America—have forgotten all about Islam. They have never come in contact with it. They take for granted that it is decaying, and that, anyway, it is just a foreign religion which will not concern them. It is, as a fact, the most formidable and persistent enemy which our civilization has had, and may at any moment become as large a menace in the future as it has been in the past. . . . Anyone with a knowledge of history is bound to ask himself whether we shall not see in the future a revival of Mohammedan political power, and the renewal of the old pressure of Islam upon Christendom.[92]

Even more intriguing is Europe's rediscovery of its Christian roots in the wake of fears about Islam today. No less a philosopher than the leftist German Jürgen Habermas has proclaimed that "Christianity, and nothing else, is the ultimate foundation of liberty, conscience, human rights, and democracy, the benchmarks of Western civilization. To this day, we have no other options [than Christianity]. We continue to nourish ourselves from this source. Everything else is postmodern chatter."[93]

In the United States, too, there has been talk of expelling Muslims. A *New York Times* report on a Christian blog provides a revealing glimpse into the fusion of deeply entrenched anti-Muslim biases and anti-immigrant resentment. On August 10, 2006, during the Israeli-Hezbollah war, bloggers wondered whether getting rid of Muslims from the United States might be the optimal solution to their nagging problem. At 11:50 a.m., one blogger, named "Resting in Him," opened the discussion by writing, "I know this is extreme, but am I wrong in thinking that we should close our borders to Muslims and [evacuate] a few who are already here? In fact, I'm wondering if all Muslim mosques, which are a haven for perpetrating hate against us, shouldn't be closed down." That afternoon, another blogger, called "Werner," acknowledged that the war was indeed against Islam, but asked, "Have you thought through the logic of this? How many Muslims are American citizens? . . . Should we force them to wear a little red crescent badge? If you can outlaw and deport Muslims then you can do the same to any religion or faith. The way to defeat Islam is to share with them the Gospel." After some debate as to whether such removals would be constitutional, one "Ole Shosty" wrote, at 8:59 p.m., "No one is suggesting they be subjected to the horrors of concentration camp, or beaten and arrested on site. But what would be wrong with at least an immediate cessation of all incoming Muslims/Arabs, and perhaps a watch list or even eventual deportation of those in the country?" About an hour later, "Livin'4Him" revealed the twin motive in the anti-immigration movement: "My daughter works at a 7-Eleven store and her boss is Muslim and he's not exactly the nicest person to work for. We just haven't had any good experiences with them." Thus, in the course of one day's blogging, the reasons for anti-Muslim bias shifted from politics and religion to typical resentment of the immigrant's economic success.

On the same day that the *Times* published this blog conversation (and the story of a one-eyed Minuteman), the *Washington Post* reported that the fate of India's Muslims—around 13 percent of the country's 1.1 billion citizens—already discriminated against in the professions and increasingly under suspicion since 9/11, is becoming more precarious. A pharmacist from the prosperous Nayanagar district in Mumbai (formerly Bombay) put it this way: "I am a Hindu and I sit and eat together with the Muslims in the next shop. They are not terrorists, they are my friends. But I'll be honest, there is a growing feeling that there is a fight in the world between the

West and Muslims. And even here, some people say it's good if Muslims are being killed; the fewer left the better."[94]

Although it is true that the history of Islam in the West and the cultural differences between Latinos and Anglos must be taken into account in any analysis of the contemporary impasse over identity issues in Europe and the United States, it is even more significant that the status of minorities in the modern world is a feature of the post-Reconquista period; it has been universalized over time and has become a fundamental feature of the modern and postmodern world orders. The current language of Islamophobia is informed both by old prejudices and rivalries and by the post-9/11 environment. For example, anti-Muslim sentiments were disproportionately high in countries such as Denmark *before* the 2005–2006 cartoon scandal erupted into global view. In the Netherlands, too, the scene of high-profile scandals such as the murder of the filmmaker Theo van Gogh in 2004, an official report published on April 11, 2006, reproached politicians for fanning an unjustified "aversion" to Islam by associating isolated acts with the whole Muslim community. "When a Dutch vegan murdered the gay right-wing politician Pim Fortuyn, the distinction between a criminal and his dietary tastes remained sharp," wrote Corey Robin in the *Nation,* "but when Mohammed Bouyeri, a Muslim with dual citizenship in the Netherlands and Morocco, murdered Dutch filmmaker Theo van Gogh, a leap was instantly made from a lone assassin to an entire religion and region." This climate has allowed the Far Right in France to take aim at Islam in all sorts of ways, some even charging the Algerian liberation movement, which is fighting against French colonialism, with "genocide" against the French people.

What, for instance, could explain the "veil mania" that has seized European politicians, when the number of girls and women wearing head scarves, much less the infamous *niqabs* or *burqas,* is so negligible as to be socially unnoticeable? What justifies the acrimonious politicking over the issue of the veil in French public schools during much of the 1990s and beyond, when empirical data show that the number of girls wearing *hijabs* in school, together with the conflict this mode of dress engenders, has actually declined? As the Sorbonne professor Esther Benbassa comments on the panic over the veil in France, how is one to seriously believe that "approximately 1,500 veiled girls could threaten the Republic"? Islam does pose serious cultural challenges in Europe, but the threat of Islamism is exaggerated. A recent comprehensive study of Muslim communities in Europe showed that no more than 400,000 Muslims held or were passively sympathetic to fundamentalist views, and most Muslims fitted into the general and historic patterns of integration. Polls have shown that the vast majority of Muslims in France and the Netherlands prefer a republican secular system. Pascal Mailhos, director of the French intelligence services, has estimated that there are only 200,000 practicing Muslims in France, with no more than 5,000 suspected of belonging to "fundamentalist Salafist groups." Even France's widely covered riots in November 2005, the nation's "worst public order crisis since the popular revolts of 1968," were not the first skirmish in Islam's long war on Europe, as fearmongers of Eurabia insinuated. Mailhos told *Le Monde* that the riots had nothing whatsoever to do with "radical Islam." As the distinguished professor Philip Jenkins notes, they were more about racism and exclusion. Two years later, in November 2007, new riots erupted in another suburban region of Paris for similar reasons. Had there been no 9/11, one might not have associated such riots with Islam, for fear of Islam had been a fringe concern until then. When Jean Raspail published *The Camp of the Saints,* an account of Europe's takeover by immigrant hordes, in 1973, Islam was not a major concern at all.[95]

Jenkins's study of religion in Europe shows that, for all the alarm about a dying Europe and a fast-rising Muslim population, in no European country, nor in Europe as a whole, do Muslims exceed 5 percent of the population. Moreover, as many former Communist states (with practically no Muslim presence) are incorporated into the European Union (EU), the additional 60 million people or so further erodes the percentage of Muslims in the continent as a whole. Even now, Muslim population percentages in Europe are significantly lower than those of minority groups such as African Americans and Hispanics in the United States. If Albania or the states comprising the former Yugoslavia are admitted into the EU, the rates may be affected further. In any case, Muslims are expected to account for 8 percent of Europe's population (excluding the former Soviet states) by 2025 and about 25 percent by 2050. Even if Turkey and Morocco (other longtime applicants) were eventually to be incorporated into the EU, the minority percentages would still be tolerable and would pose no threat to Europe's cultural identity. Not only would most of the immigrants' children be totally assimilated but there would be fewer of them: the fertility rates in North African countries, the main source of Muslim migrants to

Europe, are falling so sharply that some are matching France's own low fertility rates. The British Office for National Statistics reported in 2005 that
the country's nonwhite population had declined by 0.1 percent, ceding
ground to Chinese immigrants.[96] Finally, even if Europe's Muslim minority were to grow and become more assertive, it would only help revitalize
and expand European Christianity, as Jürgen Habermas's statement most
dramatically indicates.

Because many of the facts do not lend themselves to the doomsday
scenarios depicted by detractors of Islam, Vincent Geisser, author of *La
Nouvelle islamophobie* (2003), suggests that it is not "lived Islam" that is the
target of new Islamophobic policies, measures, and intellectual discourse
(of the Left and the Right, and of Muslims, too) but an imaginary Islam,
one that exists only as a vague, shapeless fear, much as the Jew did in previous decades and centuries: a sinister and invisible schemer bent on de-
stroying the pure nations and high civilization of Europe. For the term
Islamophobia, as Benbassa astutely remarks, conflates all Arabs in France
under a religious designation, even if many of them have nothing to do
with religion at all. Pretending to be a fear of Islam, Islamophobia is in fact
a racist ideology that excludes the North African Arab simply for being
North African. In other words, Muslim immigrants today are the embodiment of the Moors of old, as Fallaci clearly asserted in her diatribes against
Muslim immigrants.[97] They are the Moriscos (and Jews) who, despite conversion, cannot overcome their biological origins. The historian Joan Wallach
Scott is right to deduce that the panic over the scarf and "the negative por-
trayal of Islam in France" are part of an attempt to reestablish the mythical and universal pillars of French identity, which have foundered in an age
of global turbulence, massive demographic shifts, and widespread cultural
mixings.[98]

Similarly, the history of American immigration is one long tale of sorrow in which non-English and, later, non–northern European whites were
deemed inferior species of the human race and excluded by one nativist
policy after another. For the Latinos of today were the Asians of yesterday,
who themselves had been the Africans and, before them, the natives of the
land—all considered at one time or another unsuitable to be part of the
American community of (white) virtue. The very Hispanics who sang
the U.S. national anthem in Spanish during their proimmigration rallies
on May 1, 2006, across the country also broadcast Neil Diamond's song

"America," evoking the epic journey of an earlier wave of undesirables. "That song," explained the singer, "tells the immigrant story. It was written for my grandparents and the immigrants who came over in the late 1800s, the Irish, Jews and Italians. But it's the song for the modern-day Latino coming as well." The same song had been adopted by Michael Dukakis in his 1988 campaign for the presidency, and if it ever comes to be replaced by Ricardo Arjona's "Mojado" (Wetback), the idea would still remain the same.[99]

Times, certainly, are a-changing. In *The War of the World,* Niall Ferguson outlines what looks like an inevitable future of a declining Western empire, rising Asian powers, and global demographic shifts that will make the Muslim presence in Europe an incontrovertible fact. Such "ethnic confluence, economic volatility and empires on the wane" are the "fatal formula" that often leads to atrocities against alien groups. "No historian of the twentieth century," Ferguson warns, "can overlook this huge—and ongoing—secular shift."[100] Similar scenarios, with different outcomes, are envisaged by James Kurth, the Claude Smith Professor of Political Science at Swarthmore College, who foresees Europe and the United States breaking down into at least two civilizations, one of besieged, isolated Europeans and Anglos, the other of violent Muslims and Latinos. The impacts of Islamic immigration in Europe and of Hispanic immigration in the United States are not quite analogous, but the differences are ultimately not that significant:

> It is probably too much to predict that in the Anglo nation there will be a widespread fear of some kind of Latino terrorism, although young Latinos in the United States may learn from their Islamic counterparts in Europe. It is quite plausible, however, that there will be Latino urban riots and mob violence. And it is very likely that there will be a widespread fear of Latino crime. Gated communities, which are already widespread in the southwestern United States, could become an even more central part of the Anglo way of life, the distinctive architectural style and urban design of the Anglo nation.

The Western nations that have reached these new explosive demographic realities, Kurth adds, are in fact no longer nations.[101]

Although I think that predicting such apocalyptic outcomes tends to oversimplify the complex processes of history and group assimilation, the influx of Muslims and Latinos into bastions of European and Anglo supremacy vindicates John Bell's nineteenth-century warning that "blood will show itself, at the distance of centuries, when the cup of bitterness overflows, and when the oppressor least expects it." When Muslims are excluded from the benefits of full citizenship, many resort to their religious orthodoxies, often based on imagined and heavily edited histories, thereby further exacerbating the tensions between the two camps. I am not sure yet about the Hispanic response to their treatment. Christianity cannot be the answer, for that religion (particularly as the old antagonisms between Protestantism and Catholicism have faded) is the common legacy of many people on both sides of the border, the aliens and antialiens, mestizo Mexicans and white Buchanans. Moreover, to claim a Latin heritage (as distinct from an Anglo one) is to resort to yet another imagined cultural category, one that excludes America's indigenous people and Africans, who can't claim any racial or cultural affiliation with the motherland Spain or with France, which invented the designation of Latin America "in the course of a dual diplomatic offensive against the United States and Spain."[102]

Perhaps it is sufficient to say that, by their mere presence in Europe and the United States, Muslims and Hispanics are asserting their rights in a globally distorted economy, one that continues to favor the conquistador nations and marginalizes the conquered. As we shall see in the conclusion of this book, the idea of undesirable aliens in a global economy makes very little sense. Sergio Arau's 2004 film *A Day without a Mexican,* about the panic that seizes California when its entire Latin population vanishes for a day, is a comic reminder that xenophobic bravado is bad for the economy and the strength of the society anti-immigrants want to defend. With the economy in a shambles and upper-middle-class gringos left to fend for themselves, the absence of Mexicans in California leads even the most hardened nativists to reconsider their stance. By the time the Mexicans reappear, the border patrol agents are so grateful that they hail the first illegal immigrants they catch as heroes.[103] It is doubtful that major state economies would do as well if they didn't rely on the contribution of undocumented workers. In 2004, such workers added almost $18 billion to the economy of Texas and "sent $420 million more to Austin in taxes than they received in state services." "Simply put," Roger Daniels notes in his history of American immigration, "the nativist approach to immigration, which sees it as a threat, is not only illiberal but, if adopted, could be disastrous to the entire economy."[104]

Two years after *A Day without a Mexican* was released, Tahar Ben Jelloun, the celebrated Moroccan writer and commentator on immigrant affairs in France and Europe, wrote "Le Dernier immigré" (The Last Immigrant), a short story about the expulsion of the last Arab immigrant from France and its consequences. At first, the French breathe a sigh of relief at not having to endure the odor of spicy cuisine or strange North African customs. However, this euphoric moment is soon followed by an irreparable sense of loss, beginning with the right-wing, anti-immigration movements, which have lost the very foundations of their political platform. Whole occupations are left unfilled, too, but the coup de grâce is the erasure of Arab words from the French language, including dictionaries, leaving gaping holes in France's cultural traditions. Soon, the French realize that, just as Arab ideas and words had entered their culture without border controls or visas, the expelled immigrants should also be allowed to return, to restore what in essence are France's hybrid traditions. The head of state appears on national television and gives a bilingual speech that begins and ends with the greeting "Asslâm alikoum" (Peace be upon you) and bombastic salutes to both France and the Maghreb—in Arabic.[105]

Perhaps no recent artistic production brings together the fear of Islam and Mexican immigrants better than the Academy Award–winning film *Babel* (2006), directed by Alejandro González Iñárritu.[106] Richard and Susan Jones, a white couple from San Diego, leave their two children with a Mexican nanny to travel in Morocco, hoping to patch up their troubled relationship following the sudden death of their third child. While the couple is on a tourist bus driving through the isolated villages of the Atlas Mountains, a Moroccan shepherd aims his father's new rifle at the bus, mostly to try out its shooting range. When a bullet hits Susan Jones, the shooting is quickly elevated to a terrorist incident, leading to the besiegement of the boy's family and the death of his brother. Because this dramatic event keeps the Joneses away from home, the Mexican nanny takes the two children in her care to Tijuana to attend her son's wedding. On the way back, a series of incidents leave her stranded in the desert. She eventually seeks help from the U.S. Border Patrol, upon which she is found to be illegally in the country and ordered deported back to Mexico, even though she has resided in the United States for sixteen years. Thus, an incident involving an American in a Muslim country leads to the deportation of a Mexican woman in California. I am not sure to what extent this meaning was intended, but the film clearly connects the fear of Islam and of Hispanics, as we see heavily armed law enforcement officers chasing shepherds in Morocco and immigrants in California.

Fiction—in film and in print—is thus giving us the chance to imagine what might happen if we succumbed to the passions that were supposed to unite Spain in the fifteenth and sixteenth centuries and to preserve the cultural purity of the nations that were inspired by King Ferdinand's Machiavellian model. There was no cultural purity or political unity then, let alone in the twenty-first century, when the tentacles of globalization are constantly forcing people and cultures into and out of the same geographical spaces. To believe that the fences that are now being built across the globe to keep illegal immigrants or threatening neighbors at bay is a solution to our fears and failed neighborly policies is to delay thinking about new solutions to our demographic realities. Fences, whether on the edges of or within nations, "stand as sentinels to unsolved problems, such as economic disparity, inadequate law enforcement, and ethnic and religious hatred," comments the *Christian Science Monitor*.[107] When the world is supposed to be reveling in its globalization, such "walls of shame," as Juan Goytisolo, the eminent Spanish writer, called them in relation to the Berlin Wall, remind us that we are still beholden to archaic notions of identity and security that do nothing but exacerbate our collective suffering.[108] To be sure, well-educated professionals roam the globe in the comfort of jet seats and world-class hotels, but the poor are condemned to confinement and even death. For those who are determined to cross borders will not be stopped by walls, barbed wire, or mighty oceans. The European trawlers that empty Senegalese waters of their fish stocks leave few income options to the Senegalese fishermen and other young people who embark on perilous journeys across the ocean with the hope of reaching Spain's coasts. This may explain why a popular saying in Senegal (in French and Wolof) is quite explicit about those who sail to Spain illegally: "Barcelone ou barxax," meaning "Barcelona or death." As one Sudanese from Darfur explained to a reporter in 2007, dying while trying to reach Europe by sea from Libya was no worse than staying home: "We were already dead when we were in Sudan and Libya. If we died on the boat, it's all the same."[109] Similarly, no fence would deter Mexicans trying to cross the border, as a Mexican *corrido* has it:

Now they are putting up barriers in front of us so we don't return
but that is not going to block us from crossing into the United States
We leap them like deer, we go under them like moles.[110]

Like his fellow desperate immigrants from other continents and nations, one Mexican said, "Prefiero morir que seguir con la miseria que tengo allí" (I'd rather die than continue living miserably back home).[111]

Even if all immigrants were deported and the border were sealed, would social and economic life be one iota better than it is now for native (white) Americans? asks Roberto Rodriguez.[112] The only outcome of such an expulsion would be finding yet another group to blame for the nation's social ills and fragmentation. Given the escalating tragedies produced by fences and unequal opportunities, it would be far better and more consistent with our liberal aspirations to imagine a world in which all humans moved and worked freely on a planet that was deeded to no one.

We Are All Moors

More like the stranger described by Georg Simmel, the Muslim is not a person that "today comes and tomorrow goes, but he who today comes and tomorrow stays."

—STEFANO ALLIEVI, "Islam in Italy"

If we have any hope of moving beyond the bloody past of the last half millennium of nation-building, then we must acknowledge the path from which we have come and from which we hope to learn and divert.

—ANTHONY W. MARX, *Faith in Nation*

Catholic Spain, with its political philosophy and treatment of minorities, gave shape to the modern world, but the unified nation could never exorcise the ghost of its own *mestizaje,* the genetic mixing that no myth of blood purity could eradicate. It was this anxiety about the perceived lack of purity, religious and political unity, and even orthodox Christianization that gave the Inquisition its frightening powers. Despite the "burning pile of the bigot," in Musa Ben Abil's words, Spain was never able to shake its Moorish heritage. Alexandre Dumas, the nineteenth-century French author of, among many other works, *The Count of Monte Cristo* and *The Three Musketeers,* famously said that "Africa begins at the Pyrenees." As late as 1908, Havelock Ellis, the British doctor and social reformer, could write, "Spain is a great, detached fragment of Africa, and the Spaniard is the first-born child of the ancient white North African," and "the land of Spain and the physical traits of Spaniards lead us back to Africa. If we take a more penetrating survey we shall find that there is much in the character of the Spaniard which we may also fairly count as African."[1] "Everyone knows," wrote the Brazilian historian Gilberto Freyre in the mid-twentieth century, that "Spain and Portugal, though conventionally European states, are not orthodox in all their European and Christian qualities, experiences, and conditions of life, but are in many important respects a mixture of Europe and Africa, of Christianity and Mohammedanism."[2] Even Oriana Fallaci explained Spain's tolerance of its Muslim immigrants by referring to this indelible connection. "Too many Spaniards," she complained before her death, in 2006, "still have the Koran in the blood."[3]

Spain's ambivalence toward the Moors and the way Spaniards use the Moors as a hidden text to describe any oppressive power or regime is best illustrated in the mock battles between Moors and Christians, called *moros y cristianos,* that now dot the calendar of fiestas in Spain. From the very start, even before 1492, fighting Moors was a complex affair. In Zaragoza, a mock battle had King Jaume of Aragon-Catalonia place "a kiss of peace on the face of the [defeated] Moorish captain," thereby signaling the start of a festive dance joining Christians and converted Moors, an intriguing detail that led Max Harris, in his invaluable study of the genre, to suspect that "from the beginning, the Spanish *moros y cristianos* were more about a yearning for peace and *convivencia* than they were about war." Sometimes, as in the festival at Sant Feliu de Pallerols, *caballetes* (sawhorses) are used to divide Christians and Saracens, who are almost indistinguishable and who don't seem to care about who wins. In 1996, when Harris asked the performers who won, they replied, "No one, we just keep fighting."[4]

In Mexico, ambivalence toward the Moor was displayed with great pomp in the 1539 pageant *The Conquest of Jerusalem,* "arguably the most spectacular and intellectually theatrical event in post-contact sixteenth-century Mexico," which at the time was an Indian region governed by Indians loyal to the Spanish monarch. The armies of Spain (led by an Indian), European soldiers in the service of the Holy Roman Emperor, and the armies of New Spain (whose weakest elements were the Caribs) were arrayed against the Moors, led, most intriguingly, by "the Great Sultan" Hernando Cortés and his commander, Pedro de Alvarado. After a protracted battle during which each side tried but failed to break through the Moorish fortress, the archangel Michael appeared to give the Moors a final chance to repent and convert, sparing them a worse fate, because the Moors had "showed reverence for the Holy Places," a view commonly shared by the Franciscans who preached in Tlaxcala and reported on the events of the play. Sultan

Cortés and his people were thus welcomed into the pope's fold "with great affection."[5]

As such plays adapted to local cultures, the outcome became less clear, almost deliberately suspended. Sometimes, as in the "carnival week of Hue-jotzingo" in Puebla, Christians were given no role whatsoever, even though a wide cast of characters, including "Chichmeca, Apaches, Turks, bandits, mountain Indians, and soldiers of North Africa," took part. When Harris wondered about this curious omission, one performer explained that they were all Aztecs and that "the Spaniards have been defeated." This sort of subversion may have been noted by Alonso Ponce, whose travels across Mexico, Guatemala, El Salvador, and Nicaragua between 1584 and 1589 were recorded by his secretary, Antonio de Ciudad Real, in *Tratado curioso y docto de las grandezas de la Nueva España*. Not a single *moros y cristianos,* according to Real's account, ended with a clear Christian victory: "Spaniards were absent, nightfall interrupted the play, the Moors had to finish their wine, or, in Tlaxcala, just four days before the Puebla *moros y cristianos,* whether by accident or design, the stage castle went up in flames and the performance had to be canceled."[6]

Back in Spain, in 1561, the appointment of eighteen-year-old Luis Hurtado de Mendoza as mayor of the Alhambra, the Moorish palace in Granada, was celebrated by a *moros y cristianos* in which the mayor, the traditional protector of the Moriscos against the schemes of Granada's twenty-six-member chancery that had jurisdiction over the province, played the role of a Moorish leader (thereby identifying with his Morisco subjects) and won. This would be the first—and only—instance in which Moriscos took part in such mock battles. This spirit soon faded and yielded to the persecutions, fed by fears of the depredations of Turks in the eastern Mediterranean. On Christmas Eve of 1568, a few Alpujarran Moriscos (residents of the high mountains), dressed as Turks, attacked the city of Granada. Soon the Morisco Revolt, "the most brutal war to be fought on European soil" during the sixteenth century, according to Henry Kamen, led to systematic ethnic cleansing and the eradication of all traces of Moorish civilization from the kingdom. The fear of the Turk became a staple of the festivals, and even today, "of the twenty festivals of Moros and Christians still staged in Granada, 'fifteen allude to a landing of the Turks on the southern coast [although no real Turkish vessel had come to the Moriscos' rescue].'" Yet even this tragic episode did not eliminate the kiss of peace, the implicit fraternal affection, or the yearning for *convivencia,* Harris suspects. "I am persuaded," Harris writes, "that Spain's festivals of Moors and Christians, by rewriting the country's most prolonged ethnic conflict so that it ends not in exile but in reconciliation, express that yearning." Tellingly, in Válor today, the play ends with the Moorish king telling his counterpart, "Yesterday you were my enemy, / Today you will be my affectionate brother."[7]

Even more telling is the "Capture of Motecuzoma," a dramatization of the conquest of Mexico and the capture of Motecuzoma, in which appears "Mawlay Muhammed, governor of Tetouan and Chechaouen, subject of the Sharif, king of Fez and of Morocco, to the lord high governor of Alcalá de los Gazules [near Tarifa]," who comes to participate in the play as a token of appreciation for his good treatment while a prisoner. In these two towns facing Morocco (both free of Moorish rule since the thirteenth century and therefore lacking a Morisco population), the mock battle "Capture of Motecuzoma" is the only "instance of a large-scale Spanish *moros y cristianos* being given over entirely to a Mexican theme,"[8] as well as the only one unequivocally linking the Mexican and Moroccan leaders' fates. Political reasons have been proposed for the strong and explicit Mexican motif, but one might also surmise that because Tarifa and its extension, Alcalá, almost touch Morocco, the notion of contact (and conflict) with a sovereign Moorish nation (whose mountains are visible from the coast) is more palpable here than in any other part of Spain. Contact with Moors/Moriscos in the rest of Spain may have generated a different effect (and imagination) based on the nature of existing power relations, but Spain's southernmost point, which almost abuts Morocco, is a different matter. One cannot live on either coast of the narrow stretch of the Mediterranean known as the Straits of Gibraltar, as I did when growing up in Tangier, without constantly being reminded of the other side.

As the attraction of *moros y cristianos* started to decline for Spanish royalty, the pageants turned into popular festivals reenacting the country's complex history for the masses. In places such as Valencia, or Alcoy and Villena in Alicante, they have never been more popular. And the themes of *convivencia,* the kiss of peace, the syncretism of Spanish culture, and the idea that the enemy is myself are still there to behold. The Moors in Villena (always better dressed than the Christians) now appear in several companies *(comparsas)* during the production, including Old Moors, New Moors, and Moroccan Moors, greatly outnumbering Christians. The patron saint of Villena, Our Lady of the Virtues, known as *la morenica* because of her dark skin, appears to popular acclaims of "Long live the Virgin! Long live *la morenica*!" (One thinks here of dark, Mexican Guadalupe, the patron saint of the Americas.) At the start of the fiesta, Christians lose control of the castle overlooking the town, and Mohammed (intriguingly feminized here as *la mahoma*) takes control. Now the devotees of *la morenica* and *la mahoma* face each other in battle. The Moors predictably lose and convert, and *la morenica* blesses all before she is escorted out of the town she has once again saved from destruction (or from secular fiestas, one of Harris's friends told him at the scene, because a Christian defeat would mean a whole year of fiestas). What happens, in the end, is conversion and assimilation, an acknowledgment of Spain's mestizo culture, if not the ineradicable presence of the Moor. Villena's patron saint might as well be called *la mora*, or the Moor, which would make the fight between two Moorish armies, not between a Christian and a Moor. Moreover, people who attend this festival know that the Moors are not merely a symbol but part of their own identity. "They are something in us. Look at our faces. Many are Moorish," one of Harris's friends at the event said. "The Moors are not bad," one *festero* (partaker in the fiesta) added. "We are all Moors," confessed another.[9]

Although Muslims continue to protest the negative depictions of their faith and prophets throughout Europe, and managed to persuade Spanish authorities at Santiago de Compostela to remove the image of slaughtered Moors at the feet of one of Spain's most revered saints, Santiago Matamoros (St. James the Moorslayer) in 2004, the Villena festival has been perfectly acceptable to the local Muslim community, because *mahoma* is accorded the same reverence given the Virgin.[10] Thus, the *moros y cristianos* has been transformed from an expression of Catholic triumphalism into a strategy of dialogue and coexistence. Eva Borreguero comments:

> "Moors and Christians" captures the racial and cultural crossroads of contemporary Spain; it is a point of convergence where past and present, apprehensions and opportunities meet. Although the festival recreates an historical confrontation of the Cross and the Crescent and could be seen as an updated version of the clash of civilizations, the celebration has an essentially playful nature. From the psychological perspective, it helps cope with cultural anxiety through games and re-enactments. At the same time, it also endorses closeness to "the other" through the scenic representation of those fears. It

is a catharsis for tensions and violent instincts, if any exist: a game in which, although there are champions and defeated, there are no winners or losers, no good guys or bad guys; above all, people identify with one another, as they all participate on both sides. What was yesterday's conflict, has now been transformed into the celebration of an encounter, or, as a participant pointed out, "a war for friendship."[11]

Spain's ambivalence is sometimes echoed in other Mediterranean countries as well, including Italy, despite Oriana Fallaci's claim to the contrary. Just as Spain recalls its history with the Moor in ominous expressions such as *moros en la costa* (Moors on the coast), Italy's encounter with Islam is remembered in the popular expression of fear "Mamma, li turchi!"; games like *giostre del Sarracino,* in which the Saracen (Muslim) is the target of attack; and structures such as the Saracen towers *(torri saracene)* that dot the Italian coast, built to watch out for pirates and, presumably, sneaky Turks. But, like Spain, Italy has had an ambivalent attitude toward Islam, as when Mussolini, who liked to think of himself as the "protector" of Islam and even "liked to be represented with the 'sword of Islam' in his hand," described Italy to the National Assembly in 1928 as a "great Muslim power."[12]

Hardwired prejudices, at least in Spain, are gradually being attenuated by official policies reversing centuries of conflict, animosity, and discrimination. On July 23, 1989, Spain's Ministry of Justice recognized Islam as a national religion. "The Islamic religion," wrote A. Fernández González and D. Llamazares Fernández on behalf of the Advisory Board for Religious Freedom of the ministry,

> has been present in Spain since the 8th century, with significant diffusion in the earlier centuries, and a greater or lesser presence thereafter depending on the period and historical circumstances, and has remained so uninterruptedly to present times. The Islamic communities cover a great part of the Spanish territory. Their presence is especially significant in the lower third of the Iberian Peninsula and in the Spanish territories in North Africa. There is, in our opinion, a clear awareness among Spanish citizens that the Islamic religion is one of the spiritual beliefs that historically has had a presence in Spain, a presence which continues until present times.[13]

This ruling finally became law on November 10, 1992, five hundred years after the surrender of Granada, the last Islamic stronghold in Spain. In 2003, the Spanish city of Seville hosted the first world congress of an estimated 10 million Spanish-speaking Muslims. In October 2006, when alarm bells were ringing throughout Europe about the dangers of Muslim immigration, the Parliament of Andalusia, the southernmost state in Spain, started the process of establishing a law that could grant 5 million Moroccans of Morisco origin, as well as the descendants of Moriscos scattered throughout the Mediterranean, preferential access to Spanish citizenship.[14]

Perhaps in the fullness of time, such consciousness may spill over into the rest of Europe, which was first imagined as an anti-Muslim (and anti-Jewish) sphere. That French right-wing organizations would deliberately load their soups with pork products and call themselves "pig eaters" when feeding the homeless (as happened in 2006) shows that, despite their successful integration into European culture, Jews are still inadvertently connected to Muslims in the European "genocidal passion." After reading about this form of culinary xenophobia, a woman from Chicago wrote that "French·Muslims and Jews now have reason to unite and proclaim liberty, equality and fraternity, by opening a joint halal/kosher soup kitchen!"[15] Comical as the soup incident may be to some, this act of exclusion is part of a larger and more systematic attempt by Europe to reclaim its heritage, including the Christian one. Who is to say that the current pope's insistent calls for the re-Christianization of the continent in order to contain the Islamic menace and give Europe its historic identity could not bring back a new era of ethnic cleansing? When the European Union undertook to address the twin scourges of anti-Semitism and Islamophobia through the European Monitoring Centre, in 2002–2003, Robert Purkiss, the center's management board chairman, was quite clear about the effects of the Christian heritage:

Our conceptions of European identity are significant drivers of anti-Semitism and Islamophobia. One of the similarities between anti-Semitism and Islamophobia is their historical relationship to a Europe perceived as exclusively Christian. Jews have of course suffered the most unspeakable crimes by European Christians. But it is true that *all* other religions, including Judaism and Islam, have been excised from Europe's understanding of Europe's identity as Christian and white. Both Islam and Judaism have long served as Europe's "other," as a symbol for a distinct culture, religion and ethnicity.[16]

Again, this is not to claim that European consciousness has not changed in the last few decades, or that Jews and Muslims occupy the same place in the new European order; but the patterns of European history have so often treated Jews and Muslims as part of a threatening difference that we simply cannot take the present conditions for granted. In fact, a Pew survey undertaken in early 2008 revealed that, although Muslims are viewed far less favorably than Jews across Europe, negative views of Jews rose in a number of European countries (with Spain in the lead) between 2004 and 2006. This survey draws attention to the fact that the social groups who have a low opinion of Muslims tend to be the same ones who don't like Jews.[17]

To be sure, as odious as the policies and statements of right-wing xenophobes in Europe may sound, one must acknowledge that the sudden and massive irruption of difference within any community provokes legitimate concerns and anxieties about the future. Still, changing demographics could revitalize traditions even as they unsettle old social patterns. As Oriana Fallaci was expressing concern about the erosion of an authentic Italian way of life, Arab immigrants from Tunisia and Jordan were emerging as some of the best chefs of traditional Italian cuisine in the country. In 2008, the first prize for cooking Rome's traditional carbonara (a pasta dish that includes eggs, pecorino cheese, and *guanciale,* or cured pig cheek) went to Nabil Hadj Hassen, an immigrant from Tunisia, and the second prize went to an Indian.[18] So, instead of regressing to old and dangerous arrangements, hasn't the time come, as Aristide Zolberg suggests, to wonder about the limits of inclusion and exclusion and to ask on what rational basis they are determined?[19]

The more one thinks about the networked world we live in, the more difficult it is to believe that we can still inhabit the nations and adopt the ideologies bequeathed on the world by Spain in the sixteenth century. Identities of any sort are often more fictional than real. "Identity," wrote Stuart Hall, "far from the simple thing we think it is (ourselves always in the same place), understood properly is always a structure that is split: it always has ambivalence within it. The story of identity is a cover story. A cover story for making you think you stayed in the same place, though with another bit of your mind you do know that you've moved on." It is a *"process of identification . . .* something that happens over time, that is never absolutely stable, that is subject to the play of history and the play of difference."[20]

Just as identities are unstable, so is the concept of race. As Mae Ngai, following Paul Gilroy, reminds us, race and racism are "historically specific" notions that change with time. Moreover, as Arjun Appadurai notes in *Fear of Small Numbers,* his insightful treatise on the "geography of anger," as globalization intensifies the incompleteness of national unity and diminishes the power of traditional citizens, minorities become "the major site for displacing the anxieties of many states about their own minority or marginality (real or imagined) in a world of a few megastates, of unruly economic flows and compromised sovereignties."[21]

Barring more genocides and episodes of ethnic cleansing, there is no doubt at all that the identity structures of old must yield to a new consciousness of the Other. In such a consciousness, as in the mock battles of *moros y cristianos,* the enemy would appear as oneself, not the Other; or, even better, the Other would finally emerge as oneself, eliminating the need for devising elaborate but futile mechanisms of social exclusion and persecution. Needless to say, Muslims in their home countries would be obligated to reciprocate in kind, to see their cultural identity as part of an initial act of religious differentiation from previous monotheistic religions, and so to do away with the anxiety over Jewish, Christian, and even Western influence once and for all.

The same would apply in the United States in regard to its non-Anglo-Saxon and nonwhite populations. (Although the Irish and Mexicans constituted the largest national groups of illegal immigrants from the 1960s to the 1980s, the apprehension and deportation of the former was laughably negligible compared to that of the latter. Commenting on the forty-seven deportable Irish aliens the government captured in 1997, Roger Daniels writes that "it could have found more than that in a Saturday night surveillance of one of the more popular Irish bars in New York or Boston, or at an Irish or Irish American soccer game.")[22] Just as Spain eventually came to accept that Islam, introduced into the Iberian Peninsula in 711, is part of its legacy, the United States must face the even more poignant fact that the Iberians (including Moors) explored and settled parts of the United States long before the Anglo-Saxons—credited by Samuel Huntington, Patrick Buchanan, and others for being uniquely able to devise liberal systems of freedom and prosperity—ever dreamed of reinventing their biblical land of promise on a continent pacified for them by hardened Spanish conquistadors. I remember being told by patrons in a sushi bar in San Diego in the early 1990s that illegal immigration from Mexico was a major threat to the state. When I casually observed that I found it interesting that Mexicans were trying to get access to places with Spanish names—such as San Diego, Los Angeles, and, of course, California itself—the group made no attempt at serious reflection. Such questions, like the topics of slavery and Native Americans, are often met with a "here we go again" attitude, an impatience with bringing up issues considered to be long gone (perhaps even resolved) and no longer applicable in America's here and now. One could find innumerable cases to illustrate the paradox of Spanish-speaking people immigrating illegally into lands once part of their national heritage. In any case, my question shows that Mexican culture cannot possibly be alien to the United States, for it was in the country before there was even an Anglo-Saxon tradition, let alone a nation called the United States. Mexican and Hispanic cultures are part of the fabric of Americanness; to pretend otherwise is to invite more confusion and to fuel the xenophobic tendencies that have given strength to nativists and sanctioned violence.

Just as racial categories can no longer justify discrimination (one might imagine what could happen if we all checked our DNA for genetic lineages), one must now wonder whether the national paradigm established by Spain in the sixteenth century is still a viable model for the twenty-first century, particularly when people are not infrequently joined together by forces beyond their control. In 2006, when Mexicans and Hispanics were protesting the draconian bill to criminalize illegal immigrants and their supporters, Moisés Naím, the editor of *Foreign Policy* magazine and author of *Illicit: How Smugglers, Traffickers, and Copycats Are Hijacking the Global Economy,* commented that it was absurd to still peg the increasingly antiquated notion of sovereignty to physical barriers: "Traditional borders are violated daily by countless means, and virtual borders seem even more permeable and misunderstood. 'Closing the border' may appeal to nationalist sentiments and to the human instinct of building moats and walls for protection. But when threats travel via fiber optics or inside migrating birds, and when finding ways to move illegal goods across borders promises unimaginable wealth or the only chance of a decent life, unilateral security measures have the unfortunate whiff of a Maginot line."[23]

One might more accurately talk about boundaries (in Arabic, *hudud*) in the sense explored by the Moroccan feminist and civil rights activist Fatima Mernissi, in her book *Dreams of Trespass,* for, despite the rise of new technologies that make the notion of walls and fences seem obsolete, the current model of globalization has maintained, if not intensified, the segregation between those with access to resources and those without.[24] Still, Naím is right to point out that the physical shape of nationalism looks hopelessly out of sync with global realities today. What this approach to preserving a people's identity and sovereignty does is reflect the gradual collapse of the old world order through the inexorable march of globalization. That American politicians, for instance, spent a considerable amount of time introducing bills about English-language-only policies and mandating the construction of fences in the single year of 2006 is proof that Samuel Huntington and Oriana Fallaci were speaking to deeply entrenched anxieties about the nature of nation-states and sovereignty in an age when neither unity of faith nor racial homogeneity—the twin pillars of sixteenth-century Spain's nationalism—could be sustained. Moreover, one-language-only policies contravene the 1996 Universal Declaration of Linguistic Rights, which affirms that "everyone has the right to carry out all activities in the public sphere in his/her language," and the 1992 European Union charter mandating the protection of minority languages across the continent. (By 2007, the number of official European languages, written in three alphabets—Latin, Greek, and Cyrillic—reached twenty-three.) The pillars of Spanish nationalism—linguistic, religious, cultural, and racial—no longer hold in a world of strangers. The real discussion is therefore about the mounting tension "between the nation-state and Babel's growing tower," as Edward Rothstein, the *New York Times* cultural observer, puts it.[25]

Aristide Zolberg has noted that not only do borders (and, one might add, boundaries as well) serve to affirm state sovereignty and maintain democracy, but, as "economic modeling suggests," they also guard against the redistribution of wealth and an empowered international labor movement. Although the inequalities of the global economic system will continue to drive immigration, Zolberg warns, nativist responses pose "a more immediate threat to liberal democracy," for "the elimination of unauthorized immigration would require no less than the transformation of the United States and other affluent democracies into police states, protected by a new iron curtain or a Berlin wall." As a "steel curtain" stretching from the Pacific to the Rio Grande descends on America, Americans and their nation are inviting more trouble, not less, according to two searing editorial indictments by the *New York Times* in March 2008. Listing the various ruthless and self-defeating measures being considered in Congress to punish illegal immigration, the *Times* commented thus: "Maybe some people do not mind that immigration zealotry is sending the country down a path of far greater intrusion into citizens' lives, into a world of ingrained suspicion, routine discrimination and economic disruption," but this prospect, in the end, would be quite "frightening." There is, therefore, no option other than "the maintenance by the affluent democracies of relatively open borders" if they want to live in a "more liberal world." Put another way, it's preferable to live with the "imperfections" of "unauthorized immigration" (it is, after all, the unskilled and persecuted poor who are forced to move away from their local environments for better prospects elsewhere) rather than to condemn one's society to a dark future of illiberalism.[26] A liberal, cosmopolitan approach that allows people to "vote with their feet" is a better option than locking up people behind border fences. We know what happened when countries refused to admit Jews in the 1930s. Moreover, this cosmopolitan approach helps raise questions about the suitability of the European state system worked out in the seventeenth century (known as the Westphalian model), including whether "national sovereignty as the dominant principle of international organization is in keeping with our dawning awareness of the interdependence of all the segments of the human species, arising from the global nature of the thermonuclear threat and of environmental degradation."[27]

When the Irish, fleeing the Great Hunger in the nineteenth century, were met with intense xenophobia and nativism on the American side of the Atlantic, Herman Melville, who had served as a sailor on an immigrant ship, called for their more enthusiastic welcome and, indeed, for welcoming anybody who wished to come to America: "Let us waive the agitated national topic, as to where such multitudes of foreign poor should be landed on our American shores; let us waive it, with the only one thought that if they can get here, they have God's right to come; though they bring all Ireland and her miseries with them. For the whole world is the patrimony of the whole world; there is no telling who does not own a stone in the Great Wall of China."[28] Melville was expressing the optimism of post–Civil War America, when the country was still imagined as a cosmopolitan refuge welcoming all the world's races and ethnicities. "We are the heirs of all time," he wrote in *Redburn*, "and with all nations we divide our inheritance. On this Western Hemisphere all tribes and peoples are forming into one federated whole; and there is a future which shall see the estranged children of Adam restored as to the old hearthstone in [an American] Eden. . . . The seed is sown, and the harvest must come."[29]

Other Americans, in twentieth-century America, shared Melville's optimism. In 1915, the philosopher Horace Kallen, thought to have coined the phrase "cultural pluralism," imagined the United States not as a melting pot but as an "orchestra," a "democracy of nationalities." Louis Adamic, author of the 1945 book *A Nation of Nations,* expressed a similar sentiment when he wrote, "The United States is great. . . . Its greatness consists of two elements: the idea it brought into government—that all men are created equal and have a voice in how they are governed—and the variegated texture of its makeup. . . . Such an interplay was in line with the major direction in which the world has been moving—from the clan through the tribe, through the nation and race toward denationalization, Americanism (democracy), internationalism, humanity."[30] Adamic's cosmopolitan spirit, however, was dampened by the cold war. As in our own time, political conflicts and war invariably took America back to its most unproductive social instincts.

What Zolberg calls the "Melville principle" is an excellent expression for the fundamental human right to free movement, shifting the burden onto unrepentant nativists, for one surely needs to explain what is natural about state structures, in rich and poor countries alike, that confine the movements of billions of people worldwide while giving unrestricted access to a select group of people to live and play anywhere they want. Melville's vision, echoed in Walt Whitman's poetry, is a far better prospect to imagine than the persistence of a primitive form of nationalism based on exclusion and expulsion, or a social model of gated communities antagonizing the poor by keeping them out of bounds. These are simply not rational long-term solutions for an already besieged planet. If Moors or Moriscos are the residual prototype of Gypsies, Native Americans, Africans, Jews, Hispanics, and, in general, the West's undesirables since 1492, we might as well avoid the tragedies that dogmatic concepts of national identities have engendered—the expulsion of Jews in 1492; the expulsion of Moriscos in 1609; the scapegoating of minorities as infidels in the nation's holy body politic; and the horrors of genocide visited on various non-Europeans and on Jews in Nazi Germany—by accepting our true nature as mestizos in a world where national, racial, ethnic, and cultural boundaries are dangerous illusions.

Should we make a conscious effort to attain a state of irreversible *mestizaje,* there is no better group than the Mexicans to lead the way. It is not insignificant that it was a Mexican intellectual who coined the expression "cosmic race" early in the twentieth century. As the reliably insightful *Los Angeles Times* columnist and author Gregory Rodriguez has shown in his masterful study *Mongrels, Bastards, Orphans, and Vagabonds: Mexican Immigration and the Future of Race in America* (2007), although Mexicans are the "largest immigrant group in the history of the United States," the Mexican culture of *mestizaje* impels them toward inclusion through intermarriage and adaptation. "There is no private Mexican American college in the United States. In Los Angeles, there is no ethnic-Mexican hospital, cemetery, college, or broad-based charity organization," Rodriguez notes.[31]

Miscegenation, or, rather, *mestizaje,* characterized the birth of modern Mexico, from the moment Spanish conquistadors encountered the Aztec empire. Malinali, better known as Doña Marina, Hernán Cortés's translator and lover (who was reviled as a traitor after Mexican independence from Spain), was emblematic of this period of conquest. More than bilingual, she delivered Mexico to a new nation of mixed offspring and a mestizo destiny.[32]

If racial purity was difficult in Mexico, it was even harder on the northern edges of New Spain, in outposts such as New Mexico, Texas, Arizona, and California. As early as the eighteenth century, Spanish authorities in Florida welcomed slave refugees from the Carolinas and Georgia, leading to the establishment of the town Gracia Real de Santa Teresa de Mosé, in St. Augustine, "the first legally sanctioned free black community in what is now the United States."[33] By 1821, the 200,000 Africans who had come— mostly as slaves—to Mexico were blended into the mestizo population; their children, if born to indigenous women, were born free, as stipulated by law. In Mexican Texas, free blacks enjoyed equal rights with whites, a fact often noted and condemned by white Texans who found ways to circumvent the Mexican law and introduce slaves. In February 1836, Gen. Antonio López de Santa Anna complained about the fate of such enslaved blacks. "Shall we permit those wretches," he wrote to Mexico's minister of war, "to moan in chains any longer in a country whose kind laws protect the liberty of man without distinction of caste or color?"[34] When Texas became independent, slaves often dashed across the Rio Grande into Mexico, where some rose to positions of prominence. So widespread was this perception, especially north of the border, that a common saying in Texan bars had it that "a nigger in Mexico is just as good as a white man."[35] Still, many, like present-day migrants crossing the border in the opposite direction, died or starved on their way to freedom.[36]

Like other Latinos, Mexican Americans remain a hopeful lot. The great contemporary Mexican American writer Richard Rodriguez expressed his cosmic identity best when he wrote, "I take it as an Indian achievement that I am alive, that I am Catholic, that I speak English, that I am American. My life began, it did not end, in the sixteenth century."[37]

Given the persistence of our identity structures and deeply entrenched fear of change, one suspects that strangers will continue to suffer the wrath of nativists, the self-appointed or popularly acclaimed defenders of the purity of nations and guardians of exclusive ways of life. Even as globalization continues to spin its wheels, sublimating what Richard Sennett calls the "specter of uselessness" into "ethnic or race prejudice," one doesn't yet see any attempt to question the legacy that Spanish crusaders handed down to an expanding Europe, or the insecurities generated by the global economic system. "The fear of loss of control," Sennett writes in *The Culture of the New Capitalism*, "now has a target close at hand [i.e., immigrants]. And in that perverse work of the imagination, it does not register that persecuting these close-by weak outsiders does little to make one's job secure."[38]

In 1883, the poet Emma Lazarus, a descendant of Sephardic Jews, composed two poems that bridge the historical gaps between 1492, when the contours of the modern world were being shaped by the Catholic Monarchs, Ferdinand and Isabella, and the late nineteenth century, when the United States was emerging as an industrial powerhouse. In both historical periods, Jews, whether in Spain or in Russia, were the undesirable lot in Europe. In the poem "1492," Lazarus gave a greeting to immigrants entering the New World that welcomed all without distinction to race: "Ho, all who weary, enter here! / There falls each ancient barrier that the art / Of race or creed or rank devised, to rear / Grim bulwarked hatred between heart and heart!" America, alas, was nevertheless soon imprinted by the worst prejudices of the Old World. But the poet was undaunted by history. In "The New Colossus," she continued to imagine America as a refuge to the "huddled masses, yearning to breathe free," "the wretched refuse of your teeming shore," and "the homeless, tempest-tost" approaching our "golden door," words that are now immortalized on the Statue of Liberty.[39] Politicians and ideologues may continue to appeal to national essences based on imagined ethnicities or races to exclude new groups of undesirables, but there is, in the end, no escaping the fact that "we are all Moors," that we are all minorities in a world of diversities. It is high time we banish the specter of the Moor from our consciousness and embrace the differences that enrich us all. It is far more sensible to start preparing for a new golden age when every human being on earth and every cultural tradition will be embraced with the love and care now accorded to any species threatened with extinction. For the margin between life and death seems to have narrowed considerably in the last few years.

NOTES

INTRODUCTION

1. Fareed Zakaria, *The Post-American World* (New York: Norton, 2008), 1, 20, 26; Niall Ferguson, *The War of the World: Twentieth-Century Conflict and the Descent of the West* (New York: Penguin, 2006), xli.

2. For a succinct account of this thesis, see Abbas Hamdani, "Columbus and the Recovery of Jerusalem," *Journal of the American Oriental Society* 99, no. 1 (1979): 39–48.

3. See Denis Guénoun, *Hypothèses sur l'Europe: Un essai de philosophie* (Belfort, France: Circé, 2000), 63–65, 287–89.

4. See David Levering Lewis, *God's Crucible: Islam and the Making of Europe, 570–1215* (New York: Norton, 2008), xxiii, 123, 172–73.

5. Samuel Huntington, *The Clash of Civilizations and the Remaking of the World Order* (New York: Simon & Schuster, 1996), 207.

6. Emily C. Bartels, *Speaking of the Moor: From "Alcazar" to "Othello"* (Philadelphia: University of Pennsylvania Press, 2008), 5.

7. L. P. Harvey, "The Political, Social, and Cultural History of the Moriscos," in *The Legacy of Muslim Spain,* ed. Salma Khadra Jayyusi (Leiden, Neth.: Brill, 1992), 212.

8. See Huntington, *Clash of Civilizations,* 39.

9. See Daniel Martin Varisco, *Reading Orientalism: Said and the Unsaid* (Seattle: University of Washington Press, 2007).

10. Huntington, *Clash of Civilizations,* 89, 51, 186–92, 198–206.

11. Henry Kamen, *The Disinherited: Exile and the Making of Spanish Culture, 1492–1975* (New York: Harper, 2007), 59.

12. Francisco López de Gómara, *Historia general de las indias* (1552), quoted in Barbara Fuchs, *Mimesis and Empire: The New World, Islam, and European Identities* (Cambridge: Cambridge University Press, 2001), 7.

13. Tomás Ortiz, quoted in Tzvetan Todorov, *The Conquest of America: The Question*

of the Other, trans. Richard Howard (1984; repr., Norman: University of Oklahoma Press, 1999), 151.

14. See Robert Dannin, *Black Pilgrimage to Islam* (New York: Oxford University Press, 2002), 6, 4, 12, 16.

15. Malcolm X, quoted in Richard Brent Turner, *Islam in the African-American Experience* (Bloomington: Indiana University Press, 1997), 221.

16. Simon Wolf, quoted in Michael B. Oren, *Power, Faith, and Fantasy: America in the Middle East, 1776 to the Present* (New York: Norton, 2007), 265.

17. See Joseph Pérez, *History of a Tragedy: The Expulsion of the Jews from Spain,* trans. Lysa Hochroth (Urbana: University of Illinois Press, 2007), 36.

18. See Gil Anidjar, *Semites: Race, Religion, Literature* (Stanford, Calif.: Stanford University Press, 2008), 6, 31–32, 114–15n37.

19. Obviously, Zionism is nowadays so closely associated with the West in its conflict with Muslims and Arabs that their historical cultural kinship, like the once paradigmatic concepts of Semites and Aryans, has vanished from view. See ibid., 33.

20. See Karl Marx and Friedrich Engels, *Selected Letters: The Personal Correspondence, 1844–1877,* ed. Fritz J. Raddatz, trans. Ewald Osers (Boston: Little, Brown, 1981), 2.

21. See Rafael A. Guevara Bazán, "Muslim Immigration to Spanish America," *Muslim World* 56, no. 3 (1966): 175; and Matti Bunzl, ed., *Anti-Semitism and Islamophobia: Hatreds Old and New in Europe* (Chicago: Prickly Paradigm, 2007), 11–24.

22. Matt Carr, "You Are Now Entering Eurabia," *Race & Class* 48, no. 1 (July 2006): 17.

23. Oriana Fallaci, *The Rage and the Pride* (New York: Rizzoli, 2002), 41. Fallaci was adamant about translating her own book into English so as not to dilute the tone and style of her message; but does such insistence on originality of voice allow for misspellings like "mistery" (71) or "fellony" (99)?

24. Ibid., 40–41, 30–32, 47–48, 84, 93–94, 126.

25. Ibid., 114, 127, 173–81, 182, 87.

26. Mark Steyn, *America Alone: The End of the World as We Know It* (Washington, D.C.: Regnery, 2006), 177–78. For an interesting article on President George W. Bush's preference for right-wing authors, including Steyn, see Jim Lobe, "Bush's Book List Gets More Islamophobic," March 16, 2007, CommonDreams.org, http://www .commondreams.org/headlines07/0316-01.htm.

27. Fallaci, *Rage and the Pride,* 45. See also Margaret Talbot, "The Agitator," *New Yorker,* June 5, 2006.

28. Bernard-Henri Lévy, "Oriana Fallaci: L'Inacceptable provocation," *Le Point* (Paris), May 30, 2002, quoted in Vincent Geisser, *La Nouvelle islamophobie* (Paris: La Découverte, 2003), 46; Oriana Fallaci, *The Force of Reason (La Forza della ragione)* (New York: Rizzoli, 2006), 276.

29. See Tunku Varadarajan's interview with Fallaci, "Prophet of Decline," *Wall Street Journal,* June 23, 2005.

30. Fallaci, *Force of Reason,* 305, 273, 280, 285, 307, 283, 294, 304.

31. Steyn, *America Alone*, 123.

32. Fallaci, *Force of Reason*, 185, 34, 38, 51–52, 138, 144, 67, 81, 83–84, 93–96, 111–18, 135–36.

33. Ibid., 160, 44, 40, 41.

34. Ibid., 103, 197–98.

35. Patrick J. Buchanan, *State of Emergency: The Third World Invasion and Conquest of America* (New York: Dunne, 2006), 200.

36. Ira Stoll, "The Faith of an Atheist," review of *The Force of Reason,* by Oriana Fallaci, *New York Sun,* March 15, 2006.

37. Ana Maria Manzanas Calvo, "Contested Passages: Migrants and Borders in the Río Grande and the Mediterranean Sea," *South Atlantic Quarterly* 105, no. 4 (Fall 2006): 813, 808.

38. Elaine Sciolino, "Immigration, Black Sheep, and Swiss Rage," *New York Times,* October 8, 2007.

39. Dan Bilefsky, "Bickering Belgians Find a Point of Unity in Toughening Borders," *New York Times,* October 10, 2007.

40. George W. Bush, quoted in Elisabeth Bumiller, "In Immigration Remarks, Bush Hints He Favors Senate Plan," *New York Times,* April 25, 2006.

41. President Bush repeated: "Some in this country argue that the solution is to deport every illegal immigrant and that any proposal short of this amounts to amnesty. I disagree. It is neither wise nor realistic to round up millions of people, many with deep roots in the United States, and send them across the border." The full transcript of the speech was published by the *Washington Post* on May 15, 2006.

Estimates of the number of illegal immigrants in the United States vary, but 12 million is often cited as a plausible figure. See Wendy Koch, "Outcry Grows over House-Passed Immigration Bill," *USA Today,* March 9, 2006. "Nearly 12 million now live in the USA," Koch wrote, "with 500,000 entering each year since 2000, says a new study by the Pew Hispanic Center." For a discussion of the exact number of illegal aliens in the United States, see Brad Knickerbocker, "Illegal Immigrants in the US: How Many Are There?" *Christian Science Monitor,* May 16, 2006.

42. Nick Costantino, letter to the editor, *New York Times,* May 18, 2006.

43. See, for instance, Jonathan Weisman, "House Votes to Toughen Laws on Immigration," *Washington Post,* December 17, 2005. For a summary of the bill's provisions, see the Library of Congress, http://thomas.loc.gov/cgi-bin/bdquery/z?d109:HR04437:@@@D&summ2=1&.

44. See "Interfaith Statement in Support of Comprehensive Immigration Reform," National Immigration Forum, http://www.immigrationforum.org/documents/PressRoom/InterfaithCIRStatement.pdf. The statement was issued on October 14, 2005, and updated on February 1, 2006.

45. Roger Mahony, "Called by God to Help," *New York Times,* March 22, 2006; Jill Serjeant, "Cardinal Leads Fast for Humane Immigration," *Washington Post,* April 5, 2006.

46. See, for instance, the *New York Times* editorial "The Gospel vs. H.R. 4437," *New York Times,* March 3, 2006.

47. Teresa Watanabe and Hector Becerra, "500,000 Pack Streets to Protest Immigration Bills," *Los Angeles Times,* March 26, 2006; Michelle Keller and Anna Gorman, "High School Students Leave School to Protest Immigration Legislation," *Los Angeles Times,* March 25, 2006.

48. Sonya Geis and Michael Powell, "Hundreds of Thousands Rally in Cities Large and Small," *Washington Post,* April 11, 2006.

49. Andrew S. Grove, "Keep America, America," *Wall Street Journal,* January 26, 2006.

50. Nina Bernstein, "After a Fight to Survive, One to Succeed," *New York Times,* March 9, 2008; N. C. Aizenman, "Immigration Debate Wakes 'Sleeping Latino Giant,'" *Washington Post,* April 6, 2006.

51. Nicholas Riccardi, "Anti-Illegal Immigration Forces Share a Wide Tent," *Los Angeles Times,* March 4, 2006.

52. Gustavo Arellano, "O.C. Can You Say . . . 'Anti-Mexican'?" *Los Angeles Times,* May 8, 2006; Mireya Navarro, "The Mexican Will See You Now," *New York Times,* June 24, 2007.

53. See Marc Shell, "Babel in America; or, The Politics of Language Diversity in the United States," *Critical Inquiry* 20, no. 1 (Summer 1993): 117, 125.

54. Martin Miller, "'Nuestro Himno' Foes Say U.S. Song Should Be in English," *Los Angeles Times,* April 29, 2006. To hear and read the full text of the national anthem in Spanish, see "A Spanish Version of 'The Star-Spangled Banner,'" aired on *Day to Day,* April 28, 2006, National Public Radio, http://www.npr.org/templates/story/story.php?storyId=5369145.

55. "The German National Anthem in Turkish?" *Der Spiegel,* May 2, 2006. Part of the problem for Germany's 2.6 million Turks might be verses such as "German women, German loyalty, German wine and German song"!

56. See Rachel L. Swarns, "Children of Hispanic Immigrants Continue to Favor English, Study of Census Finds," *New York Times,* December 8, 2004; "Press One for English," *New York Times,* May 20, 2006. On the day following the latter article, the *Times* reported that fewer than half the world's nations have an official language but that Canada has two, English and French. See Henry Fountain, "In Language Bill, the Language Counts," *New York Times,* May 21, 2006.

57. Paul Harris, "The Hispanic Panic," *Guardian,* April 27, 2006.

58. "'If It Ain't Dutch, It Ain't Much,'" *Der Spiegel,* January 24, 2006.

59. Marlse Simons, "Muslim's Loss of Dutch Citizenship Stirs Storm," *New York Times,* May 18, 2006. (The newspaper later clarified that Ali was a "former Muslim," not a Muslim.) For a sympathetic account of Ali's sudden fall from grace, see Melanie Phillips, "The Scapegoat," *Los Angeles Times,* May 20, 2006; for a more skeptical account of her rise to stardom, see Haroon Siddiqui, "Why the Jig Is Up for Hirsi Ali in Holland," *Toronto Star,* May 21, 2006.

60. Shell, "Babel in America," 110–11.

61. Rupert Cornwell, "At Last, America Has an Official Language (and Yes, It's English)," *Independent,* May 20, 2006.

62. Benjamin Franklin, "Observations concerning the Increase of Mankind" (1751), quoted in Roger Daniels, *Guarding the Golden Door: American Immigration Policy and Immigrants since 1882* (New York: Hill & Wang, 2004), 8. Franklin's failed newspaper venture is mentioned in Shell, "Babel in America," 109.

63. Daniels, *Guarding the Golden Door,* 8–9.

64. Richard Cohen, "My History of English-Only," *Washington Post,* May 30, 2006.

65. Lawrence Mead, "Why Anglos Lead," *National Interest,* Winter 2005–2006.

66. Robert Pear, "Proposals from Both Sides Fail in Immigration Debate," *New York Times,* June 28, 2007; Jeff Zeleny, "Immigration Bill Prompts Some Menacing Responses," *New York Times,* June 28, 2007; Robert Pear and Carl Hulse, "Immigrant Bill Dies in Senate: Defeat for Bush," *New York Times,* June 29, 2007; Julia Preston, "Defeat Worries Employers Who Rely on Immigrants," *New York Times,* June 29, 2007; Robert Pear, "Little-Known Group Claims a Win on Immigration," *New York Times,* July 15, 2007. Representative Tom Tancredo is quoted in Kirk Johnson, "Anxiety in the Land of Anti-Immigration Crusader," *New York Times,* June 24, 2007.

67. See "Rising Tide," American Israel Public Affairs Committee, http://www.aipac .org/documents/risinger060903.html; David Sharrock and Adam LeBor, "Jews Welcome the Support of Muslims," *Times* (London), May 19, 2003; François Musseau, "'Nous, les Juifs marocains, n'allons pas capituler," *Libération* (Paris), May 21, 2003; Serge Berdugo, "Morocco: A Model of Muslim-Jewish Ties," *Christian Science Monitor,* January 9, 2007.

68. "Maguy Kakon, femme, citoyenne, et juive," *Le Matin du Sahara et du Maghreb* (Casablanca, Morocco), August 31, 2007. For a good sketch of the shrinking but still dynamic and proud Moroccan Jewish community, see Marc Perelman, "From Royal Advisers to Far-Left Militants, Moroccan Jews Embody Coexistence," *Jewish Daily Forward,* October 10, 2007, http://www.forward.com/articles/11792.

69. "In Morocco, a Festival Where Tolerance Is Traditional and Jews Pray Together with Muslims," *International Herald Tribune,* July 8, 2008; Etgar Lefkovits, "Yad Vashem to Showcase Muslims Who Saved Jews from Nazis," *Jerusalem Post,* October 29, 2007; "Muslims Save Baghdad's Jewish Community Centre from Looters," *Sydney Morning Herald,* April 14, 2003.

70. Chris Lowney, *A Vanished World: Muslims, Christians, and Jews in Medieval Spain* (New York: Oxford University Press, 2005), 129–43.

71. "Marruecos: El hermano infiel," *El Mundo* (Madrid), July 2002; Giles Tremlett, *Ghosts of Spain: Travels through Spain and Its Silent Past* (New York: Walker, 2006), 228, 235.

72. Joaquín Costa, quoted in Kamen, *Disinherited,* 88.

73. Juan Goytisolo, "Moros en la costa," *El País* (Madrid), July 21, 2002.

1. PIOUS CRUELTY

1. Pierre Chaunu, "Minorités et conjuncture: L'Expulsion des Moresques en 1609," *Revue Historique* 225 (1961): 94; Henry Kamen, "The Mediterranean and the Expulsion of Spanish Jews in 1492," *Past and Present* 119 (May 1988): 44.

2. See James Reston Jr., *Dogs of God: Columbus, the Inquisition, and the Defeat of the Moors* (New York: Doubleday, 2005), 50–52, 261, 264, 268–69.

3. Henry Charles Lea, *The Moriscos of Spain: Their Conversion and Expulsion* (1901; repr., New York: Greenwood, 1968), 20–21.

4. Reston, *Dogs of God,* 174.

5. Peter Martyr, quoted in J. N. Hillgarth, *The Spanish Kingdoms, 1250–1516,* vol. 2, *1410–1516: Castilian Hegemony* (Oxford: Clarendon, 1978), 392.

6. See Hillgarth, *Spanish Kingdoms, 1250–1516,* 482, 605, 393; Reston, *Dogs of God,* 240–44, 294.

7. Lea, *Moriscos of Spain,* 29–30, 32, 38, 43.

8. Ibid., 29, 57, 82–83.

9. Ibid., 129–33, 137–55, 190–99, 266.

10. Ibid., 270, 292–93, 294.

11. L. P. Harvey, "The Political, Social, and Cultural History of the Moriscos," in *The Legacy of Muslim Spain,* ed. Salma Khadra Jayyusi (Leiden, Neth.: Brill, 1992), 209.

12. Ibid., 204–12, 106. For the full text of the Oran Fatwa of 1504, addressed to Muslim *al-guraba* (strangers) in Spain, see Lea, *Moriscos of Spain,* 61–63. Also see Roger Boase, "The Muslim Expulsion from Spain," *History Today,* April 2002, 22.

13. Yunes Benegas's story was collected by the Young Man of Arévalo and is quoted in Harvey, "Political, Social, and Cultural History," 219. Another example of the despair felt by Muslims after the first Alpujarras uprising was expressed in a poem-letter addressed to the Ottoman sultan Bayazid II: "Peace be with you in the name of the slaves who remain / in al-Andalus, in the West, the land of exile, / who are bordered by the shimmering Mediterranean / and the bottomless, deep, and tenebrous Ocean." Quoted in Henry Kamen, *The Disinherited: Exile and the Making of Spanish Culture, 1492–1975* (New York: Harper, 2007), 56.

14. Harvey, "Political, Social, and Cultural History," 219.

15. Rodrigo de Zayas, *Les Morisques et le racisme d'état* (Paris: La Différence, 1992), 238–39.

16. L. P. Harvey, *Muslims in Spain, 1500–1614* (Chicago: University of Chicago Press, 2005), 113–15, 204; Raphaël Carrasco, *L'Espagne classique, 1474–1814* (Paris: Hachette, 1999), 65.

17. John of Austria, quoted in Kamen, *Disinherited,* 58.

18. The letter is from Luis de Marmol y Carvajal, *Historia del rebellion y castigo de los moriscos del reyno de Granada,* quoted in Zayas, *Les Morisques et le racisme d'état,* 234.

19. Mateo López Bravo and Fadrique Furió Ceriol, *Concejo y consejeros del principe* (1559), cited in Henry Méchoulan, *Le Sang de l'autre; ou, L'Honneur de Dieu: Indiens, juifs, morisques dans l'Espagne du siècle d'or* (Paris: Fayard, 1979), 230, 235–37.

20. Mary Elizabeth Perry, *The Handless Maiden: Moriscos and the Politics of Religion in Early Modern Spain* (Princeton, N.J.: Princeton University Press, 2005), 145–46.

21. Méchoulan, *Le Sang de l'autre,* 257.

22. Benjamin Ehlers, *Between Christians and Moriscos: Juan de Ribera and Religious*

Reform in Valencia, 1568–1614 (Baltimore, Md.: The Johns Hopkins University Press, 2006), 6–7, 80, 105.

23. *Viaje de Turqía,* quoted in Joseph Pérez, *History of a Tragedy: The Expulsion of the Jews from Spain,* trans. Lysa Hochroth (Urbana: University of Illinois Press, 2007), 108.

24. Quoted in Ehlers, *Between Christians and Moriscos,* 91.

25. Quotations in this paragraph are from Ehlers, *Between Christians and Moriscos,* 103–5, 134, 140–41. On Bleda and Ribera's approach to the Moriscos, also see James B. Tueller, *Good and Faithful Christians: Moriscos and Catholicism in Early Modern Spain* (New Orleans: University Press of the South, 2002), 117, 199, 122, 123.

26. Ehlers, *Between Christians and Moriscos,* 127 (my emphasis).

27. Ibid., 151–53, 155.

28. Lea, *Moriscos of Spain,* 296, 297–98, 299, 300–301, 304–5, 307–8, 313, 308, 312–13.

29. Harvey, "Political, Social, and Cultural History," 226, 227, 230; Lea, *Moriscos of Spain,* 315.

30. Chaunu, "Minorités et conjuncture," 94.

31. Ibid., 96–97.

32. Kamen, *Disinherited,* 59.

33. Boase, "Muslim Expulsion from Spain," 24–26; see also Zayas, *Les Morisques et le racisme d'état,* 243–62.

34. Lea, *Moriscos of Spain,* 303.

35. Ibid., 325, 329, 363, 394. Rodrigo de Zayas's estimate, in *Les Morisques et le racisme d'état,* is 600,000, but in a later article based on the book, he gives the number as 500,000. See Rodrigo de Zayas, "L'Expulsion des morisques d'Espagne," *Le Monde diplomatique,* March 1997, 14. L. P. Harvey's guess for the number of Moriscos expelled is 300,000–330,000. See Harvey, *Muslims in Spain,* 12. Most recent figures stay in the 300,000 range.

36. Harvey, *Muslims in Spain,* 331.

37. Philip III, quoted in Tueller, *Good and Faithful Christians,* 199.

38. Harvey, "Political, Social, and Cultural History," 230.

39. Henry Charles Lea, quoted in Richard Hitchcock, "Cervantes, Ricote, and the Expulsion of the Moriscos," *Bulletin of Spanish Studies* 81, no. 2 (2004): 177.

40. Lea, *Moriscos of Spain,* 367, 368–77, 384, 395, 399, 397.

41. Ibid., 22.

42. Harvey, *Muslims in Spain,* 13.

43. Voltaire is quoted in ibid., 308; and Richelieu in Lea, *Moriscos of Spain,* 365.

44. M. Dánvila y Collado, *La Expulsión de los moriscos españoles* (1889), quoted in Anwar G. Chejne, *Islam and the West: The Moriscos, a Cultural and Social History* (Albany: State University of New York Press, 1983), 15.

45. Raymond Carr, introduction to *Spain: A History,* ed. Raymond Carr (New York: Oxford University Press, 2000), 8–9.

46. Niccolò Machiavelli, *The Prince,* trans. and ed. Robert M. Adams (New York: Norton, 1977), 63 (my emphasis).

47. Giovanni Botero, *Practical Politics* [*Della ragion di stato*], trans. and ed. George Albert Moore (Chevy Chase, Md.: Country Dollar Press, 1949), 116–18.

48. José Antonio Maravall, "The Origins of the Modern State," *Journal of World History* 6 (1961): 798, 800, 802, 797.

49. Charles Tilly, "States and Nationalism in Europe," *Theory and Society* 23, no. 1 (February 1994): 135.

50. Pérez, *History of a Tragedy*, 100, 107.

51. Heather Rae, *State Identities and the Homogenisation of Peoples* (Cambridge: Cambridge University Press, 2002), 3–4.

52. Aristide Zolberg, quoted in ibid., 7.

53. Max Weber's view is mentioned in Talal Asad, *On Suicide Bombing* (New York: Columbia University Press, 2007), 14.

54. Anthony W. Marx, *Faith in Nation: Exclusionary Origins of Nationalism* (Oxford: Oxford University Press, 2003), 109, 3, 113, 115.

55. Ibid., 200.

56. Ibid., 199–200.

57. Joseph Pérez, *The Spanish Inquisition: A History*, trans. Janet Lloyd (New Haven, Conn.: Yale University Press, 2005), 1.

58. Carrasco, *L'Espagne classique*, 101.

59. Ibid., 62.

60. On the Inquisition and witchcraft, see Pérez, *Spanish Inquisition*, 79–85.

61. Carrasco, *L'Espagne classique*, 3, 19.

62. See Malek Chebel, *Dictionnaire amoureux de l'islam* (Paris: Plon, 2004), 334. Chebel states that 250,000 Muslims were forced into exile after the fall of Granada, a far greater number than that of the Jews.

63. Carrasco gives two different dates in *L'Espagne classique*; see pp. 18 and 120.

64. Ibid., 20, 18–19, 120–21.

65. The letter is quoted in Hillgarth, *Spanish Kingdoms*, 622.

66. Fadique Furió Ceriol and Luis de Granada are both quoted in Henry Kamen, "Toleration and Dissent in Sixteenth-Century Spain: The Alternative Tradition," *Sixteenth Century Journal* 19, no. 1 (Spring 1988): 17, 20–21, 23.

67. See Zayas, *Les Morisques et le racisme d'état*, 45.

68. Francisco Márquez Villanueva, quoted in Harvey, *Muslims in Spain*, 199.

69. Vicente Espinel, *Vida del escuedro Marcos de Obregón* (1618), translated and quoted in Harvey, *Muslims in Spain*, 200.

70. Raymond Carr, introduction, 6–7.

71. Eva Borreguero, "The Moors Are Coming, the Moors Are Coming! Encounters with Muslims in Contemporary Spain," *Islam and Christian-Muslim Relations* 17, no. 4 (October 2006): 420.

72. Pérez, *History of a Tragedy*, 8–9.

73. Richard Ford, *Handbook for Travellers in Spain*, and Gerald Brennan, *The Spanish Labyrinth*, are both quoted in Carr, introduction, 6.

74. Carr, introduction, 7; Felipe Fernández-Armesto, "The Improbable Empire," in Carr, *Spain*, 146.

75. Fernández-Armesto, "Improbable Empire," 177, 133; Carr, introduction, 8–9.

76. Borreguero, "Moors Are Coming," 422.

77. Olivares is quoted in Carr, introduction, 6.

78. Chaunu, "Minorités et conjuncture," 82. For foreign views of Spanish Christianity and violence, see Kamen, "Toleration and Dissent," 4n5.

79. Zayas, *Les Morisques et le racisme d'état*, 120, 123, 124, 672n174, 130; see also Pérez, *Spanish Inquisition*, 21.

80. Zayas, *Les Morisques et le racisme d'état*, 265, 268, 273–74, 278, 281.

81. Ibid., 194–95; Zayas, "L'Expulsion des morisques," 14.

82. See Harvey, *Muslims in Spain*, 7n4.

83. Carrasco, *L'Espagne classique*, 105; *Vox* is quoted on p. 6. Harvey, *Muslims in Spain*, 7n4, 8, 9.

84. Georges Bensoussan, *Europe, une passion génocidaire: Essai d'histoire culturelle* (Paris: Mille et une nuits, 2006), 19, 20, 102, 106–7.

85. Aimé Césaire, *Discourse on Colonialism*, trans. Joan Pinkham (New York: Monthly Review Press, 2000), 36.

86. Bensoussan, *Europe, une passion génocidaire*, 28. Despite striking similarities, Hitler's Nuremberg laws of 1935 were worse than the Inquisition, because they made conversion impossible. See Raymond P. Scheindlin, *A Short History of the Jewish People: From Legendary Times to Modern Statehood* (New York: Macmillan, 1998), 204.

87. Bensoussan, *Europe, une passion génocidaire*, 422; also see 389–434.

88. Ibid., 449, 451, 456.

89. See, for instance, Youssef Elidrissi, "Les Racines de l'exclusion," *Maroc Hebdo International,* July 26–August 1, 2002, 30.

90. Méchoulan, *Le Sang de l'autre*, 204, 206–7, 199, 215, 207, 216–17, 205, 217, 213–14.

91. Joseph Pérez, quoted in ibid., 196.

92. Henry Méchoulan, "Communauté de destin," *Los Muestros*, April 10, 1993, http://www.sefarad.org/publication/lm/010/mechoula.html.

93. Matti Bunzl, ed., *Anti-Semitism and Islamophobia: Hatreds Old and New in Europe* (Chicago: Prickly Paradigm, 2007), 45.

94. See Brian Klug's response to Bunzl, "A Contradiction in 'the New Europe,'" in Bunzl, *Anti-Semitism and Islamophobia*, 57.

95. Joseph Banister, *England under the Jews* (1901), quoted in Klug, ibid., 60.

2. NEW WORLD MOORS

1. Simon Romero, "Hispanics Uncovering Roots as Inquisition's 'Hidden' Jews," *New York Times,* October 29, 2005. One possible sign of a Hispanic's Jewish heritage is the painful presence of autoimmune diseases such as *pemphigus vulgaris* (PV), common among certain Jews. For a full study of crypto-Judaism in New Mexico, see Stanley M. Hordes, *To the End of the Earth: A History of the Crypto-Jews of New Mexico* (New

York: Columbia University Press, 2005). The pejorative origins of the term *Marrano,* as well as the presence of PV among Hispanics, is discussed on pp. 5–7, 271–73, and 281.

2. Trying to answer the question of how he got to have a "white" name, Brent Staples, the *New York Times* editorial observer, had his DNA tested and found out that one-quarter of his genes are European and one-fifth are Asian. Brent Staples, "Why Race Isn't as 'Black' and 'White' as We Think," *New York Times,* October 31, 2005. More interestingly, a geneticist at the University of Arizona has speculated, based on DNA testing, that the family lineage of Thomas Jefferson, the author of the Declaration of Independence, could be traced to Sephardic Jews in Morocco or the Middle East. Jefferson's Y chromosome matched perfectly with that of a Moroccan Jew. See Nicholas Wade, "Study Raises Possibility of Jewish Tie for Jefferson," *New York Times,* February 28, 2007.

3. When white people's tests turn out negative for Native American DNA, they typically become quite angry. Meanwhile, a nursing home director raised as a Christian hired a lawyer to sue Israel for denying him citizenship without conversion. This man reported that a Los Angeles rabbi's response to his claim was "DNA, schmeeNA." See Amy Harmon, "Seeking Ancestry in DNA Ties Uncovered by Tests," *New York Times,* April 12, 2006.

4. In a remarkable twist of fate, increasing numbers of people and even entire communities in Spain are recasting themselves as Jewish to capitalize on this new trend. See Renwick McLean, "With Jewish Roots Now Prized, Spain Starts Digging," *New York Times,* November 5, 2006. This article features a photograph of a Moorish-style synagogue in Toledo but somehow omits the connections between the Jews' golden age in Spain and the Islamic civilization that allowed it. This is one more instance of Muslims' disappearing from history despite the overwhelming evidence (such as in architecture) of their vital presence. The case of Jews and Spain will be discussed more fully in chapter 3.

5. Jodi Wilgoren, "Islam Attracts Converts by the Thousand, Drawn before and after Attacks," *New York Times,* October 22, 2001.

6. Daniel J. Wakin, "Growing Number of Latino-Americans Turn to Islam," *New York Times,* January 2, 2002.

7. Fidel Castro, quoted in Hisham Aidi, "Let Us Be Moors: Islam, Race, and 'Connected Histories,'" *Middle East Report* 229 (Winter 2003): 43.

8. Ibid., 43–46.

9. John V. Tolan, *Saracens: Islam in the Medieval European Imagination* (New York: Columbia University Press, 2002), 282.

10. Emily C. Bartels, "Making More of the Moor: Aaron, Othello, and Renaissance Refashionings of Race," *Shakespeare Quarterly* 41, no. 4 (Winter 1990): 433–54.

11. Michael Neill, "'Mulattos,' 'Blacks,' and 'Indian Moors': Othello and Early Modern Constructions of Human Difference," *Shakespeare Quarterly* 49, no. 4 (Winter 1998): 364–65.

12. Richard Hakluyt, *The Principal Navigations, Voyages, Traffiques, & Discoveries of the English Nation* (1589), quoted in Bartels, "Making More of the Moor," 440.

13. Jan Huyghen van Linschoten, *Discours of Voyages into ye Easte & West Indies* (1598), quoted in Neill, "'Mulattos,' 'Blacks,' and 'Indian Moors,'" 367.

14. Mansur Xu Xianiong, "From Moors to Moros: The North African Heritage of the Hui Chinese," *Journal of Muslim Minority Affairs* 16, no. 1 (January 1996): 21–29.

15. Patricia Seed, *Ceremonies of Possession in Europe's Conquest of the New World, 1492–1640* (Cambridge: Cambridge University Press, 1995), 186n15.

16. Samuel Purchas, *Hakluytus Posthumus; or, Purchas His Pilgrimes* (1625), cited in Neill, "'Mulattos,' 'Blacks,' and 'Indian Moors,'" 368–69.

17. See Mercedes García-Arenal, introduction to *Al-Andalus allende el-Atlántico*, ed. Mercedes García-Arenal (Paris: Ed. UNESCO, 1997), 29; and J. N. Hillgarth, *The Spanish Kingdoms, 1250–1516*, vol. 2, *1410–1516: Castilian Hegemony* (Oxford: Clarendon, 1978), 386. On the foundation of Santa Fe, see Eladio Lapresa Molina, *Santafé, historia de una ciudad del siglo XV* (Granada, Spain: Universidad de Granada, 1979), 23–37; on the origins of the *castrum*, see George Kubler, *Mexican Architecture of the Sixteenth Century* (New Haven, Conn.: Yale University Press, 1948), 94, 99.

18. Luis Weckmann, *La Herencia medieval de México*, quoted in Tomás Lozano, *Cantemos al alba: Origins of Songs, Sounds, and Liturgical Drama of Hispanic New Mexico*, ed. and trans. Rima Montaya (Albuquerque: University of New Mexico Press, 2007), 316. Relying on the *Diccionario de la lengua española*, Lozano translates *alfaqui* as a sage or doctor, *zaquizamíes* as a "Syrian ceiling and the name given in Egypt to a coffered ceiling," and *alfarjes* as "ceilings of carved wood, artistically interwoven" (321).

19. See Antonio Garrido Aranda, *Moriscos e indios: Precedentes hispánicos de la evangelización en México* (Mexico City: Universidad Nacional Autónoma de México, 1980), 90, 70.

20. Ibid., 94–98, 100–104.

21. Antonio Domínguez Ortiz and Bernard Vincent, *Historia de los moriscos: Vida y tragedia de una minoría* (Madrid: Revista de Occidente, 1978), 98.

22. Gaspar Pérez de Villagrá, *Historia de la Nueva Mexico* (1610), quoted in ibid., 163. Also see Lozano, *Cantemos al alba*, 316.

23. Rafael A. Guevara Bazán, "Muslim Immigration to Spanish America," *Muslim World* 56, no. 3 (1966): 177.

24. Ibid., 175–81.

25. Quoted in ibid., 182.

26. Quoted in ibid., 185.

27. Ibid., 186–87.

28. Rafael A. Guevara Bazán, "Some Notes for a History of the Relations between Latin America, the Arabs, and Islam," *Muslim World* 61, no. 4 (October 1971): 289.

29. Henry Kamen, "Toleration and Dissent in Sixteenth-Century Spain: The Alternative Tradition," *Sixteenth Century Journal* 19, no. 1 (Spring 1988): 6.

30. Abdelhamid Lotfi, *Muslims on the Block: Five Centuries of Islam in America* (Ifrane, Morocco: Al Akhawayn University Press, 2002).

31. Abd El Hadi Ben Mansour, "Magreb–Península ibérica en los siglos XVI–XVII: Eslabón y confluencias transatlánticas," in García-Arenal, *Al-Andalus allende*

el-Atlántico, 116–17. Another Moroccan coastal town, Safi, was renowned in New Spain for its honey and wax, from which wax candles, much used in European churches, were made.

32. See Frederick Webb Hodge, *History of Hawikuh, New Mexico, One of the So-Called Cities of Cíbola* (Los Angeles: Southwest Museum, 1937), 1–4; James Reston Jr., *Dogs of God: Columbus, the Inquisition, and the Defeat of the Moors* (New York: Doubleday, 2005), 302; and *The Narrative of the Expedition of Coronado by [Pedro de] Castañeda,* ed. Frederick W. Hodge, in *Spanish Explorers in the Southern United States, 1528–1543* (New York: Scribner's, 1907), 276, 285–87. Castañeda reported that Nuño de Guzmán also founded the present-day cities of Jalisco and Guadalajara during this early expedition (287).

33. Hodge, *History of Hawikuh,* 38.

34. Max Harris, *Aztecs, Moors, and Christians: Festivals of Reconquest in Mexico and Spain* (Austin: University of Texas Press, 2000), 162.

35. Rayford W. Logan, "Estevancio: Negro Discoverer of the Southwest; A Critical Reexamination," *Phylon* 1, no. 4 (1940): 306.

36. Michael A. Gomez, *Black Crescent: The Experience and Legacy of African Muslims in the Americas* (New York: Cambridge University Press, 2005), 6, 45, 43, 146. "The equating of the Mande with Satan," says Gomez, "is, at one level, a reflection of the Iberian attitude toward Islam as well as the Spanish experience with African Muslims both in al-Andalus and the Americas." The Mandingas and other Muslim Senegambians were too pervasive, though, in places such as Colombia and Peru. "Él que no tiene de Inga tiene de Mandinga" (He who is not descended from the Incas is a Mandinga), goes a popular Peruvian saying (26).

37. G. Aguirre Beltran, "Races in 17th Century Mexico," *Phylon* 6, no. 3 (1945): 212–18.

38. Allan D. Austin, *African Muslims in Antebellum America: Transatlantic Stories and Spiritual Struggles* (New York: Routledge, 1997), 22. Such estimates may change as further research sheds more light on the subject.

39. See ibid., 5–6, 33, 50–62.

40. Thomas Tea, quoted in Gomez, *Black Crescent,* 170.

41. Richard Brent Turner, *Islam in the African-American Experience* (Bloomington: Indiana University Press, 1997), 40; Austin, *African Muslims in Antebellum America,* 129–56.

42. Richard Robert Madden, quoted in Gomez, *Black Crescent,* 57.

43. Austin, *African Muslims in Antebellum America,* 66–77.

44. Ibid.; Gomez, *Black Crescent*; Sylvanie A. Diouf, *Servants of Allah: African Muslims Enslaved in the Americas* (New York: New York University Press, 1998); Turner, *Islam in the African-American Experience*; Robert Dannin, *Black Pilgrimage to Islam* (New York: Oxford University Press, 2002); Sherman A. Jackson, *Islam and the Blackamerican: Looking toward the Third Resurrection* (New York: Oxford University Press, 2005).

45. Turner, *Islam in the African-American Experience,* 44–45.

46. Gomez, *Black Crescent,* 16–18.

47. Ibid., 131–47, 148–51.

48. Ibid., 173–82.

49. Gilberto Freyre, *New World in the Tropics: The Culture of Modern Brazil* (1959; repr., New York: Knopf, 1971), 56.

50. Ibid., 59, 72.

51. Gomez, *Black Crescent*, 80.

52. Turner, *Islam in the African-American Experience*, 45–46.

53. David Walker, *Appeal to the Colored Citizens of the World, but in Particular, and Very Expressly, to Those of the United States of America* (1829), quoted in Jackson, *Islam and the Blackamerican*, 127.

54. John Henry Smyth, quoted in Turner, *Islam in the African-American Experience*, 60.

55. Edward Wilmot Blyden, *Christianity, Islam, and the Negro Race* (1888), quoted in Turner, *Islam in the African-American Experience*, 51–52.

56. Clifton E. Marsh, *The Lost-Found Nation of Islam in America* (Lanham, Md.: Scarecrow, 2000), 9; Alex Haley, "The Malcolm X Interview," *Playboy*, May 1963, available online at http://www.unix-ag.uni-kl.de/~moritz/Archive/malcolmx/malcolmx .playboy.pdf. Haley's interview was ranked by the *Guardian* as the ninth-greatest interview of the twentieth century. See "Great Interviews of the 20th Century," *Guardian*, http://www.guardian.co.uk/theguardian/series/greatinterviews.

57. Turner, *Islam in the African-American Experience*, 47–67.

58. Ibid., 83, 88, 90.

59. Ibid., 96.

60. Quoted in Gomez, *Black Crescent*, 266.

61. Peter Lamborn Wilson, *Sacred Drift: Essays on the Margins of Islam* (San Francisco: City Lights Books, 1993), 16.

62. Turner, *Islam in the African-American Experience*, 71–72.

63. Ibid., 101–7; also see Gomez, *Black Crescent*, 203–75. Both Turner and Gomez offer fascinating accounts of Noble Drew Ali's movement.

64. See Turner, *Islam in the African-American Experience*, 109–46. Muhammad Sadiq is quoted on pp. 121 and 122.

65. Gomez, *Black Crescent*, 278, 282.

66. Walker, *Appeal to the Colored Citizens of the World*, quoted in ibid., 306.

67. W. E. B. Du Bois, *The World and Africa: An Inquiry into the Part Which Africa Has Played in World History* (New York: International Publishers, 1965), 23.

68. Aimé Césaire, *Discourse on Colonialism*, trans. Joan Pinkham (New York: Monthly Review Press, 2000), 36.

69. Gomez, *Black Crescent*, 318–30.

70. Malcolm X, quoted in Turner, *Islam in the African-American Experience*, 193.

71. *By Any Means Necessary: Speeches, Interviews, and a Letter by Malcolm X*, ed. George Breitman, 12th ed. (New York: Pathfinder, 1987), 37–38, quoted in Gomez, *Black Crescent*, 354.

72. Haley, "Malcolm X Interview"; Gomez, *Black Crescent*, 352.

73. Gomez, *Black Crescent,* 337, 333.

74. Ibid., 365–70.

75. See Patrick Condon, "Minnesota Sends First Muslim to Congress," *Guardian,* November 10, 2006; and Neil MacFarquhar, "Muslim's Election Is Celebrated Here and in Mideast," *New York Times,* November 10, 2006.

76. See the editorial "Fear and Bigotry in Congress," *New York Times,* December 23, 2006.

77. Bazán, "Some Notes for a History," 290. Also see Antonello Gerbi, "The Earliest Accounts on the New World," in *First Images of America: The Impact of the New World on the Old,* ed. Fredi Chiappelli (Berkeley and Los Angeles: University of California Press, 1976), 37–43.

3. MUSLIM JEWS

1. Tom Reiss, *The Orientalist: Solving the Mystery of a Strange and Dangerous Life* (New York: Random House, 2006), xxiii, 7–8.

2. Quoted in ibid., 34.

3. Ibid., 37, 40–41, 5.

4. Ibid., 63, 66, 71.

5. Ibid., 80; Joseph Pérez, *The Spanish Inquisition: A History,* trans. Janet Lloyd (New Haven, Conn.: Yale University Press, 2005), 222–25.

6. Lev Nussimbaum, quoted in Reiss, *Orientalist,* 120–21.

7. Reiss, *Orientalist,* 124–25.

8. Ibid., 132, 177, 178, 185, 189.

9. Nussimbaum, quoted in ibid., 193.

10. Reiss, *Orientalist,* 193, 198–99, 201, 203, 212.

11. Ibid., 209–10, 265.

12. Ibid., 215, 256–60, 267, 339, 300–301.

13. Ibid., 331.

14. Gil Anidjar, "Postface: Réflexions sur la question," in *Juifs et musulmans: Une histoire partagée, un dialogue à construire,* ed. Esther Benbassa and Jean-Christophe Attias (Paris: La Découverte, 2006), 130.

15. Inga Clendinnen, *Reading the Holocaust* (Cambridge: Cambridge University Press, 1999), 35.

16. Elie Wiesel, "Stay Together, Always," *Newsweek,* January 16, 1995, 58.

17. Primo Levi, *Survival in Auschwitz: The Nazi Assault on Humanity,* trans. Stuart Woolf (New York: Collier, 1993), 90.

18. Emil Fackenheim, quoted in Gil Anidjar, *The Jew, the Arab: A History of the Enemy* (Stanford, Calif.: Stanford University Press, 2003), 141.

19. Yehiel Feiner, quoted in Anidjar, *The Jew, the Arab,* 147–49.

20. Clendinnen, *Reading the Holocaust,* 35; Giorgio Agamben, *Remnants of Auschwitz: The Witness and the Archive,* trans. Daniel Heller-Roazen (New York: Zone, 1999), 44–45, 52.

21. Quoted in Anidjar, *The Jew, the Arab,* 142.

22. Agamben, *Remnants of Auschwitz*, 45.

23. Anidjar, "Postface," 115, 125, 127.

24. Ibid., 129.

25. A recent DNA study revealed that Jewish women accompanied Jewish men as they made their way into Europe, a fact that undercuts the belief that Jewish men migrated alone and married locally. See Nicholas Wade, "New Light on Origins of Ashkenazi in Europe," *New York Times,* January 14, 2006.

26. Raymond P. Scheindlin, *A Short History of the Jewish People: From Legendary Times to Modern Statehood* (New York: Macmillan, 1998), 23.

27. Bernard Lewis, *The Jews of Islam* (Princeton, N.J.: Princeton University Press, 1984), 76–77; Joseph Pérez, *History of a Tragedy: The Expulsion of the Jews from Spain,* trans. Lysa Hochroth (Urbana: University of Illinois Press, 2007), 11, 21.

28. Scheindlin, *Short History of the Jewish People,* 81–82; Lucien Gubbay, *Sunlight and Shadow: The Jewish Experience of Islam* (New York: Other Press, 2000), 4.

29. Lewis, *Jews of Islam,* 81, 79–80, 85, 21, 84, 92, 87.

30. See the chapter "The Jews in the Islamic World: From the Rise of Islam to the End of the Middle Ages (632 to 1500)," in Scheindlin, *Short History of the Jewish People,* 71–95.

31. Ibn Khaldun, quoted in Bernard Lewis, *Semites and Anti-Semites: An Inquiry into Conflict and Prejudice* (New York: Norton, 1986), 130.

32. Scheindlin, *Short History of the Jewish People,* 210, 134; also see the chapter "The Jews in the Ottoman Empire and the Middle East (1453 to 1948)," 123–47.

33. Quoted in Lewis, *Jews of Islam,* 135–36.

34. Edward Said, *Orientalism* (New York: Pantheon, 1978). Said considered orientalism the "Islamic branch" of anti-Semitism and recognized that "Western anti-Semitism has always included both the Jews and Muslims. The latter have yet to be released from that ideological prison." See Ivan Davidson Kalmar and Derek J. Penslar, "Orientalism and the Jews: An Introduction," in *Orientalism and the Jews,* ed. Ivan Davidson Kalmar and Derek J. Penslar (Waltham, Mass.: Brandeis University Press / Hanover, N.H.: University Press of New England, 2005), xv, xxxv.

35. Lewis, *Jews of Islam,* 72–73.

36. Pierre Lory, "Le Judaïsme et les juifs dans le Coran et la tradition musulmane," in Benbassa and Attias, *Juifs et musulmans,* 16, 20–22, 18; Gubbay, *Sunlight and Shadow,* 17–18; Lewis, ibid., 10, 25, 28, 32.

37. Georges Bensoussan, *Europe, une passion génocidaire: Essai d'histoire culturelle* (Paris: Mille et une nuits, 2006).

38. Lory, "Le Judaïsme et les juifs," 19; Lewis, *Semites and Anti-Semites,* 50, 55–57, 44.

39. Karen Armstrong, "We Cannot Afford to Maintain These Ancient Prejudices against Islam," *Guardian,* September 18, 2006.

40. Allan Harris Cutler and Helen Elmquist Cutler, *The Jew as Ally of the Muslim: Medieval Roots of Anti-Semitism* (Notre Dame, Ind.: University of Notre Dame Press, 1986), 6.

41. Ibid., 7–8, 12, 121, 344n2, 13–14.

42. Ibid., 28, 22, 32, 65–66; Jeremy Cohen, "The Muslim Connection; or, On the Changing Role of the Jew in High Medieval Theology," in *From Witness to Witchcraft: Jews and Judaism in Medieval Christian Thought,* ed. Jeremy Cohen (Wiesbaden, Ger.: Harrassowitz, 1997), 151–53; John V. Tolan, *Saracens: Islam in the Medieval European Imagination* (New York: Columbia University Press, 2002), 148, 154–55, 275.

43. Tolan, *Saracens,* 117.

44. Cutler and Cutler, *Jew as Ally of the Muslim,* 389, 338n14, 92–94, 196, 96, 204; also see Tolan, ibid., 195–98.

45. Cohen, "Muslim Connection," 143–44.

46. Ibid., 144.

47. Peter the Venerable, quoted in ibid., 155.

48. Cohen, "Muslim Connection," 159; Norman F. Cantor, *The Civilization of the Middle Ages* (New York: HarperCollins, 1993), 339.

49. Benjamin Braude, "'Jew' and Jesuit at the Origins of Arabism: William Gifford Palgrave," in *The Jewish Discovery of Islam: Studies in Honor of Bernard Lewis,* ed. Martin Kramer (Tel Aviv, Isr.: Moshe Dayan Center for Middle Eastern and African Studies, Tel Aviv University, 1999), 79.

50. Richard W. Southern, *Western Views of Islam in the Middle Ages* (Cambridge, Mass.: Harvard University Press, 1962), 3, quoted in ibid., 145.

51. Cohen, "Muslim Connection," 147.

52. Cutler and Cutler, *Jew as Ally of the Muslim,* 183.

53. See Anidjar, *The Jew, the Arab,* 187–88n136.

54. Todros Abulafia, "There's Nothing Wrong in Wanting a Woman," in *The Dream of the Poem: Hebrew Poetry from Muslim and Christian Spain, 950–1492,* trans. and ed. Peter Cole (Princeton, N.J.: Princeton University Press, 2007), 260.

55. Christopher Marlowe, *The Jew of Malta* (Manchester, Eng.: Manchester University Press, 1997), 58–59.

56. Heinrich Heine, *Almansor,* quoted in Martin Kramer, introduction to Kramer, *Jewish Discovery of Islam,* 5.

57. Friedrich Wolf, *Mohammed,* quoted in Kramer, introduction, 25.

58. John M. Efron, "Orientalism and the Jewish Historical Gaze," in Kalmar and Penslar, *Orientalism and the Jews,* 82–84; also see Jacob Lassner, "Abraham Geiger: A Nineteenth-Century Jewish Reformer on the Origins of Islam," in Kramer, *Jewish Discovery of Islam,* 105, 109. Although Geiger highlighted the similarities between Judaism and Islam, he was also aware of Islam's anxiety to differentiate itself as a new faith (126–29).

59. Efron, "Orientalism and the Jewish Historical Gaze," 85–87, 83.

60. See the interview with Albert Hourani in Nancy Elizabeth Gallagher, *Approaches to the History of the Middle East: Interviews with Leading Middle East Historians* (Reading, Eng.: Ithaca, 1994), 40, 42, quoted in ibid., 240–41n19.

61. Efron, "Orientalism and the Jewish Historical Gaze," 89–90.

62. Ibid., 93, 92.

63. Ignaz Goldziher, quoted in ibid., 92; see also Lawrence I. Conrad, "Ignaz

Goldziher on Ernest Renan: From Orientalist Philology to the Study of Islam," in Kramer, *Jewish Discovery of Islam*, 137, 163, 143, 148, 147, 144, 167; and Kramer's introduction, 14–16.

64. Ignaz Goldziher, quoted in Daniel Martin Varisco, *Reading Orientalism: Said and the Unsaid* (Seattle: University of Washington Press, 2007), 183.

65. Minna Rozen, "Pedigree Remembered, Reconstructed, Invented: Benjamin Disraeli between East and West," in Kramer, *Jewish Discovery of Islam*, 50. Russell Schweller, in "'Mosaic Arabs': Jews and Gentlemen in Disraeli's Young England Trilogy," *Shofar: An Interdisciplinary Journal of Jewish Studies* 24, no. 2 (2006), writes that Disraeli "converted to Christianity at the age of twelve" (56).

66. Benjamin Disraeli, quoted in Kalmar and Penslar, "Orientalism and the Jews," xxxi. Interestingly, Disraeli's father had published an English version of the popular Arab love story *Mejnooun and Leila, the Arabian Petrarch and Laura,* in 1797 (xxx).

67. Schweller, "'Mosaic Arabs,'" 58.

68. William Gladstone, quoted in Rozen, "Pedigree Remembered, Reconstructed, Invented," 49.

69. Lord Cromer, cited in Kramer, introduction, 7.

70. Benjamin Disraeli, quoted in Kramer, introduction, 7.

71. Benjamin Disraeli, *Coningsby; or, The New Generation,* quoted in Rozen, "Pedigree Remembered, Reconstructed, Invented," 60.

72. Benjamin Disraeli, *Tancred; or, The New Crusade,* quoted in Varisco, *Reading Orientalism,* 216.

73. Disraeli, *Tancred,* quoted in Kramer, introduction, 63–64.

74. Quoted in Varisco, *Reading Orientalism,* 210.

75. Russell Schweller, quoted in Kramer, introduction, 69.

76. See Braude, "'Jew' and Jesuit," 77, 85.

77. Ivan Davidson Kalmar, "Moorish Style: Orientalism, the Jews, and Synagogue Architecture," *Jewish Social Studies: History, Culture, and Society* 7, no. 3 (2001): 84–86, 69.

78. G. Gustalla, quoted in ibid., 77–78.

79. Ludwig Förster, quoted in Kalmar, "Moorish Style," 78–79.

80. Accademia delle Arti del Disegno, quoted in Kalmar, "Moorish Style," 86.

81. Paul de Lagarde, quoted in Kalmar, "Moorish Style," 89.

82. Kalmar, "Moorish Style," 89, 71.

83. Martin Buber, quoted in ibid., 90.

84. Kalmar, "Moorish Style," 91–93.

85. Aladar Deutsch, quoted in ibid., 93.

86. Quoted in Reiss, *Orientalist,* 240.

87. Martin Buber, quoted in ibid., 241.

88. See Anidjar, *The Jew, the Arab,* 120, 130.

89. Judd Ne'eman and M. Z. Feierberg (from *Whither?*) are quoted in Ranen Omer-Sherman, "The Cultural and Historical Stabilities and Instabilities of Jewish Orientalism," introduction to *Shofar: An Interdisciplinary Journal of Jewish Studies* 24, no. 2 (2006): 2–3.

90. See Arthur Hertzberg, *The Fate of Zionism: A Secular Future for Israel and Palestine* (San Francisco: HarperSanFrancisco, 2003), 169–70.

91. See, for instance, Michael Berkowitz, "Rejecting Zion, Embracing the Orient: The Life and Death of Jacob Israel de Haan," in Kalmar and Penslar, *Orientalism and the Jews*, 109–24. For many European Zionists imbued with the same colonial and orientalist mind-set as Europe's gentiles, the Haredim, or ultra-Orthodox Jews, were as much an obstacle as the Arabs, if not more so, before 1931. The Haredim, under the leadership of the Dutch-born homosexual writer and legal scholar Jacob Israel De Haan (1881–1924), the victim of the first political assassination in Jerusalem, at the age of forty-three, rejected any distinction not based on faith alone (110).

92. Amnon Raz-Krakotzkin, "The Zionist Return to the West and the Mizrahi Jewish Perspective," in Kalmar and Penslar, *Orientalism and the Jews*, 167, 169.

93. Yehouda Shenhav, *The Arab Jews: A Postcolonial Reading of Nationalism, Religion, and Ethnicity* (Stanford, Calif.: Stanford University Press, 2006), 197, 26–27. (An earlier, Hebrew version of this book was published in Israel in 2003.)

94. Ibid., 89.

95. Ibid., 70–76, 104–5.

96. David Ben-Gurion, quoted in Raz-Krakotzkin, "Zionist Return to the West," 171, 172, 173, 175.

97. Quoted in Shenhav, *Arab Jews*, 192.

98. Shenhav, *Arab Jews*, 193–96.

99. Raz-Krakotzkin, "Zionist Return to the West," 176, 180.

100. David Shasha, quoted in Omer-Sherman, "Cultural and Historical Stabilities and Instabilities," 7.

101. Martin Kramer, "The Road from Mecca: Muhammad Asad (Born Leopold Weiss)," in Kramer, *Jewish Discovery of Islam*, 228.

102. Muhammad Asad, *The Road to Mecca* (New York: Simon & Schuster, 1954), 98.

103. Kramer, "Road from Mecca," 230.

104. Ibid., 233, 232, 235, 239, 243.

105. Tudor Parfitt, "The Use of the Jew in Colonial Discourse," in Kalmar and Penslar, *Orientalism and the Jews*, 62–63, 235–36n40, 67.

106. Kalmar and Penslar, "Orientalism and the Jews," xxxii–xxxv.

107. Adolf Wahrmund, quoted in ibid., xxxv.

108. Lewis, *Semites and Anti-Semites*, 176. For an interesting review of recent literature on the little-known history of Zionism, see Geoffrey Wheatcroft, "Zion Story: Jabotinsky, Weizmann, and the Roots of the Most Contentious Communal Struggle on Earth Today," *Times Literary Supplement*, February 20, 2008.

109. Ma'ruf al-Russafi, quoted in Lewis, *Semites and Anti-Semites*, 202.

110. Dan Kurzman, *Genesis 1948: The First Arab-Israeli War* (New York: Signet, New American Library, 1972), 209, quoted in Cutler and Cutler, *Jew as Ally of the Muslim*, 84–85.

111. Uri Zvi Greenberg, "The Word of the Son of Blood" [in Hebrew], in *Shield Area and the Word of the Son of Blood* (Tel Aviv, 1930), quoted in Omer-Sherman, "Cultural and Historical Stabilities and Instabilities," 4. Omer-Sherman describes Greenberg's

lines as "unfortunate" for their condescending view, but I don't see it as such. Such a view anticipates King Abdullah's statement quoted earlier.

112. Kalmar and Penslar, "Orientalism and the Jews," xl.

113. Patrick Klugman, comment in "Juifs et Arabes: Comment, après les accords de Genève, dialoguer aujourd'hui en France sur le conflit israélo-palestinien?" in Benbassa and Attias, *Juifs et musulmans,* 101.

114. Eric H. Yoffie, quoted in Neil MacFarquhar, "Abandon Stereotypes, Muslims in America Say," *New York Times,* September 4, 2007.

115. *Fitna,* film, directed by Scarlet Pimpernel (Scarlet Pimpernel, 2008); Cnaan Liphshiz, "Dutch Jews Louder than Muslims in Condemning 'Fitna' Film," *Haaretz,* April 2, 2008, http://www.haaretz.com/hasen/spages/970768.html.

116. See Eric Hobsbawm, "Benefits of Diaspora," *London Review of Books,* October 20, 2005.

4. UNDESIRABLE ALIENS

1. Samuel P. Huntington, *The Clash of Civilizations and the Remaking of the World Order* (New York: Simon & Schuster, 1996), 149, 312.

2. Samuel P. Huntington, *Who Are We? The Challenges to America's National Identity* (New York: Simon & Schuster, 2004), 37, xv–xvi, 40.

3. Ibid., xvii, 20, 30, 12, 38. The other two components are "culture (most notably language and religion) and ideology" (12).

4. Porter, Zangwill, and Kallen are cited in ibid., 38–47, 49–57, 128–31.

5. Huntington, *Who Are We?* 141–77.

6. Milton M. Gordon, *Assimilation in American Life: The Role of Race, Religion, and National Origins* (New York: Oxford University Press, 1964), quoted in ibid., 183.

7. Roger Daniels, *Guarding the Golden Door: American Immigration Policy and Immigrants since 1882* (New York: Hill & Wang, 2004), 25.

8. Geraldo Rivera, *HisPanic: Why Americans Fear Hispanics in the U.S.* (New York: Celebra, 2008), 262.

9. Daniels, *Guarding the Golden Door,* 178–220.

10. Ibid., 225, 227.

11. Morris Janowitz, quoted in ibid., 246.

12. National Council of La Raza, quoted in Daniels, *Guarding the Golden Door,* 253.

13. Daniels, *Guarding the Golden Door,* 221–56.

14. Huntington, *Who Are We?* 364–65; John Updike, *Rabbit at Rest* (New York: Knopf, 1990), 259.

15. T. R. Reid, *The United States of Europe: The New Superpower and the End of American Supremacy* (New York: Penguin, 2004); Jeremy Rifkin, *The European Dream: How Europe's Vision of the Future Is Quietly Eclipsing the American Dream* (New York: Tarcher/Penguin, 2004).

16. Aristide R. Zolberg, *A Nation by Design: Immigration Policy in the Fashioning of America* (New York: Russell Sage Foundation; Cambridge, Mass.: Harvard University Press, 2006), 437.

17. John Higham, *Strangers in the Land: Patterns of American Nativism, 1860–1925* (1955; repr., New Brunswick, N.J.: Rutgers University Press, 1988), 95–96.

18. Quoted in ibid., 4.

19. Higham, *Strangers in the Land,* 4.

20. Cited in Kenneth C. Davis, "The Founding Immigrants," *New York Times,* July 3, 2007.

21. Higham, *Strangers in the Land,* 5–7, 10–11.

22. Quoted in ibid., 23.

23. Higham, *Strangers in the Land,* 42, 41, 55.

24. Ibid., 75.

25. Ibid., 75–76.

26. Ibid., 76, 85, 90–91, 93.

27. Ibid., 108, 109, 110, 121, 124, 125.

28. Ibid., 138–39.

29. Ibid., 140, 146, 147–48.

30. Ibid., 160–61.

31. Ibid., 180, 184, 186.

32. Ibid., 194–212, 218, 157.

33. Ibid., 231, 233.

34. Ibid., 262, 264.

35. Ibid., 273–77.

36. Ibid., 277.

37. Ibid., 297.

38. Ibid., 293.

39. Ibid., 295, 301.

40. Ibid., 317, 323, 300, 330; Mae M. Ngai, *Impossible Subjects: Illegal Aliens and the Making of Modern America* (Princeton, N.J.: Princeton University Press, 2004), 4–5, 61. On the illegal alien, Ngai writes: "The illegal alien that is abstractly defined is something of a specter, a body stripped of individual personage" (61).

41. David H. Bennett, *The Party of Fear: From Nativist Movements to the New Right in American History* (Chapel Hill: University of North Carolina Press, 1988). For the full citations for books by Higham, Daniels, Ngai, and Zolberg, see earlier notes in this chapter.

42. See Marion Lloyd, "Harvard Scholar Who Warned of Threat from Hispanic Immigration Gets Hostile Greeting in Mexico," *Chronicle of Higher Education,* September 24, 2004. Huntington was also called racist by Manuel Ángel Núñez Soto, the governor of the state of Hidalgo. When Huntington was told about the Stephen King comment, he asked, "Who's Stephen King?"

43. Mark Fiore, "Migraphobia," April 4, 2006, MarkFiore.com, http://www.mark fiore.com/migraphobia_0.

44. See Gregory Rodriguez, "A Sanitized Betrayal of America's History," *Los Angeles Times,* June 11, 2007; Rosa Brooks, "How Immigrants Improve the Curve," *Los Angeles Times,* June 29, 2007; Julia Preston, "California: Study of Immigrants and Crime," *New York Times,* February 26, 2008.

45. Reuters, "Survey Finds Protestants Losing Membership," July 20, 2004.

46. Simon Romero, "A Texas Newspaper Bets on Español, Not Assimilation," *New York Times,* January 31, 2005; "A Senate Speech Says Si, Gonzales," *New York Times,* February 3, 2005; D'Vera Cohn and Tara Bahrampour, "Of U.S. Children under 5, Nearly Half Are Minorities," *Washington Post,* May 10, 2006; Sam Roberts, "In Name Count, Garcias Are Catching Up to Joneses," *New York Times,* November 17, 2007; Anushka Asthana, "Demographer's Art of Prediction Often Imitates Life," *Washington Post,* July 27, 2006; Sam Roberts, "A Nation of None and All of the Above," *New York Times,* August 17, 2008.

47. Patrick J. Buchanan, *State of Emergency: The Third World Invasion and Conquest of America* (New York: Dunne, 2006), 11–12, 21–22, 29–31, 48–49, 88–89, 105–6, 135, 201, 235, 239–40, 248.

48. "Border Illusions," *New York Times,* May 16, 2006.

49. Cristina Rodríguez, "E Pluribus Unum: How Bilingualism Strengthens American Democracy," *Democracy,* no. 4 (Spring 2007): 36–37.

50. On July 22, 2005, Brazilian Jean Charles de Menezes was shot seven times in the head, execution-style, and even accused posthumously of having raped a woman in 2002. He was cleared after samples from his body were tested against those from the rape scene. On August 1, 2007, an official investigative report blamed a high-ranking officer for twisting the facts related to the innocent man's death. The Colombian Rigoberto Alpizar, of Florida, was shot eleven times. See Vikram Dodd and Rosie Cowan, "Brazil Warns of Climate of Fear over the Tube Shoot-to-Kill Policy," *Guardian,* September 30, 2005; "Menezes Is Cleared of Rape Accusation," *Daily Mail* (London), April 26, 2006; David Sanderson, "Police Persecuted Me, Says De Menezes Whistleblower," *Times* (London), May 8, 2006; David Mills, "Getting Away with Murder," *Guardian,* August 1, 2007; Abby Goodnough, "Man Killed by Air Marshals Was Shot 11 Times," *New York Times,* May 24, 2006.

51. John Quincy, quoted in Lars Schoultz, *Beneath the United States: A History of U.S. Policy toward Latin America* (Cambridge, Mass.: Harvard University Press, 1998), 5.

52. Quoted in Juan Gonzalez, *Harvest of Empire: A History of Latinos in America* (New York: Viking, 2000), 18.

53. See Gonzalez, *Harvest of Empire,* 13, 31.

54. Quoted in ibid., 33.

55. Gonzalez, *Harvest of Empire,* 34.

56. Quoted in Schoultz, *Beneath the United States,* 19.

57. Ibid., 26.

58. Sam Houston and Stephen Austin are quoted in Michael L. Krenn, *The Color of Empire: Race and American Foreign Relations* (Washington, D.C.: Potomac, 2006), 32.

59. Washington Hunt, quoted in Krenn, *Color of Empire,* 32.

60. John C. Calhoun, quoted in Krenn, *Color of Empire,* 36. (On April 14, 2005, CNN pundit and middle-class populist Lou Dobbs suggested that leprosy was spreading in the United States because of illegal immigration. See David Leonhardt, "Truth, Fiction, and Lou Dobbs," *New York Times,* May 30, 2007.)

61. John Bell, quoted in Schoultz, *Beneath the United States,* 37.
62. Gonzalez, *Harvest of Empire,* 43.
63. Quoted in ibid., 49.
64. Ulysses S. Grant, quoted in ibid., 44.
65. Daniels, *Guarding the Golden Door,* 178.
66. Quoted in Gonzalez, *Harvest of Empire,* 100.
67. Gonzalez, *Harvest of Empire,* xii.
68. For chilling reports, see Anti-Defamation League, "Extremists Declare 'Open Season' on Immigrants: Hispanics Target of Incitement and Violence," May 23, 2006, http://www.adl.org/main_Extremism/immigration_extremists.htm; and David Holthouse and Mark Potok, "The Year in Hate: Active U.S. Hate Groups Rise to 888 in 2007," Spring 2008, Southern Poverty Law Center, http://www.splcenter.org/intel/intelreport/article.jsp?aid=886.
69. Albert Johnson, quoted in Daniels, *Guarding the Golden Door,* 47–48.
70. Ngai, *Impossible Subjects,* 3.
71. Johnson, quoted in Daniels, *Guarding the Golden Door,* 55.
72. John C. Box, quoted in Daniels, *Guarding the Golden Door,* 62.
73. Daniels, *Guarding the Golden Door,* 63; Ngai, *Impossible Subjects,* 8.
74. Nina Bernstein, "100 Years in the Back Door, Out the Front," *New York Times,* May 21, 2006.
75. Joseph W. Swing, quoted in Ngai, *Impossible Subjects,* 155.
76. Gonzalez, *Harvest of Empire,* 203.
77. See Buchanan, *State of Emergency,* 88–89. Buchanan is relying here on Peter Brimelow's *Alien Nation: Common Sense about America's Immigration Disaster* (New York: Random House, 1995).
78. See Daniels, *Guarding the Golden Door,* 224–30.
79. Gonzalez, *Harvest of Empire,* 194–95, 206.
80. Zolberg, *Nation by Design,* 396; Daniels, *Guarding the Golden Door,* 242–44; Gonzalez, *Harvest of Empire,* 190–91.
81. Schoultz, *Beneath the United States,* xvii; also see 374.
82. Theodore Roosevelt, quoted in Gonzalez, *Harvest of Empire,* 375–76.
83. Richard Morse, quoted in Schoultz, *Beneath the United States,* 379.
84. Schoultz, *Beneath the United States,* 384.
85. John Perkins, *Confessions of an Economic Hit Man* (New York: Plume, 2006), xvi.
86. Quoted in Margaret Talbot, "The Agitator," *New Yorker,* June 5, 2006.
87. Mark Steyn, *America Alone: The End of the World as We Know It* (Washington, D.C.: Regnery, 2006), 170.
88. Juan Gonzalez, "Democrats Cowed by GOP Scare Tactics on Immigrants," *New York Daily News,* November 15, 2007.
89. Gaby Hinsliff, "Britain Shuts the Door on New Wave of Migrants," *Observer* (London), October 22, 2006; Jonathan Brown and Andy McSmith, "Lies, Damned Lies, and Immigration," *Independent* (London), August 22, 2006; Steve Lee Myers, "In Anti-immigrant Mood, Russia Heeds Gadfly's Cry," *New York Times,* October 22, 2006;

Sophia Kishkovsky, "Attackers Pillage Moscow Art Gallery and Beat Activist Owner," *New York Times,* October 22, 2006.

90. Kate Heneroty, "Mexico President Calls US Border Wall 'Embarrassment,'" *Jurist,* October 27, 2006, http://jurist.law.pitt.edu/paperchase/2006/10/mexico-president-calls-us-border-wall.php.

91. Shireen T. Hunter and Simon Serfaty, introduction to *Islam, Europe's Second Religion: The New Social, Cultural, and Political Landscape,* ed. Shireen T. Hunter (Westport, Conn.: Praeger, 2002), xv.

92. Hilaire Belloc, *The Great Heresies* (New York: Sheed & Ward, 1938), quoted in Philip Jenkins, *God's Continent: Christianity, Islam, and Europe's Religious Crisis* (New York: Oxford University Press, 2007), 3.

93. Jürgen Habermas, quoted in Philip Jenkins, "Europe's Christian Comeback," *Foreign Policy* (Web exclusive), May–June 2007, http://www.foreignpolicy.com/.

94. See Tom Zeller Jr., "A Christian Site Grapples with Muslim Mysteries," *New York Times,* August 14, 2006; Mike Davis, "Vigilante Man," May 6, 2005, TomDispatch.com, http://www.tomdispatch.com/post/2378/mike_davis_on_the_return_of_the_vigilante; Charlie LeDuff, "Poised against Incursions, a Man on the Border, Armed and Philosophical," *New York Times,* August 14, 2006; Pamela Constable, "Muslims in India 'Targeted with Suspicion,'" *Washington Post,* August 14, 2006. Muslims in India, many of whom are descendants of converts from the lower Hindu castes, are literally becoming the untouchables of the new economy, as they are "lagging behind" in education, employment, and wealth. See Somini Sengupta, "Report Shows Muslims Near Bottom of Social Ladder," *New York Times,* November 29, 2006.

95. Jean-Pierre Stroobants, "L' 'Aversion injustifiée' des Néerlandais pour l'islam," *Le Monde,* April 15, 2006; Corey Robin, "Strangers in the Land," *Nation,* April 10, 2006; Naima Bouteldja, "The Dutch Have Reached a New Level of Authoritarianism," *Guardian,* November 21, 2006; Esther Benbassa, "Xenophobia, Anti-Semitism, and Racism: Europe's Recurring Evils?" in *Anti-Semitism and Islamophobia: Hatreds Old and New in Europe,* ed. Matti Bunzl (Chicago: Prickly Paradigm, 2007), 87; Arno Tausch et al., *Why Europe Has to Offer a Better Deal towards Its Muslim Communities: A Quantitative Analysis of Open International Data,* Entelequia eBooks, no. b001 (Malaga, Spain: Entelequia y Grupo Eumed.net, Universidad de Málaga, 2006), http://ideas.repec.org/b/erv/ebooks/b001.html; Matt Carr, "You Are Now Entering Eurabia," *Race & Class* 48, no. 1 (July 2006): 5, 12–13; Jenkins, *God's Continent,* 174, 234; Xavier Ternisien, "Villiers-le-Bel, radioscopie d'un 'ghetto social,'" *Le Monde,* November 30, 2007.

96. Jenkins, *God's Continent,* 14–17, 115, 199, 256–58, 260–65, 288; Carr, "You Are Now Entering Eurabia," 18; Simon Kuper, "The Crescent and the Cross," *Financial Times* (London), November 10, 2007.

97. Vincent Geisser, *La Nouvelle islamophobie* (Paris: La Découverte, 2003), 9–12, 19–22, 115–16; Dan Diner, "Reflections on Anti-Semitism and Islamophobia," in Bunzl, *Anti-Semitism and Islamophobia,* 49–50; Benbassa, "Xenophobia, Anti-Semitism, and Racism," 86; Oriana Fallaci, *The Rage and the Pride* (New York: Rizzoli, 2002), 96–97, 136.

98. Joan Wallach Scott, "Veiled Politics," *Chronicle Review*, November 23, 2007, B10–11.

99. Ann Powers, "Latinos Give New Life to Neil Diamond Anthem," *Los Angeles Times*, May 9, 2006.

100. Niall Ferguson, *The War of the World: Twentieth-Century Conflict and the Descent of the West* (New York: Penguin, 2006), xli, lxviii.

101. James Kurth, "One-Child Foreign Policy," *American Conservative*, August 27, 2007.

102. See Roberto Márquez, "*Raza, Racismo, e Historia*: 'Are All My Bones from There?'" *Latino(a) Research Review* (Winter 2000): 17; and Juan Marichal, "The New World from Within: The Inca Garcilaso," in *First Images of America: The Impact of the New World on the Old*, ed. Fredi Chiappelli (Berkeley and Los Angeles: University of California Press, 1976), 59.

103. *A Day without a Mexican*, DVD, directed by Sergio Arau (2004; Xenon Pictures, 2004).

104. John Moritz, "Study: Illegal Immigrants Boost Economy, Drain Services," *Fort Worth (Tex.) Star-Telegram*, December 8, 2006; Daniels, *Guarding the Golden Door*, 266.

105. Tahar Ben Jelloun, "Le Dernier immigré," *Le Monde diplomatique*, August 2006, 24.

106. *Babel*, DVD, directed by Alejandro González Iñárritu (2006; Paramount, 2007).

107. "A World of Fences," *Christian Science Monitor*, October 19, 2006.

108. Juan Goytisolo, "Les Boucs émissaires de l'Espagne européenne," *Le Monde diplomatique*, October 1992, 12.

109. Jason DeParle, "Rising Breed of Migrant: Skilled and Welcome," *New York Times*, August 20, 2007; Meg Bortin, "Migrants, Bound for Spain, Set Off a Boom," *New York Times*, June 19, 2006; Ian Fisher, "For African Migrants, Europe Gets Further Away," *New York Times*, August 26, 2007; Sharon Lafraniere, "Europe Takes Africa's Fish, and Boatloads of Migrants Follow," *New York Times*, January 14, 2008.

110. See Randal C. Archibold, "Far from Home, Mexicans Sing Age-Old Ballads of New Life," *New York Times*, July 6, 2007.

111. Quoted in Ana Maria Manzanas Calvo, "Contested Passages: Migrants and Borders in the Río Grande and the Mediterranean Sea," *South Atlantic Quarterly* 105, no. 4 (Fall 2006): 809.

112. Roberto Rodriguez, "Without Mexicans, Who Would Americans Blame for Their Country's Problems? Us vs. Them in the Immigration Debate," *CounterPunch*, May 25, 2007, http://www.counterpunch.org/rodriguez05252007.html.

CONCLUSION

1. Havelock Ellis, quoted in George M. Foster, *Culture and Conquest: America's Spanish Heritage* (Chicago: Quadrangle, 1960), 26.

2. Gilberto Freyre, *New World in the Tropics: The Culture of Modern Brazil* (1959; repr., New York: Knopf, 1971), 40.

3. Oriana Fallaci, quoted in Margaret Talbot, "The Agitator," *New Yorker,* June 5, 2006.

4. Max Harris, *Aztecs, Moors, and Christians: Festivals of Reconquest in Mexico and Spain* (Austin: University of Texas Press, 2000), 38–39, 50–51.

5. Ibid., 132–47.

6. Ibid., 157–59.

7. Ibid., 208–11; Henry Kamen's statement, from *Philip of Spain* (New Haven, Conn.: Yale University Press, 1997), is quoted on p. 210.

8. Harris, *Aztecs, Moors, and Christians,* 215.

9. Ibid., 216–26.

10. Philip Jenkins, *God's Continent: Christianity, Islam, and Europe's Religious Crisis* (New York: Oxford University Press, 2007), 239; Eva Borreguero, "The Moors Are Coming, the Moors Are Coming! Encounters with Muslims in Contemporary Spain," *Islam and Christian-Muslim Relations* 17, no. 4 (October 2006): 428.

11. Borreguero, "The Moors Are Coming," 430.

12. Stefano Allievi, "Islam in Italy," in *Islam, Europe's Second Religion: The New Social, Cultural, and Political Landscape,* ed. Shireen T. Hunter (Westport, Conn.: Praeger, 2002), 78.

13. A. Fernández González and D. Llamazares Fernández, quoted in Bernabé López García and Ana I. Planet Contreras, "Islam in Spain," in Hunter, *Islam, Europe's Second Religion,* 168–69, 173n8.

14. Hisham Aidi, "Let Us Be Moors: Islam, Race, and 'Connected Histories,'" *Middle East Report* 229 (Winter 2003): 43. For a special report on Moroccans of Morisco origin, see Juan Carlos de la Cal, "Los Hijos de al Andalus," *El Mundo* (Madrid), August 27, 2006. For an account of the citizenship-law proposal, see "La Mesa exige mayoría cualificada para debatir la propuesta de IU sobre derecho preferente de moriscos a la nacionalidad," October 7, 2006, Noticias Ya.com, http://noticias.ya.com/local/andalucia/7/10/2006/mesa-propuesta-iu.html.

15. Craig G. Smith, "Poor and Muslim? Jewish? Soup Kitchen Is Not for You," *New York Times,* February 28, 2006; Miriam Joyce, letter to the editor, *New York Times,* March 7, 2006.

16. Robert Purkiss, quoted in Matti Bunzl, ed., *Anti-Semitism and Islamophobia: Hatreds Old and New in Europe* (Chicago: Prickly Paradigm, 2007), 9–10.

17. See Pew Global Attitudes Project, "Unfavorable Views of Jews and Muslims on the Increase in Europe," Pew Research Center, September 17, 2008, at http://pewglobal.org/reports/display.php?ReportID=262. I thank Michael Morris for bringing this news item to my attention.

18. Ian Fisher, "Is Cuisine Still Italian Even if the Chef Isn't?" *New York Times,* April 7, 2008.

19. See Aristide Zolberg, *A Nation by Design: Immigration Policy in the Fashioning of America* (New York: Russell Sage Foundation; Cambridge, Mass.: Harvard University Press, 2006), 16–17.

20. Stuart Hall, "Ethnicity and Difference," in *Becoming National: A Reader,* ed. Geoff Eley and Ronald Grigor Suny (New York: Oxford University Press, 1966), 344.

21. Mae M. Ngai, *Impossible Subjects: Illegal Aliens and the Making of Modern America* (Princeton, N.J.: Princeton University Press, 2004), 7; Arjun Appadurai, *Fear of Small Numbers: An Essay on the Geography of Anger* (Durham, N.C.: Duke University Press, 2006), 43.

22. Roger Daniels, *Guarding the Golden Door: American Immigration Policy and Immigrants since 1882* (New York: Hill & Wang, 2004), 140–41.

23. Moisés Naím, "Borderline," *Washington Post,* May 28, 2006.

24. Fatima Mernissi, *Dreams of Trespass: Tales of a Harem Girlhood* (Reading, Mass.: Addison-Wesley, 1994).

25. Edward Rothstein, "In the U.S. and Europe, Tensions between a National and Minority Languages," *New York Times,* May 29, 2006; John Tagliabue, "Soon, Europe Will Speak in 23 Tongues," *New York Times,* December 6, 2006.

26. Zolberg, *Nation by Design,* 14, 450–51, 457; "Border Insecurity," *New York Times,* March 4, 2008; "The Road to Dystopia," *New York Times,* March 13, 2008.

27. Zolberg, *Nation by Design,* 454.

28. Herman Melville, *Redburn* (Harmondsworth, UK: Penguin, 1976), 382, quoted in ibid., 455.

29. Melville, *Redburn,* quoted in John Higham, *Strangers in the Land: Patterns of American Nativism, 1860–1925* (1955; repr., New Brunswick, N.J.: Rutgers University Press, 1988), 21.

30. Louis Adamic, quoted in Ngai, *Impossible Subjects,* 233.

31. Gregory Rodriguez, *Mongrels, Bastards, Orphans, and Vagabonds: Mexican Immigration and the Future of Race in America* (New York: Pantheon, 2007), xvi.

32. Ibid., 33–54.

33. Ibid., 87.

34. Antonio López de Santa Anna, quoted in ibid., 83.

35. Rodriguez, *Mongrels, Bastards, Orphans, and Vagabonds,* 87.

36. Ibid., 86.

37. Richard Rodriguez, *Days of Obligation: An Argument with My Mexican Father* (1992), quoted in ibid., xi.

38. Richard Sennett, *The Culture of the New Capitalism* (New Haven, Conn.: Yale University Press, 2006), 90, 167.

39. Emma Lazarus, "1492" and "The New Colossus," in *The Norton Anthology of American Literature,* ed. Nina Baym, shorter 7th ed. (New York: Norton, 2008), 1601–2.

INDEX

INDEX 219

and symbolic function as Other and outsider of, 62; Renaissance representations of, 63–65; as symbol or metaphor for anyone not considered part of social mainstream, 5

Moors of Granada: Alpujarras uprisings (1499 and 1568–1570), 33, 36; deportation of, 36–37; under Ferdinand and Isabella, 32–33; objections to persecutions of, 36–37

Morisco Revolt (1568), 163

Moriscos: association with Arab and Berber conquerors of 711, 54; attempts to convert forcibly baptized, 38–39; Christianization of, 49; defined in *Vox* (Spanish-language dictionary), 54; denial of privileges of conversion, 57; expulsion from Spain (1609–1614), 1, 9, 10, 31, 39–42, 122, 183n35; fears of fertility rates of, 37–38, 42; in Mexico, 72; in *moros y cristianos*, 163; opposition coalition against expulsion from Spain (1609–1614), 49–50; racialization of, 39; recast by Ribera as dangerous Moors, 39; in sixteenth-century literature, 49–50

Moriscos of Spain, The (Lea), 40

Moritz, John, 200n104

Morocco: African heritage of, 28; Drew Ali's claim to Moroccan ancestry, 78–80; sense of kinship with its ancient Semitic heritage, 25–26; Spanish-Moroccan dispute over uninhabited rock in Mediterranean (2002), 27, 28; treatment of Jews in, 99, 122

Moros (Muslims from Philippines), 64

moros y cristianos (mock battles between Moors and Christians), 162–67; acknowledgment of Spain's mestizo culture in, 165; fiesta in Villena, Spain, x–xi, 164–65; transformed into strategy of dialogue and coexistence,

165–66; yearning for peace and *convivencia* in, 162, 163–64

Morse, Richard, 148, 198n83

Mosaic Arabs (Jews), 11, 110, 115, 121

Moses, 100

Moses of Huesca (Petrus Alfonsi), 102

Moslem Sunrise, The (magazine), 80

Mothers against Illegal Aliens, 20, 149

Mudéjarism, 31

Muhammad, Elijah (Elijah Poole), 81, 83, 84

multiculturalism: era of, 125; global, based on homogeneous, well-defined national cultures, 127; precursors of, 133

Münzer, Hieronymous, Dr., 32

Muselmann, Muselmänner, Muselweiber, 92–94

Muslim Jews, 87–122; anti-Semitism as corollary of Crusades against Islam and, 11–12, 100–105; disdain for Christian culture binding Jews and Muslims, 105–10; Disraeli, 11, 109–11, 113, 115, 118, 121, 193n66, 193n70–73; Jewish orientalists, 108–9, 114–15; lingua franca of Arabic, impact on Hebrew philology, 95–96; Moorish heritage asserted through architecture, 11, 112–13; *Muselmann*, doomed Jews of Holocaust, 92–94; Nussimbaum, 87–93, 107, 118, 190n6; Sephardim welcomed by Ottomans after expulsion from Spain, 96–98; Zionism and, 113–22

Muslims: African American, 10–11, 60, 72–85; assertion of their rights in globally distorted economy, 156; conflation of Hispanics and, 142; disdain for Christian culture binding Jews and, 105–10; in Europe and United States, expulsion contemplated for, 150–51; Jews and, 35, 56–57; Jews and, in Christian imaginary, 40, 94,

Anouar Majid is author of *A Call for Heresy: Why Dissent Is Vital to Islam and America* (Minnesota, 2007). He is professor of English and founding director of the Center for Global Humanities at the University of New England in Maine and editor of *Tingis,* a Moroccan-American magazine of ideas and culture.